WE Make Stuff HAppen (WEMSHA)©
TAPUniversity's Project Management Workbook V 3.01

by Laura Hilkemann, PhD, PMP®
and David Kohrell, MA, PMP®, CISA®, CBAP®

May 12, 2009
Edition 3.01

© 2009 TAPUniversity Publishing
ISBN # – 978-0-578-02450-9
Publisher
TAPUniversity Publishing via www.lulu.com

TECHNOLOGY
AS PROMISED

Preface

In the summer of 2004 I discovered the meaning of the street we live on in Lincoln, Nebraska – Wemsha Street. Our home was built in the late 1990's. The street was completed about two years before our home was built. Apparently the subdivision was taking its toll on the creative naming ability of its developers. The founding fathers and mothers of Lincoln, Native American tribes, letters of the alphabet and a smattering of United States presidents had long since been taken within our city. Within the twenty or so streets that feed the Regents Heights neighborhood relatives (Nancy or Eric Drive) and numbers and courts (81st) had consumed the final bit of available street names.

So, as I discovered from a very knowledgeable post office official, the developers were at a creative bypass. There was one remaining east-west street to be named. In a quandary they apparently leveraged their catch phrase "We Make Stuff Happen". They had a different "S" word in mind but in keeping this project management workbook family friendly, we'll stay with "Stuff."

After several months of disappointment of knowing my family and I lived on an "acronym" street – it dawned on me. My profession and the profession of those we help is all about "Making Stuff Happen." It's what we do. Remove the clutter of excess methodology, management fades of the year and overtired cliché and acronyms – we make stuff happen says it quite well. It also helps to keep project managers' egos grounded (then again, managing a project is usually sufficient for that). When we taste the elixir of executive power, when we touch the sky on the "big project," when visions of upward mobility greet us at our office (OK cubicle) – it's important to remember we are the ones counted on to make stuff happen.

The purpose of this workbook is to help you progress from the "what" of project management to the "how." That's the essence of our training at our corporate learning portal - TAPUniversity. Our goal is to help you "tap" into mastering the what-to-how transition. Over 1,000 professionals have accessed TAPUniversity and the first and second edition of the WEMSHA workbook.

In our third edition of this workbook we have dramatically increased the amount of "how-to" help. My business partner, Laura Hilkemann, has taken the how-to challenge to the next level by developing and refining over 110 exercises.

TECHNOLOGY
AS PROMISED

Our mission with this workbook is NOT to rehash either the Guide to the Project Management Body of Knowledge, 4th Edition or the plethora of PMP/ PMBOK Study Guides in terms of straight ahead narrative. Rather our mission IS to provide a gateway for a deeper understanding by having students apply the essential project management concepts. In so doing we have included at least one exercise per the forty-two processes articulated in the Guide to the PMBOK, 4th Edition.

We hope you enjoy this workbook and we look forward to hearing how it has worked for you.

David Kohrell

Table of Contents

Exercise Index

Exercises and Processes

Exercise 1. Projects, Programs, and Ongoing Operations
    Introductory Concepts

Exercise 2. Why Do Projects Come Into Existence?
    4.1 Develop Project Charter

Exercise 3. Inputs / Tools & Techniques / Outputs
    Introductory Concepts

Exercise 4. Practicing Process Patterns
    Introductory Concepts

Exercise 5. TAPUniversity Organizational Assessment
    Introductory Concepts

Exercise 6. Organizational Types
    Introductory Concepts

Exercise 7. Stakeholders
    Introductory Concepts

Exercise 8. Create Portfolio
    4.1 Develop Project Charter

Exercise 9. Benefit-to-Cost and Payback Period
    4.1 Develop Project Charter

Exercise 10. NPV Exercise
    4.1 Develop Project Charter

Exercise 11. Financial Selection Techniques
    4.1 Develop Project Charter

Exercise 12. More Practice on Financial Selection Techniques
    4.1 Develop Project Charter

Exercise 13. Force Field Analysis
    4.1 Develop Project Charter

Exercise 14. SWOT Analysis
    4.1 Develop Project Charter

Exercise 15. Pairwise Chart
    4.1 Develop Project Charter

Exercise 16. Movie Pairwise Chart
        4.1 Develop Project Charter

Exercise 17. Organizational Process Assets versus Enterprise Environmental Factors
        Introductory Concepts

Exercise 18. SOW
        4.1 Develop Project Charter

Exercise 19 Stakeholder Analysis
        10.1 Identify Stakeholders

Exercise 20. Stakeholder Register
        10.1 Identify Stakeholders

Exercise 21. Stakeholder Management Strategy
        10.1 Identify Stakeholders

Exercise 22. Major Project Documents
        4.1 Develop Project Charter
        4.2 Develop Project Management Plan
        5.2 Define Scope

Exercise 23. Collect Requirements – Group Decision Making Techniques
        5.1 Collect Requirements

Exercise 24. Collect Requirements – Questionnaire
        5.1 Collect Requirements

Exercise 25. Collect Requirements – Traceability Matrix
        5.1 Collect Requirements

Exercise 26. Project Charter Sample Internet Portal
        4.1 Develop Project Charter

Exercise 27. Scope Development Checklist – Sample Internet Portal
        5.2 Define Scope

Exercise 28. Scope / Charter
        4.1 Develop Project Charter
        5.2 Define Scope

Exercise 29. Vacation WBS
        5.3 Create Work Breakdown Structure

Exercise 45. Sample Resource and Staffing Plan for Internet Portal
      9.1 Develop Human Resource Plan
      6.3 Estimate Activity Resources

Exercise 46. Sample Budget Overview for Internet Portal
      7.2 Determine Budget

Exercise 47. Determine Budget – Cost Performance Baseline
      7.2 Determine Budget

Exercise 48. Quality Plan for Internet Portal
      8.1 Plan Quality

Exercise 49. Plan Quality – Cost of Quality
      8.1 Plan Quality

Exercise 50. Plan Quality – Quality Checklists
      8.1 Plan Quality

Exercise 51. Sample Responsibility Assignment Matrix (RAM) for the Internet Portal
      9.1 Develop Human Resource Plan

Exercise 52. Sample Responsibility / Authority Balance for Internet Portal
      9.1 Develop Human Resource Plan

Exercise 53. Develop Human Resource Plan – Maslow's Hierarchy
      9.1 Develop Human Resource Plan

Exercise 54. Develop Human Resource Plan – Profiling
      9.1 Develop Human Resource Plan

Exercise 55. Communication Formula
      10.2 Plan Communications

Exercise 56. Plan Communication – Communication Methods
      10.2 Plan Communications

Exercise 57. Sample Communication Plan for Internet Portal
      10.2 Plan Communications

Exercise 58. Project Updates
      10.2 Plan Communications

Exercise 59. Sample Escalation Plan for Internet Portal
      10.2 Plan Communications

TECHNOLOGY
AS PROMISED

Exercise 60. Plan Risk Responses – Strategies
    11.1 Plan Risk Management

Exercise 61. Risk Management Plan Sample
    11.1 Plan Risk Management

Exercise 62. The Risk Processes
    11.1 Plan Risk Management
    11.2 Identify Risks
    11.3 Perform Qualitative Risk Analysis
    11.4 Perform Quantitative Risk Analysis
    11.5 Plan Risk Responses
    11.6 Monitor and Control Risks

Exercise 63. Plan Procurements – Make or Buy Analysis
    12.1 Plan Procurements

Exercise 64. Sample Specific Contract Requirements for Internet Portal
    12.1 Plan Procurements

Exercise 65. Identify Contract Type
    12.1 Plan Procurements

Exercise 66. Plan Procurements - Contract Types
    12.1 Plan Procurements

Exercise 67. Plan Procurements - Specific Contract Types
    12.1 Plan Procurements

Exercise 68. Direct and Manage Project Execution – Change Requests
    4.3 Direct and Manage Project Execution

Exercise 69. Perform Quality Assurance – Spaghetti Diagram
    8.2 Perform Quality Assurance

Exercise 70. Perform Quality Assurance – SIPOC Analysis
    8.2 Perform Quality Assurance

Exercise 71. Keep Everyone in the Loop – Internet Portal
    4.2 Develop Project Management Plan
    5.2 Define Scope
    11.1 Plan Risk Management
    10.2 Plan Communications
    8.1 Plan Quality

Exercise 72. Status Reports Process for Internet Portal
    10.2 Plan Communications

Exercise 73. Acquire Project Team - Resource Calendars
> 9.2 Acquire Project Team

Exercise 74. Develop Project Team – Team Building Activities
> 9.3 Develop Project Team

Exercise 75. Develop Project Team – Recognition and Rewards
> 9.3 Develop Project Team

Exercise 76. Manage Project Team – Resolving Conflict
> 9.4 Manage Project Team

Exercise 77. Manage Project Team – Tools and Techniques
> 9.4 Manage Project Team

Exercise 78. Manage Stakeholders Expectations – Issue Log
> 10.4 Manage Stakeholders Expectations

Exercise 79. Procurement
> 12.1 Plan Procurements
> 12.2 Conduct Procurements

Exercise 80. Monitor and Control Project Work
> 4.4 Monitor and Control Project Work

Exercise 81. Perform Integrated Change Control
> 4.5 Perform Integrated Change Control

Exercise 82. Verify Scope
> 5.4 Verify Scope

Exercise 83. Change Control Triple Constraint
> 5.5 Control Scope
> 6.6 Control Schedule
> 7.3 Control Costs

Exercise 84. Earned Value Scrimmage
> 7.3 Control Costs

Exercise 85. Earned Value Basics
> 7.3 Control Costs

Exercise 86. Earned Value Practice
> 7.3 Control Costs

Exercise 87. The Normal Distribution Curve
    8.3 Perform Quality Control

Exercise 88. Construct a Fishbone Diagram
    8.3 Perform Quality Control

Exercise 89. Control Chart
    8.3 Perform Quality Control

Exercise 90. Pareto Diagram
    8.3 Perform Quality Control

Exercise 91. Scatter Plot
    8.3 Perform Quality Control

Exercise 92. Report Performance – Forecasting
    10.5 Report Performance

Exercise 93. Report Performance – Variance Analysis
    10.5 Report Performance

Exercise 94. Administer Procurements
    12.3 Administer Procurements

Exercise 95. Thirty Questions on Nine Processes
    4.3 Direct and Manage Project Execution
    8.2 Perform Quality Assurance
    4.4 Monitor and Control Project Work
    4.5 Perform Integrated Change Control
    5.4 Verify Scope
    5.5 Control Scope
    6.6 Control Schedule
    8.3 Perform Quality Control
    11.6 Monitor and Control Risks

Exercise 96. Project Close-Out
    4.6 Close Project or Phase

Exercise 97. Sample Project Post Mortem for Internet Portal
    4.6 Close Project or Phase

Exercise 98. Close Procurements for the Banana Farm
    12.4 Close Procurements

Exercise 99. Where Did I Come From?
    Many Processes

Exercise 100. Process Sort
      All Processes

Exercise 101. Inputs, Tools and Techniques, and Outputs
      All Processes

Exercise 102. Integration Area Inputs, Tools and Techniques, and Outputs
      4.1 Develop Project Charter
      4.2 Develop Project Management Plan
      4.3 Direct and Manage Project Execution
      4.4 Monitor and Control Project Work
      4.5 Perform Integrated Change Control
      4.6 Close Project or Phase

Exercise 103. Scope Inputs, Tools and Techniques, and Outputs
      5.1 Collect Requirements
      5.2 Define Scope
      5.3 Create Work Breakdown Structure
      5.4 Verify Scope
      5.5 Control Scope

Exercise 104. Time Inputs and Outputs
      6.1 Define Activities
      6.2 Sequence Activities
      6.3 Estimate Activity Resources
      6.4 Estimate Activity Durations
      6.5 Develop Schedule
      6.6 Control Schedule

Exercise 105. Cost Inputs, Tools and Techniques, and Outputs
      7.1 Estimate Costs
      7.2 Determine Budget
      7.3 Control Costs

Exercise 106. Quality Inputs, Tools and Techniques, and Outputs
      8.1 Plan Quality
      8.2 Perform Quality Assurance
      8.3 Perform Quality Control

Exercise 107. Human Resource Inputs, Tools and Techniques, and Outputs
      9.1 Develop Human Resource Plan
      9.2 Acquire Project Team
      9.3 Develop Project Team
      9.4 Manage Project Team

TECHNOLOGY
AS PROMISED

Exercise 108. Communications Inputs, Tools and Techniques, and Outputs
      10.1 Identify Stakeholders
      10.2 Plan Communications
      10.3 Distribute Information
      10.4 Manage Stakeholders Expectations
      10.5 Report Performance

Exercise 109. Risk Inputs and Outputs
      11.1 Plan Risk Management
      11.2 Identify Risks
      11.3 Perform Qualitative Risk Analysis
      11.4 Perform Quantitative Risk Analysis
      11.5 Plan Risk Responses
      11.6 Monitor and Control Risks

Exercise 110. Procurement Inputs, Tools and Techniques, and Outputs
      12.1 Plan Procurements
      12.2 Conduct Procurements
      12.3 Administer Procurements
      12.4 Close Procurements

Exercise 111. Code of Ethics
      Ethics

PMP Scrimmage® Curriculum, Edition 3.01   *Page 17*
www.tapuniversity.com
TECHNOLOGY
AS PROMISED

Introduction

In the early 1990's there were four or five project management books on the market. Today there are close to four or five hundred. Why the explosion in interest?

Getting stuff done without direct control, the more formal name for that is "project management."

Project management focuses on getting stuff done with people that you may not necessarily supervise directly. Despite the fallout at the end of the dot.com/telecoms/Y2k/post 9-11 era, project management's acceptance and growth continued this decade due to an increasing weave of international projects, dependencies and relationships - outsourcing, off shoring to just name two. That trend continues during the current global Recession. Organizations are pressed to do more with less; oftentimes through a series of supply chain relationships that, in the 1990's, would have been done all within the same organization.

Today, you are expected to "get stuff done," usually without direct control of the resources. This book has been designed to help you get stuff done in a variety of ways.

Its purpose is to assist those preparing for project management certification (Project Management Professional, administered by the Project Management Institute). Also, it is meant as a practical workbook for day to day project management.

The dialog can continue at www.tapuniversity.com – just register, reference this book and you will be given access to the TAPUniversity Community at no charge. At TAPUniversity, you can receive support in the way of courses (e.g., TAPUniversity's PMP® Scrimmage and numerous other classes) as well as sample PMP® exam questions. Please join our LinkedIn and Facebook groups and follow us at Twitter (@tapuniversity). Once you have earned your PMP® we are here to help maintain your important credential through our TAPUniversity subscription program. Ultimately we just want to help "make it happen" the WEMSHA way.

Finally, this book helps you "get stuff done" by demonstrating a seminal concept of project management called "progressive elaboration." This is not an overnight effort. In fact it's been several years in the making. So, we hope you enjoy this book and please provide feedback on its content to the TAPUniversity Community.

TECHNOLOGY
AS PROMISED

Chapter 1   - Project Management Overview

As shared in the introduction, project management concerns getting stuff done with people whom you may not have direct supervisory responsibility. The key to successful project management is getting stuff done without direct control.

Project:
*Temporary,
*Start-End,
*Progressive Elaboration,
*People

This leads to the following definition that graces almost every project management book: "a project is a temporary endeavor undertaken to create a unique product, service or result." Why this definition? It's how the Project Management Institution (www.pmi.org) defines it in their *Guide to the Project Management Body of Knowledge, Fourth Edition (2008)*. This guide is commonly referred to as the PMBOK® (pronounced PEMBok). To begin, the three key elements of a project are:

1. Temporary = definite beginning and definite end date.
2. Unique = product or service is different in some distinguishing way from all other products or services.
3. Progressive Elaboration = developing in steps.

We make explicit a fourth element:
4. People = projects versus change requests involve more than one person.

Clues that you may be involved in a project are that "it" seems to have the following characteristics:

> Scheduled start and calculated end date (temporary in nature) – it's not ongoing.
> Unique purpose with well-defined objective – there's something distinctive about it.
> Requires resources from various areas – it's not just an armada of one.
> Has a primary sponsor and customer – someone has authorized its existence and someone has identified a need.

Project Management processes are not linear or discrete. The results from one part of the cycle feed into the next. Contrast projects to ongoing operations which are the business activities that do not have an end-date, but are meant to be continually performed.

Projects usually come into existence as the result of one or more of the following:
> Market demand
> Organizational need
> Customer request
> Technological advance
> Legal requirement

Projects and Programs

Individual project success can occur with a firm understanding of what lifecycle your organization uses and an appreciation of how the five process groups can provide measurement and insight regardless of which lifecycle(s) is/are deployed. Projects do not exist in isolation. Project managers can often become successful after acquiring some essential knowledge and mastering "one off" or isolated projects. What separates project managers and organizational project maturity is the ability to implement related projects and connect those to the existing production environment. That is where program management comes in. Portfolios add yet another level—they are a collection or projects or programs and other work.

Program management is the classic term for connecting inter-related projects. The PMBOK® definition is as follows:

> *"the coordinated management of a portfolio of projects which benefit from a consolidated approach and achieve a set of business objectives."*

Characteristics of programs include:
- Group of coordinated projects (e.g., Operating Systems or Office Applications for information technology; Coal Generating Power Plant Generation for public power);
- Larger in scope and may be linked to a product portfolio (e.g., Microsoft Windows is the product, Windows X.P. the program and Windows X.P. Service Pack 2 the project);
- Not necessarily time-limited.

Project Management is more than just the PMBOK®

The PMBOK® Guide is the definitive body of knowledge for project management. It is not, however, the only resource. For those pursuing the Project Management Professional (PMP®) designation, that is an important aspect to understand since a significant number of test questions are derived from outside the PMBOK®. They may come from human resource, general management, communication, organizational behavior, and other project management texts from Kerzner, Pritchard, Zells, etc.

For those with a PMP® or desire to apply the practical knowledge of project management, this aspect is important to help avoid "taking on" the PMBOK® and all of its glorious 42 processes and many "Inputs, Tools and Techniques, and Outputs" and spring them on an unsuspecting workplace. The PMBOK®, and similar bodies of knowledge, are not constructed for out-of-the-box implementation. It's overkill to expect all 42 processes to be applied on each and every project. That misses the salient point that projects need to balance scope, cost, and time; ensure objectives are met; resources are available and leveraged; risks are managed; project information shared and third party resources controlled.

Project Processes, Phases and Knowledge Areas

The PMBOK® has established five process groups that provide a framework for the 42 processes across nine knowledge areas.   Those process groups and brief descriptions of their purpose are as follows:

> ➢ Initiating: Authorizing the project or phase
> ➢ Planning: Defining or refining objectives and selecting the best course of action
> ➢ Executing: Coordinating the resources
> ➢ Monitoring and Controlling: Ensuring the objectives are met
> ➢ Closing: Formalizing acceptance

This illustration (Figure 3.2 from the third Edition PMBOK®) depicts one important aspect of the process groups: **they overlap**. Unlike a project lifecycle that may impose a set of sequential steps, the five process groups provide a feedback loop among planning, executing, and monitoring/controlling processes. The underlying premise is that projects require authorization (initiation) and then, depending upon industry, a whole set of activities to "make the stuff" happen. When all the stuff is done, the project closes.

A broad framework? Yes, but it is necessary. Within information technology alone there are over 25 different methodologies or lifecycles in use from Waterfall to RUP to Agile. Add in the distinctive nature of each organization that exists, and you end up with endless ways to get stuff done.

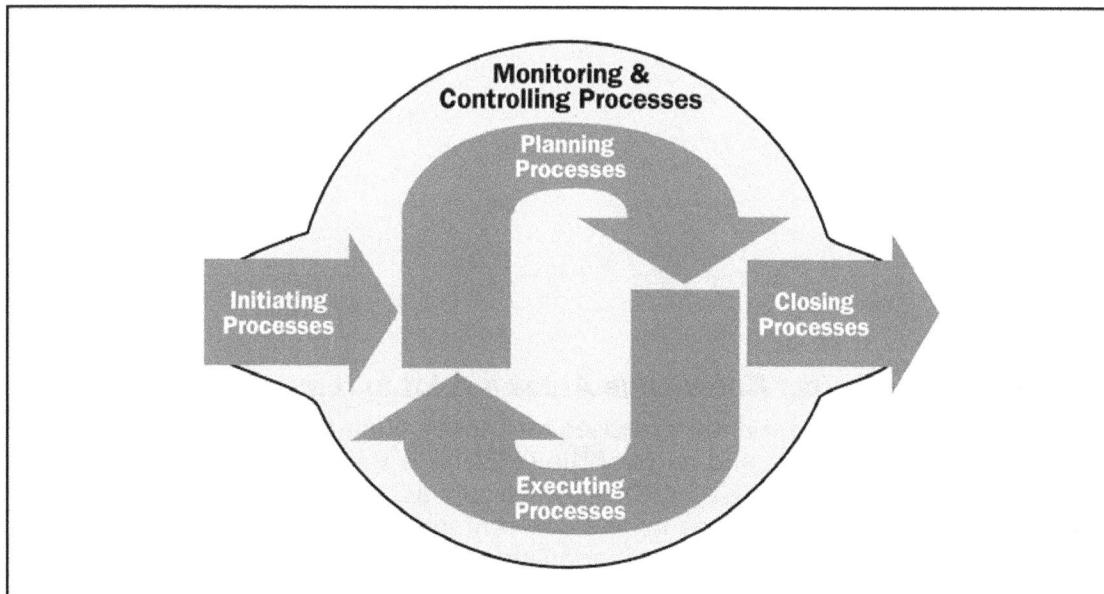

Figure 3-2. Project Management Process Groups Mapped to the Plan-Do-Check-Act Cycle

A Guide to the Project Management Body of Knowledge-Third Edition (PMBOK® Guide). ©2004 Project Management Institute, Inc. All Rights Reserved.

Illustration 1: Project Management Process Groups

TECHNOLOGY
AS PROMISED

Project Lifecycles

As referenced in the previous section, a project lifecycle is different from the five process groups defined in the PMBOK®. Process Groups and Project Lifecycles are NOT mutually exclusive; they work together. A project life cycle generally defines:

> ➤ Technical work to be done.
> ➤ Who should be involved.
> ➤ Typically four or five phases (though some have 15 to 16 for product oriented lifecycles).
> ➤ May reach beyond the conclusion of a project to include product retirement.
> ➤ Conclusion of each phase is generally marked by review of a "deliverable" also called phase exits, stage gates, or kill points.

Project Knowledge Areas

What brings together the process groups, lifecycles, and programs are the 42 processes bound within nine knowledge areas addressed in the PMBOK®. This workbook explores those processes and key accompanying input, tools and techniques, and outputs in subsequent chapters. These 42 processes are arranged within five process groups and within nine knowledge areas. The knowledge areas provide the context within a specific discipline (e.g. Risk or Quality Management) for each process. The nine knowledge areas are:

> ➤ Integration
> ➤ Scope
> ➤ Time
> ➤ Cost
> ➤ Quality
> ➤ Human Resource
> ➤ Communication
> ➤ Risk
> ➤ Procurement

Process Groups + Project Knowledge Areas = A lot to remember

One of the more challenging mental exercises for those taking the PMP® exam as well as for those implementing pieces and parts of the PMBOK® is the matrix of the process groups and knowledge areas. The PMBOK® specifically addresses how those processes connect with the five process groups in nine different knowledge areas. Add to that the plethora of Inputs, Tools and Techniques, and Outputs and it becomes a bit overwhelming. There are a couple of ways to simplify this.

The first way to simplify is keeping a left to right then top to bottom perspective as you review the Process – Knowledge Area Matrix table. (See Illustration).

PMP Scrimmage® Curriculum, Edition 3.01   *Page 22*
www.tapuniversity.com
TECHNOLOGY
AS PROMISED

Knowledge Area	Process Group				
	Initiating	**Planning**	**Executing**	**Monitoring and Controlling**	**Closing**
Integration	4.1 Develop Project Charter	4.2 Develop Project Management Plan	4.3 Direct and Manage Project Execution	4.4 Monitor and Control Project Work 4.5 Perform Integrated Change Control	4.6 Close Project or Phase
Scope		5.1 Collect Requirements 5.2 Define Scope 5.3 Create Work Breakdown Structure		5.4 Verify Scope 5.5 Control Scope	
Time		6.1 Define Activities 6.2 Sequence Activities 6.3 Estimate Activity Resources 6.4 Estimate Activity Durations 6.5 Develop Schedule		6.6 Control Schedule	
Cost		7.1 Estimate Costs 7.2 Determine Budget		7.3 Control Costs	
Quality		8.1 Plan Quality	8.2 Perform Quality Assurance	8.3 Perform Quality Control	
Human Resource		9.1 Develop Human Resource Plan	9.2 Acquire Project Team 9.3 Develop Project Team 9.4 Manage Project Team		
Communications	10.1 Identify Stakeholders	10.2 Plan Communications	10.3 Distribute Information 10.4 Manage Stakeholders Expectations	10.5 Report Performance	
Risk		11.1 Plan Risk Management 11.2 Identify Risks 11.3 Perform Qualitative Risk Analysis 11.4 Perform Quantitative Risk Analysis 11.5 Plan Risk Responses		11.6 Monitor and Control Risks	
Procurement		12.1 Plan Procurements	12.2 Conduct Procurements	12.3 Administer Procurements	12.4 Close Procurements

Illustration 2: Process Group – Knowledge Area Matrix

TECHNOLOGY
AS PROMISED

Much of the detailed work for project management occurs in the planning area processes. "Measure twice and cut once" or as George Washington said, "if I had eight hours to cut down a tree I would spend seven hours sharpening the saw."

The Executing process group's primary process occurs within the Integration Knowledge Area – "Direct and Manage Project Execution" with additional processes in Quality, Human Resources, Communication and Procurement. There are seven total processes. The "triple constraint" Knowledge Areas of Scope, Time and Cost as well as Risk do not have processes within the Execution process Group. Why is that? There are not new processes or activities that occur within Execution for those four knowledge areas (e.g., such as performing quality assurance).

The Monitoring and Controlling Process Group has touch point processes for all knowledge areas. There are 14 total processes. After our discussion concerning the Executing Process Group, this merits some additional explanation. The Monitoring and Controlling Process Group seeks out information on the project's health and progress. That touches every knowledge area. The Integration Knowledge area provides the two umbrella processes for this – Monitor and Control the Project Work and Integrated Change Control. Those processes guide the change control processes and change verification for each of the other knowledge areas.

The second way to simplify is to look for repeat patterns in the inputs, tools and techniques, and outputs. There are numerous inputs, tools and techniques, and outputs. However, many of those are reused many times and others are unique.

Triple Constraint

Every project is limited in different ways. These constraints are called Scope, Time, and Cost. The project manager must balance these often competing goals. One of the project management adages is "good, fast, and cheap, you can pick two."

> ➤ Scope (requirements): What the project manager is trying to accomplish in terms of a unique product or service.
> ➤ Time: How long will it take to complete the project?
> ➤ Cost: What should the cost be to complete the project?

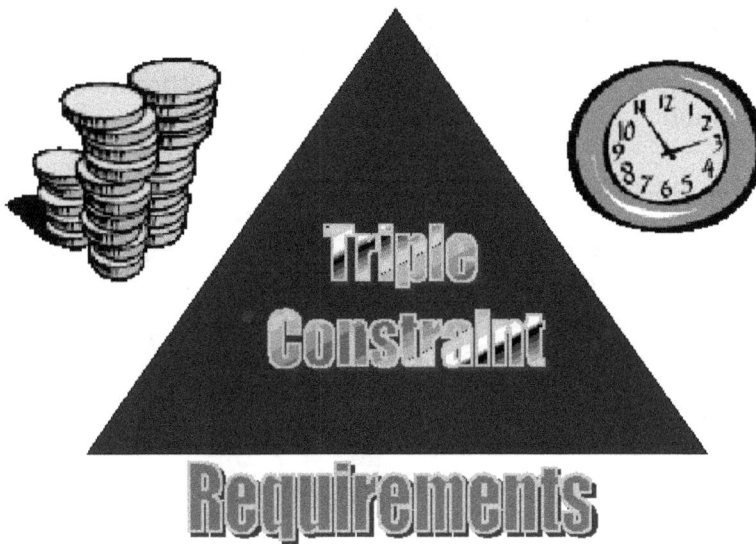

Understanding your organization and working within your organization's norms is more important than leveraging the latest management fad.

Illustration 3: Triple Constraints

Successful project managers must be able to adapt to further constraining and constricting of one side or goal. Constraining all of the goals introduces risk and reduces quality.

Organizational Behavior and Structures

Before this text launches into a deeper exploration of project mechanics, there is one additional and critical topic that factors into project management and project manager success – organizational behavior and structures. A good amount of project management concerns organizational behavior. Why? How your organization is structured and how you fit into that organization will determine a good deal of your success. Use an agile, seat-of-your-pants approach in a staid, established, guideline-driven organization and you lose. Conversely, strap down a fast-moving, new economy organization with too much rigor and structure in your project management approach and you may see passive or active aggressive resistance.

Project management deals with change. As a project manager, you are a change agent. Introduce too much change at once and the negative risk of organizational rejection escalates. A career limiting move (CLM for the acronym watchers) that some project managers make when joining a new organization is to force an approach (or more formally, project management methodology) that just will not fit. An exercise at the end of this chapter will help you assess your organizational culture and avoid that CLM.

Types of organizational structures

The PMBOK®'s focus is on organizational structure—not behavior. Four organizational structures are discussed in the PMBOK® with three derivatives of a matrix organization.

> **Pure or Functional** – pure or functional organizations are the older organizational forms – picture a traditional factory or typical military (i.e. "chain of command"). The impact on project management in this type of organization is threefold on role, authority, and communication:

- *ROLE*. The role of project manager is temporary – (e.g., someone is assigned temporary duty to organize an annual employee appreciation party but they do not relinquish their accounting job).
- *AUTHORITY.* The project manager has little or zero direct authority to accomplish the tasks (i.e., do not supervise resources or manage budget).
- *COMMUNICATION.* The project manager typically needs to route communication up and back down the chain of command to visit with team members in other organizational units.

> **Matrix** – this is where the vast number of organizations exist. Project management exists but the extent to which it is formalized and recognized varies. There are variations in terms of the extent of role, authority, and communication.

- *WEAK MATRIX.* A project coordinator/manager role may be established but the project coordinator must work through direct report managers to acquire resources and they have limited authority to ensure a project's success (though of course all of the responsibility). A key distinction between Weak Matrix and Functional organizational structures is that communication does not always have to go up and down the chain of command – direct communication with team members is assumed and allowed.

- *BALANCED MATRIX.* Often the catch all for anything in between the other types of balanced organizational structures incorporating varying levels of role, authority and communication scope. This is indeed the most common form for which project managers exist. They may have the ability to secure full-time personnel (also referred to as FTE's) and select vendors. However they may also need to coordinate with another direct report manager who manages the "people" side of that person's (direct report) existence. Challenges arise in a balanced matrix organization for resources who need to navigate the "Who do I really report to?'" phenomenon.

- *STRONG MATRIX.* This organizational structure often combines with attributes of the Fully Projectized structure but the organization has not made the complete jump into a projectized structure.

> ➤ **Projectized** – this is often perceived as an ideal state for project managers, as it establishes the role for direct leadership of projects. The organization orbits around the beautiful orb of project "managedom" and project managers often have direct report authority. This typically exists in organizations that are projectized not by the discipline of project management but rather a focus that places a strong subject matter expert, such as a leading physician, an engineer, or a consultant, as the orb for which the team members orbit around. A projectized structure is the best environment for project managers to exert their full array of project management skills.

> ➤ **Composite** – this is a hybrid form that allows and incorporates the understanding that organizations may not be uniform across all units and departments. Elements of each structure are incorporated at varying levels in different departments (e.g., business development may be strong matrix while information technology is a weak matrix).

Why does this matter? Organizational structure and design impacts team building, staff acquisition, and authority/responsibility balance. As shared in the Triple Constraint section, the exercise at the end of this chapter will help you understand the kind of organizational environment in which you fall. Project managers are typically not the "boss" of all team members, and even in Strong Matrix or Projectized organizational structures they will still need to procure resources outside the direct team. Much of project management success is determined by a manager's ability to lead a team that may only be working together on that particular project toward a common goal. Team members and the project manager will also have jobs elsewhere in theory.

In meeting those goals across a variety of organizations, project managers need to be excellent communicators. The project management team must have project management knowledge competency, project management performance competency, and personal competency.

The essence of the TAP Organizational Assessment (included as an exercise at the end of this chapter) is to help you gain a perspective of what kind of organization you work for and then how to approach the change activity based on your responses. So what is the value of this?

Change is not necessarily easier in a new, fluid organization. You may be trying to introduce stability and consistency to a fluid or "cowboy" environment — that's a change to them. Cowboy environments are typically found in founder led or early stage businesses, less than 15 years old. Heroic efforts are the expected norm. Process improvements, methodologies, and project management may be viewed skeptically.

Change in a traditional organization needs to be formal and mirror the organization in how it is introduced if it is going to be realized. Consistent communication is important in either one. How that communication is delivered needs to be tailored to your organization.

Chapter 1 Exercises

Exercise 1. Projects, Programs, and Ongoing Operations

A. Using your knowledge of Projects, Programs, and Ongoing Operations, identify each below.

1. Stuffed Friends Inc. is going to develop a new set of stuffed animals—a talking donkey and elephant that are to be on the shelves by Election Day.

    Project   Program   Ongoing Operations

2. Stuffed Friends Inc. has implemented a new policy to use a flame thrower at the end of every week to burn out the extra cotton stuffing in the machines so nothing becomes jammed from a build-up of cotton.

    Project   Program   Ongoing Operations

3. Sarah has been assigned to develop the new Flame Thrower Policy and make sure the new procedures are implemented smoothly.

    Project   Program   Ongoing Operations

4. Three new Stuffed Friends stores are being opened in Africa as part of a campaign to increase their market share overseas. A different project manager is being assigned to construct and build each store.

    Project   Program   Ongoing Operations

5. The talking elephant and donkey were so successful during the current election; that they will be produced again just before the next election.

    Project   Program   Ongoing Operations

B. Thinking of a current or past workplace, what would be an example of each of the following?

1. Project

2. Program

3. Ongoing Operations

Exercise 2. Why Do Projects Come Into Existence?

Why did this project come into existence?	Market demand	Organizational need	Customer request	Technological advance	Legal requirement
1. Because Stuffed Friends Inc. is crowded in its current headquarters, they are beginning a project to construct a larger building that will better suit their needs.					
2. A new synthetic fur-like fabric has been developed that is able to withstand fire, repels insects, has a pleasant odor, and is machine-washable. Stuffed Friends authorizes a project to gradually replace all their old stuffed animal fabric with this revolutionary fabric.					
3. A project has already been begun to redesign the unpopular stuffed shark toy. Customers have been complaining that the sharp glass teeth have been causing deep cuts, and asked that a cuddlier version be manufactured.					
4. Stuffed Friends Inc. needs a research report and implementation plan to change the stuffing of its toys to a flame-retardant material in order to comply with new federal consumer safety guidelines.					
5. The Opossum Fancier Association has requested ten thousand stuffed opossum toys be manufactured for its most loyal members. A project manager has been assigned to develop and launch this new project.					
6. Due to a recent trend in Green products, Stuffed Friends Inc. has authorized a project that will develop a feasibility report on creating a line of biodegradable native rainforest animals completely from recycled products.					
7. Unfortunately, a small project needs to be launched immediately to discreetly discontinue the jellyfish stuffed toy. Although the engineers had convinced marketing that a toy that produces a realistic electric shock would be successful, the Consumer Protection Agency deemed it unsafe.					

Exercise 3. Inputs / Tools & Techniques / Outputs

Practice conceptualizing a process's inputs, tools and techniques, and outputs. For these two processes, list as many inputs, tools and techniques, and outputs as you can.

Process Create an Apple Pie

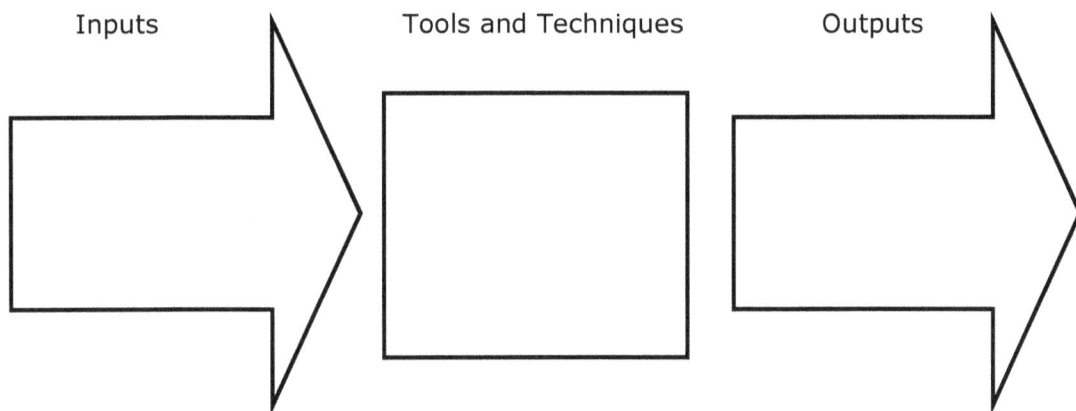

Inputs   Tools and Techniques   Outputs

Process Perform Lawn Mowing

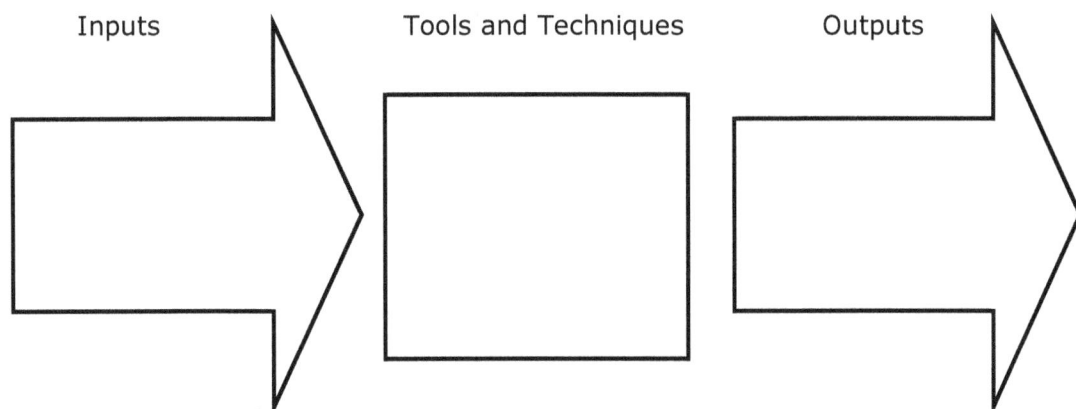

Inputs   Tools and Techniques   Outputs

Exercise 4. Practicing Process Patterns

The best way to learn the organization of the processes is to look for patterns. Using the table of 42 processes in chapter 1, answer the questions below.

1. Which is the only Knowledge Area that has processes in all five Process Groups?

2. Which two Knowledge Areas have processes in four of the five Process Groups?

3. Which is the only Process Group that has processes in all nine Knowledge Areas?

4. The three Quality processes all have what word in their name?

5. The six Risk processes all have what word in their name?

6. The four Procurement processes all have what word in their name?

7. The six Time processes all have one of which two words in their name?

8. If the word "Team" is in a process name, which Knowledge Area and Process Group must it be in?

9. If the word "Manage" is in a process name, which Process Group must it be in?

10. If the work "Plan" is in a process name, which Process Group must it be in?

11. If the work "Define" or "Estimate" is in a process name, which Process Group must it be in?

12. If the work "Close" is in a process name, which Process Group must it be in?

Exercise 5. TAPUniversity Organizational Assessment

Place an "x" where you think your organization is in each of the seven points.
- A Higher number of "x's" toward the right indicates structured, established organization.
- A Higher number of "x's" to the left indicates a changing, evolving organization. Each presents its own challenges to change.

The "right" may resist change while the left may be difficult to lasso in the "cowboy" mentality.

Duration

1. Company

New   Established

⟵─────────────────────────────────⟶

2. Project Management within the Company

New   Established

⟵─────────────────────────────────⟶

Documentation

3. Oral   Written

⟵─────────────────────────────────⟶

4. Ad Hoc   Routine

⟵─────────────────────────────────⟶

5. Individual Buckets   Central Repositories

⟵─────────────────────────────────⟶

Etiquette

Formal or casual dress code? Formal or informal titles (Sir/Ma'am, Last Name or First)? Who speaks first, rank or idea?

6. Informal   Formal

⟵─────────────────────────────────⟶

Change Agents

7. Accepted   Pushed back / out
Legitimized   *Ostracized*
Promotional material   *Temporary*

⟵─────────────────────────────────⟶

PMP Scrimmage® Curriculum, Edition 3.01   *Page 33*
www.tapuniversity.com
TECHNOLOGY
AS PROMISED

Exercise 6. Organizational Types

	Functional	Weak Matrix	Balanced Matrix	Strong Matrix	Projectized	Composite
1. Amy works at Aviary Architects where part of her job involves coordinating projects. Her team involves people from different departments and she has only limited authority over them.						
2. Ben is a project manager at Boats n' Barges. He has complete control over the project budget and has the reputation for firing team members who call their products "ships." His team members do not also have functional managers to report to and Ben reports directly to the CEO.						
3. Christine is a project manager at Comical Calendars. She has moderate authority over her team and she makes joint decisions about her team members with their functional managers. She is completely responsible for the project budget and has full-time administrative staff for the project.						
4. Diane works at Dazzling Diamonds. Although the company has a rigid hierarchy and established procedures, when a serious rhinestone mishap occurred, Diane was given the project to correct the situation. The situation was serious enough that she was given a high degree of authority over some of the best employees to form a team that was largely exempt from the standard reporting structure.						
5. Ernie is a project manager at Sesame Seeds. Although he works on projects full-time, his team members and administrative staff only work on projects part-time.						
6. Flora works at Fancy Fabrics as a project manager. She and the functional managers jointly control the project budget.						
7. George is a project manager at the corporate headquarters of Greasy Grub, a new fast-food chain. The CEO was formerly in the military and insists on a strict chain of command throughout the company. George occasionally coordinates a project that runs into difficulties because he has no authority over the team or resources.						
8. Harriet is a consultant at Hockey Help, a small sports consulting group. The company is set up so that each consultant mainly runs their own projects and has complete authority over their own team. Although the team members are assigned to only one consultant, there are a few administrative staff members in the company that provide services such as billing to all the consultants.						
9. Iris coordinates projects at Irritating In-laws, an old, well-established, large psychological counseling business. Her team only works on her projects a few hours a week and she has no authority over them. She must submit paperwork to her team's functional managers before assigning them tasks.						
10. Jake is a project manager at Just Jerky, a company specializing in unique meat products. His team members have functional managers although he does have a good deal of authority over the team. Jake reports to a Manager of Project Managers.						

Exercise 7. Stakeholders

Read the following paragraph and then identify the common stakeholders.

Jamie is an executive at Sugar-Laden Cereals. She has an idea for a new brand of cereal that is in the shape of little stalks of sugar cane. Jamie approves a project charter which names Kathy as responsible for this project. Kathy wants James and George to be on her team and to help with the more important decisions. George suggests that they sign a contract with Great Ingredients to obtain the sugar cane they need for this new cereal that they are unable to buy from their current supplier. James tells Kathy that Luis in the production department would be good to have on the team as he could be assigned to developing the shape of the cereal. Kathy negotiates with Luis' boss, Chester, to have him assigned part-time to this project. While working on her WBS, Kathy realizes she does not have the most recent template approved by Sugar-Laden Cereals. Kathy goes to the office where Katy works managing the paperwork for all projects across the organization, and Katy provides her with the most recent template. After six months, the project is a success, and shoppers are buying the new cereal in grocery stores across the globe.

Who works in the PMO?

Who is the Project Manager?

Who is the project Sponsor?

Who is a Functional Manager?

Who is on the Project Management Team?

Who is a Project Team Member (but not on the Project Management Team)?

Who are the Customers?

Who is a Vendor?

Chapter 2   - Manage your Project Portfolio

This chapter extends the concepts shared about programs and project portfolios in two ways:

1. By sharing techniques for managing a portfolio of projects and
2. By exploring tools to help select a project from among several promising candidates.

Successful program management requires robust configuration management. Why? Configuration management allows organizations and systems (human, computer or otherwise) to go from one known "state" to the next and roll-back if needed without interrupting ongoing operations. When successful program management and configuration management exist, the organizations can effectively and efficiently manage their entire *portfolio* of activities (project and operational).

The questions that should be answered include:

> ➢ Who is making changes?
> ➢ What are the changes?
> ➢ Are changes being communicated?
> ➢ Are changes necessary?

As new projects are evaluated or existing projects assessed for their next stage (also called stage gates or milestone reviews), the impact on existing operations and projects in the pipeline must be assessed.

Project Selection Techniques - Financial

Payback Period and Benefit to Cost Ratios

The two most common forms of financial selection are also less accurate than ones that consider the time value of money (based on net present value). However, since they are frequently used in the real world, we will address each one.

Payback Period

The payback period is simply when the project will break even with its initial investment and a set number of years of operation (one, two, or three years).

For example, a $100,000 project with revenue of $10,000 in each month beginning in month six of the project has a 16 month pay back period (10 months to pay it back plus six months from the beginning). Net present value (see below) can be applied to payback period to provide more precision.

Benefit to Cost Ratio

Benefit to Cost Ratio divides the benefits by the costs.　It can incorporate present values for both benefits and costs, although typically it does not.

Net Present Value (NPV)

Whether used to review the justification of a single project or used to assess multiple projects side by side – NPV is a key concept for bringing different project completion dates into an "apples to apples" view.
Benefit to Cost Ratio using:
Net Present Value (NPV) =PV (Cash Inflows) – PV (Cash Outflows)
NPV compares the value of a dollar today to the value of that same dollar in the future, taking into account inflation and returns. If the NPV of a prospective project is positive, it should be accepted. However, if NPV is negative, the project should probably be rejected because cash flows will also be negative.

For example, if a retail clothing business wants to purchase an existing store, it would first estimate the future cash flows that the store would generate, and then discount those cash flows into one lump-sum present value amount, say $565,000.

If the owner of the store was willing to sell his business for less than $565,000, the purchasing company would likely accept the offer as it presents a positive NPV investment. Conversely, if the owner would not sell for less than $565,000, the purchaser would not buy the store, as the investment would present a negative NPV at that time and would, therefore, reduce the overall value of the clothing company.[1]

The following is the "textbook" formula for Net Present Value.　Think "cints" as the word association (as in dollars and cents).

$$NPV = \sum_{t=0}^{N} \frac{C_t}{(1+i)^t} - Initial\,Investment$$

Illustration 4: NPV Formula

---

i　Project Management Institute, Guide to the Project Management Body of　Knowledge, Third Edition (2004).

Formula
C the cash flow at that point in time
i the weighted average cost of capital and
N the total length of the project (usually expressed in years)
t the amount of time (usually in years) that cash has been invested in the project

Let's simplify this just a bit.

PV = FV / (1+i)n
FV = PV * (1+i)n

Back to the $565,000 business. From existing operations the owner can anticipate growing six percent each year. The future value based on six percent interest over a five year period is $565,000 * 1.34 (rounding up) which is equal to $745,800 in year five annualized revenues. So, if you are selling your business and expect to make your replacement, revenue needs to be greater than $745,800.

Now $565,000 five years from now is not as much as it seems, even without accounting for inflation. It's worth $421,641 in today's present monetary value *(we hope we didn't just crush your retirement dreams)*.

Internal Rate of Return (IRR)

The internal rate of return (IRR) is defined as the discount rate that gives a NPV of zero. The NPV is calculated from an annualized cash flow by discounting all future amounts to the present. Due to the limitation of the IRR (setting NPV to zero), companies and investors often choose the Modified Internal Rate of Return (MIRR). The MIRR considers the cost of an organization's capitol. The key for IRR and MIRR is understanding when they are the preferred method for financial decision making.

Applying Financial Selection Techniques

The PMBOK® applies an order of magnitude or hierarchy of financial selection techniques. Know the rank order of the selection tools—IRR, NPV, Benefit-to-Cost, and lastly, Payback Period.
1. Internal Rate of Return (IRR) is the highest since it considers cost of reinvestment (Modified Internal Rate of Return, which sets IRR to 0, is not used at time of publishing of the PMBOK® or this text);
2. Net Present Value (NPV) is second since it considers the time value of money;
3. Benefit to Cost Ratio (that is not based on NPV) is third since it does give a cost of ownership in today's monetary units;
4. Payback period is the last. While this provides a quick rule of thumb to give a sense of when a cost is paid back – it does not factor present or future values of the investment or reinvestment.

Project Selection Techniques – Group Process

Project selection decisions employ other techniques to compliment or in place of financial selection techniques. Those techniques use group decision making processes ranging from group polling to nominal group technique. Here are some examples:

- Brainstorming
- Nominal Group Conference
- Force Field Analysis
- SWOT (strengths, weaknesses, opportunities, threats)
- Multi-voting

A useful tool for brainstorming and nominal group technique is a pairwise chart (see Table 5). The mission of a pairwise chart is to help a group compare competing projects or competing project requirements two at a time. The project or requirement that wins the most head to head competition, wins!

The following is an example of a pairwise chart for selecting a beverage or dessert. You can construct tables like these in MS Word, Open Office, or a spreadsheet by inserting a table with the maximum number of columns and rows you need, then formatting a line around the "stair step." In this example, the group began by voting whether that is tastes great or is less filling. The choice with the most votes is shown in bold.

Req A Tastes Great	Req A. Tastes Great			
Req B Less filling	**A** 　　B	Req B Less filling		
Req C Atkins friendly	**A** 　　C	**B** 　　C	Req C Atkins friendly	
Req D Makes you run faster	**A** 　　D	B 　**D**	C 　**D**	Req D Makes you run faster	
Req E Lets you slide into a stupor while sitting alone with the lights off in your basement wondering, "why, why me?"	**A** 　　E	B 　**E**	C 　**E**	D 　**E**	Req E Lets you slide into a stupor while sitting alone with the lights off in your basement wondering, "why, why me?"

Table 1: Sample Pairwise Chart

Chapter 2 Exercises

Exercise 8. Create Portfolio.

Select a project that you can use for this exercise. It can come from your current organization or a former one. For various classes we may decide to use a single project from a student from which everyone may learn. We've also included sample solutions for you — your project context will vary.

Step 1.

Answer the following questions to help you reflect on how your organization organizes its portfolio of activities.

If/when your current (former) organization does **not** pursue a project opportunity, what are the some of the reasons?

What are the top and bottom five clients of your organization in terms of the following items:
- Gross revenue
- Net revenue
- Growth opportunities
- People served – programs introduced (public sector/non-profit)

What does your organization do well in selecting and "juggling" multiple projects?

Step 2

Spend some time and collect what's on your task list, to do list, project list right now (today). It may include both project and operational activities (life isn't just new projects after all). The idea is to get a sense of your own personal project portfolio.

Factor	Project / Change Request #1 _____	Project / Change Request #2 _____	Project / Change Request #3 _____	Project / Change Request #4 _____
Scope				
# of people				
Return on Investment (H, M, L)				
Duration (months)				
Release date(s)				
Operational components impacted				
Compliance considerations				
Testing / QC preparation				
Current State				
Proposed State				

Exercise 9. Benefit-to-Cost and Payback Period

Practice calculating the Benefit-to-Cost Ratio and Payback Period for the following opportunities.

1. Fred believes his idea of starting a Jackalope farm will bring in $500,000. He calculates his expenses at $250,000.
> What is the benefit-to-cost ratio?
> Based on this, should he take this opportunity?

2. Lily finds that a full-page advertisement in a national journal will cost her $4,000. She estimates that it will bring her $3,500 in business.
> What is the benefit-to-cost ratio?
> Based on this, should she take this opportunity?

3. Wilma knows the gas station that has the cheapest gas around will take her 10 miles out of her way which will cost her $2 in gas. The gas there is 25 cents per gallon cheaper, and she needs ten gallons. Because she is bored she decides her time is worth nothing and should not be a factor in her calculations.
> What is the benefit-to-cost ratio?
> Based on this, should she drive to the cheapest gas station?

4. Rebecca thinks that her backyard garden will produce $500 in vegetables each year. Her expenses in the first year will be $980 as she needs to buy tools. Each year after that, she expects to pay only $20 in seeds.
> What is the Payback Period?

5. Jack's proposed project will earn nothing for three years, and after that he thinks it will earn $20,000 per fiscal quarter. It will cost $60,000 every year.
> What is the Payback Period?

6. Jill's idea for manufacturing a needed part in-house is calculated to cost $5000 per month. The first year will not produce savings, but after that the savings should be $90,000 per year.
> What is the Payback Period?

Exercise 10. NPV Exercise

#1 (**Example**) Mutant Foods Inc. is deciding whether to invest in genetically engineering a cross between carrots and broccoli (carroccoli). They will need to spend $200,000 immediately (year 0) on a special greenhouse. Cash outflow is expected to be $20,000 a year for years 1, 2, and 3. Cash inflow is expected to be $110,000 for years 1, 2, and 3. The rate of return is 10%. What is the NPV? Should the project be accepted?

Year	Inflow		Outflow		Discount Rate			Present Value
0 (	$0	-	$200,000)	/	1.10^0 =	1.00	=	-$200,000
1 (	$110,000	-	$20,000)	/	1.10^1 =	1.10	=	$81,818
2 (	$110,000	-	$20,000)	/	1.10^2 =	1.21	=	$74,380
3 (	$110,000	-	$20,000)	/	1.10^3 =	1.33	=	$67,618

NPV $23,817

1. For each year, including year 0, record the cash inflow and outflow.
2. Add 1 to the discount rate. The discount rate of .10 is added to 1, which equals 1.10.
3. This amount of the discount rate plus 1 is then raised to the power of the time of the cash flow. In this example, the time is the year. So for year 2: $1.10^2 = 1.10 * 1.10 = 1.21$.
4. For each year, subtract the outflow from the inflow and divide it by your discount rate raised to the power of the time. This is your present value. So for year 2, ($110,000 - $20,000) / 1.21 = $74,380.
5. Add all the PVs to obtain your NPV, which here is $23,817.
6. If your NPV is positive, the project should be accepted.

#2 Mutant Foods, Inc. just learned that the Veggie Gardeners Union will be demanding better benefits in the next three years, but that the forecasted demand for strange-looking and strangely-named vegetables will be greater than expected. They will still need $200,000 to get started and the rate of return is still 10%, but now cash outflow is expected to be $35,000 and cash inflow is expected to be $150,000 for each of the first three years. What is the NPV? Should the project be accepted?

Year	Inflow		Outflow		Discount Rate		Present Value
	(	-	)	/	=	=	
	(	-	)	/	=	=	
	(	-	)	/	=	=	
	(	-	)	/	=	=	

NPV

TECHNOLOGY
AS PROMISED

Exercise 11. Financial Selection Techniques.

For each of the four scenarios, choose either Project A or Project B as the better financial decision.

	Project A	Project B	Which project would you pick?
1. Net Present Value (what is the value of the project in today's monetary unit?)	$95,000	$75,000	
2. Internal Rate of Return (what is the percentage return of the project)	17%	14.5%	
3. Payback Period (how long will it take to pay off the cost of the project)	21 months	18 months	
4. Benefit Cost Ratio (what is the ratio of NPV benefits to cost?)	2.2	1.8	

Exercise 12. More Practice on Financial Selection Techniques

	Project A	Project B
1. The Polar Bear Club is trying to prevent polar bears from injuring themselves by slipping on ice. Project A involves posting signs warning of icy spots and has a benefit-to-cost ratio of 5.1. Project B involves relocating the bears to Florida and has a benefit-to-cost ratio of 1.2.		
2. The Chameleon Car Company is experimenting with cars that can change colors. Project A involves developing a special auto body metal and has a payback period of 47 months. Project B involves developing special car paint and has a payback period of 13 months.		
3. Polly Tishun is running for governor and is contemplating the best strategy to raise campaign funds. Project A focuses upon television ads and has an IRR of 61%. Project B focuses on expensive dinners and has an IRR of 92%.		
4. Kathy is deciding what type of drink she should sell to supplement the meager allowance she receives from her parents. Project A is to sell lemonade and has a NPV of $25. Project B is to sell chocolate milk and has a NPV of $11.		
5. A group of sports enthusiasts are trying to decide between two investments. Project A is to buy a well-known football team which has an IRR of 12% and a benefit-to-cost ratio of 1.5. Project B is to buy a lesser-known baseball team which has an IRR of 10% and a benefit-to-cost ratio of 2.5.		
6. Paper Dolls, Inc. is having trouble deciding on a potential new direction. Project A uses plain paper and prints colors with ink on the dolls which would be an investment of $50 K and would return $10 K for the first three months and $5 K every month after that. Project B uses colored paper which would be an investment of $80 K and would return $20 K per month.		
7. Mutant Veggies, Inc. has to determine which product will be more profitable. Project A is to develop a cross between eggplant and tomatoes "Eggmatoes" and has a payback period of 2 years and a NPV of $2.3 M. Project B is to develop a cross between carrots and broccoli "Carroccolli" and has a payback period of 22 months and a NPV of $2.1 M.		
8. Melvin and Maggie are mulling over whether to farm their land with modern machinery or a mule team. Project A, using modern machinery, has a payback period of 25 years and a benefit-to-cost ratio of 1.4. Project B, using a mule team, has a payback period of 2 months and a benefit-to-cost ratio of 53.7.		
9. Carla is wondering if getting more education would be a good investment. Project A, earning her MBA, has a benefit-to-cost ratio of 3, a NPV of $400 K, and an IRR of 300%. Project B, not getting any more education but working more hours, has a benefit-to-cost ratio of 2.5, a NPV of $200 K, and an IRR of 320%.		
10. Tropical Treats, a candy store near the equator, is selecting among projects to help cut their operating costs—specifically the outrageous expense of air conditioning. Project A, have the store open during the night when it's cooler instead of the day, has a benefit-to-cost ratio of .83 and a NPV of $ -25 K. Project B, switch the required employee uniform of a sweatshirt with the company's logo to a t-shirt with the company's logo, has a benefit-to-cost ratio of 1.3 and a NPV of $500.		

Exercise 13. Force Field Analysis

Think of a problem to solve or a potential project that is being considered. On the left side, write a driving force such as an advantage, and directly across from it write a restraining force that is the disadvantage.

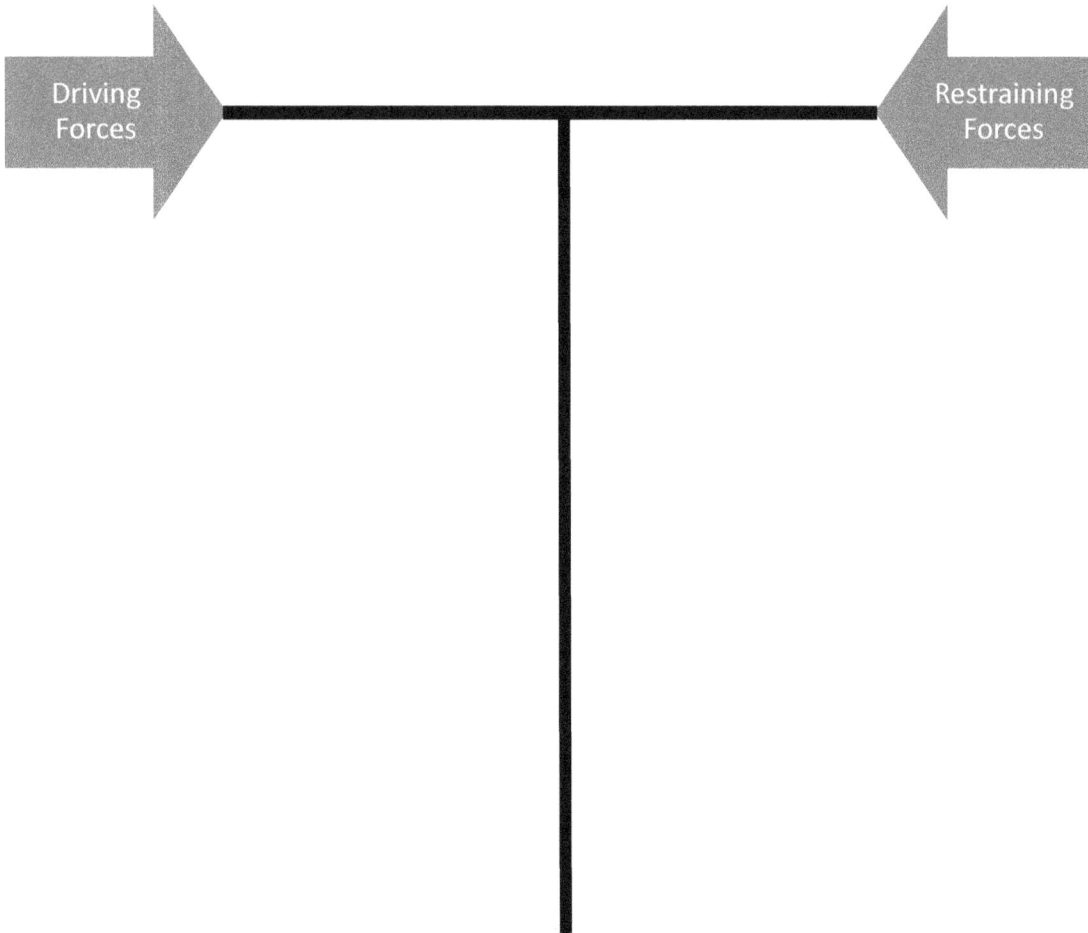

Exercise 14. SWOT Analysis

Think of an example project. It can be the project you are using as an example throughout the workbook or a different one. What are the strengths, weaknesses, opportunities and threats?

Strengths

Weaknesses

Opportunities

Threats

Exercise 15. Pairwise Chart

Complete the following pairwise chart to assess which one of the following project opportunities your team should pursue (it's a given that in real life you'll probably pursue **all** of them).   Use ROI (return on investment), fit with project delivery and new market opportunities as possible considerations.

First select five potential projects.

   For example
   - A. Insurance company portal (agents or customers)
   - B. Software for contracts
   - C. Supply chain maintenance integrated with POS
   - D. Material supply of very important utility stuff
   - E. Sarbanes Oxley compliance email path

Second, compare your project one project at a time by circling or bolding the **winner**.

Third, complete all comparisons and then review again with your team.

Project A	Project A.			
Project B	A B	Project B		
Project C	A C	B C	Project C	
Project D	A D	B D	C D	Project D
Project E	A E	B E	C E	D E	Project E

Exercise 16. *Movie Pairwise Chart*

You are on the International Cinematic Awards committee to determine which movie should receive the title of Greatest Movie of All Time. You have been asked to make a selection from six nominations. Each movie will be compared individually to all of the others for a committee vote. First, *Casablanca* will be compared to *Gone with the Wind*. Record the winner and number of votes in that box. For example, if 8 people chose *Casablanca* and two people chose *Gone with the Wind*, you would record A 8 in that box (this assumes that the same number of people will be participating in every vote). The shaded boxes are not to be filled in—they represent duplicate comparisons. Next, tally the votes in the bottom table to determine the winner.

	A. Casablanca	B. Gone with the Wind	C. Sound of Music	D. Star Wars	E. The Godfather	F. West Side Story
A. Casablanca						
B. Gone With the Wind						
C. Sound of Music						
D. Star Wars						
E. The Godfather						
F. West Side Story						

Movie	Votes	Overall Ranking
A. Casablanca		
B. Gone With the Wind		
C. Sound of Music		
D. Star Wars		
E. The Godfather		
F. West Side Story		

Chapter 3   -   Begin Project (Initiation)

Your organizational environment discerned, project fundamentals mastered, and project selected, we now move this workbook to effective ways to begin your project. There are four essential things that need to happen in order to begin a project:

1. There needs to be authorization from the sponsoring organization (i.e., your company needs to authorize it).
2. A project manager needs to be identified and their role and responsibility established.
3. The scope of the project needs to be articulated.
4. The approach that will be used to guide, plan, and update the project documents, team, and stakeholders needs to be identified.

The PMBOK® specifies two processes in the Initiation Process Group: Develop Project Charter and Identify Stakeholders. The third edition PMBOK® had another initiation process called Develop Preliminary Project Scope Statement and did not have the Identify Stakeholders process.

Develop Project Charter (4.1)

The purpose of this process is to create the project charter. Its only tool & technique is expert judgment. Notice that expert judgment is a tool & technique for all six integration processes, and it is the only tool & technique for four of those six processes.

> **Other terms for Project Charter:**
> *Project Initiation Document (PID)
> *Statement of Work (SOW)
> *Project Request

The project charter does the following:

> ➢ Recognizes formally the existence of a project.
> ➢ Provides direction for everyone involved.
> ➢ Delineates project versus department authorization and responsibilities.
> ➢ Serves as a contract between the project manager and key stakeholders.
> ➢ Clarifies purpose and establishes a mission for the project team.
> ➢ Outlines roles of functional managers from their involvement during the project (advisory or resource broker) to their role as the products of the project are placed into service or production.
> ➢ Allows the project team to understand the mission of the project. Some organizations assemble the team after the project has begun. The introduction of those team members is typically done through a project kick off.
> ➢ Allows buy-in and understanding by key stakeholders.
> ➢ Helps define the project scope statement. While treated as a separate process, primarily for focus within the PMBOK®, the project scope statement is the definition of the project – what needs to be accomplished. It is developed from

information provided by the initiator or sponsor. The project manager is actively involved in creating the scope statement.

The project charter is often prepared by the project manager (with input from stakeholders and project team) and authorized for release by another manager. The PMBOK® states this should be a manager outside the project team or sponsor. In practice the project sponsor is the one who typically issues the charter. Once the project begins, the scope of the project becomes clearer as project activities progress. In some organizations the project charter serves as the beginning and planning stages of a project. Most organizations and best practices (from PMBOK® and leading project methodologies) include a separate step for project planning.

The process of the scope becoming clearer and more fully developed is called progressive elaboration (PE). That term is often and easily confused with another term associated with a Work Breakdown Structure (WBS) – decomposition. The key distinction is that progressive elaboration further refines and develops from unknown to known; whereas decomposition subdivides and arranges that which is known. Progressive Elaboration is a bit like redecorating your living room or completing a landscape project. You know what you like, maybe have seen it in a magazine or HGTV, but you plan to work out the details with a professional as you go along. Decomposition is taking the well specified item (an 18' oval shaped fish pond), separating the deliverables and activities into more detailed parts and then organizing them all.

Identify Stakeholders (10.1)

This process is new to the fourth edition PMBOK®. Stakeholders are those who have a stake (or interest) in the outcome of a project. Stakeholders can be individuals, groups, or entire organizations. If they desire that the project be a success, they are termed positive stakeholders. If they desire that the project fail (for example, a competitor), they are termed negative stakeholders.

Stakeholders should be identified early and their relevant characteristics should be documented. Because there are often so many stakeholders, it is advantageous to categorize them into groups.

The project charter, along with procurement documents if a contract is involved, are among the inputs. Stakeholder analysis and expert judgment are the tools and techniques. The outputs from this process are the Stakeholder Register, which includes identifying information, assessment and classification of the stakeholders, and the Stakeholder Management Strategy which is a plan to increase support from the stakeholders and minimize their potential negative impact on the project.

Chapter 3 Exercises

TECHNOLOGY
AS PROMISED

Exercise 17. Organizational Process Assets versus Enterprise Environmental Factors

1. For each, decide whether it is an Organizational Process Asset or an Enterprise Environmental Factor.

	Organizational Process Asset	Enterprise Environmental Factor
Probability and impact matrix		
Marketplace conditions		
Stakeholder risk tolerances		
Commercial database		
Lessons learned documentation from old project		
Project Management Information Systems		
Proposal evaluation criteria		
Organization's building		
Strict and formal culture		
Company's defect management database		
WBS template		
Employee performance reviews		
Change control procedures		
Time reporting procedures		

2. What do you see as the key differences between Organizational Process Assets and Enterprise Environmental Factors?

Exercise 18. SOW

The Statement of Work (SOW) is an input to the Develop Project Charter process. Create a brief Statement of Work for a project (either an imaginary or a project you have been involved in).

1. What are the characteristics of the products or services that are to result from this project?

2. What is the business need for the project? (market demand, technological advance, organizational need, legal requirement, etc.)

3. How does this project fit with the organization's strategic goals?

Exercise 19. Stakeholder Analysis

Stakeholder Analysis is a tool and technique of the Identify Stakeholders process. Stakeholders may be classified in a variety of ways such as Power/Interest, Will/Skill, Power/Influence, and Influence/Impact. This exercise has a Power/Interest grid.

Think of an actual project that you've worked on. Write the names of at least five of the key stakeholders in the grid below depending on their power and interest level. Those with the most power will be in the top half, and those with the most interest will be on the right side.

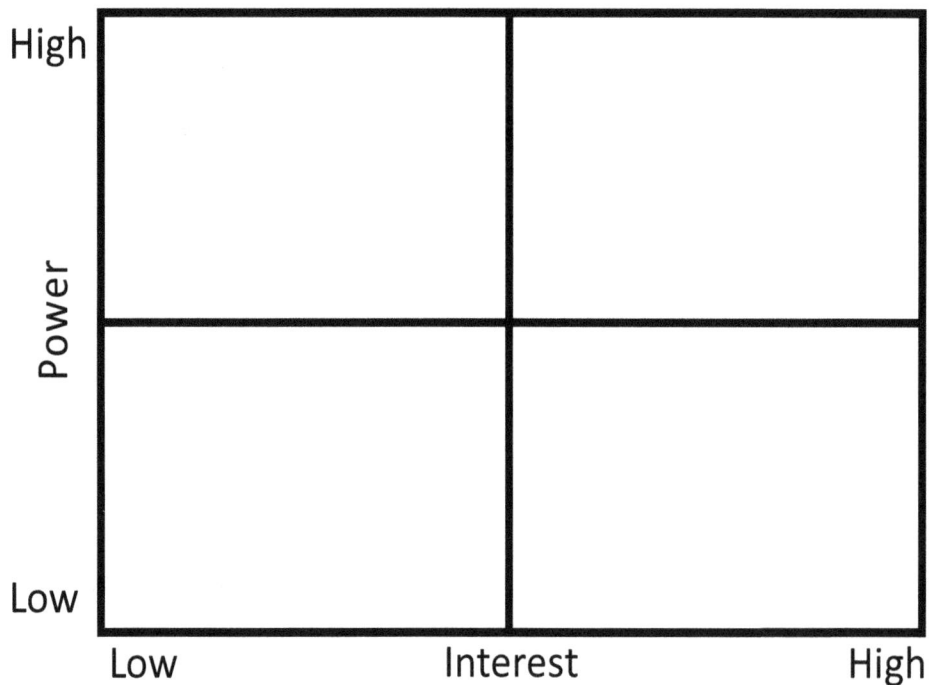

Exercise 20. Stakeholder Register

The stakeholder register is an output of the Identify Stakeholders process. It consists of Identification Information, Assessment Information, and Stakeholder Classification. The way stakeholders are classified will vary from project to project. Using the example, fill in the registry for a project of your choice.

Identification Information			Assessment Information		Stakeholder Classification
Name of Stakeholder	**Job Title**	**Role in Project**	**Expectations for project**	**Influence on Project**	**Classification**
Mr. Jones	Lead Archeologist	Determine direction	Find treasure and fame	High—ability to cancel	Internal

Exercise 21. Stakeholder Management Strategy

The stakeholder management strategy is an output of the Identify Stakeholders process. It is designed to document ways to increase support and minimize negative impacts of stakeholders. Only key stakeholders are included here along with a note on their interest and potential impact on the project.

Name of Key Stakeholder	Interest in Project	Assessment of Impact	Potential Strategies for Gaining Support or Reducing Obstacles
Mr. Jones	Personal Fame	High—has ability to end project	Remind him often that when the treasure he finds as the result of this project is placed in a museum, there will be a plaque next to it with his name.

Chapter 4　　-　　Plan your Project (Planning)

Congratulations, you are the proud parent of a failed project. Wait a minute; no one has ever just flat out said that. But do you ever wonder? Does it ever feel like you're the project manager of misfit projects (toys) on that 1960's Christmas Animation classic, "Rudolph the Red nose Reindeer?" You know with team members that look like they could be Cornelius Bill, Jack in the Box, or the Abominable Snow Monster. If your project beginning, initiation, and chartering experiences feel as productive as running under a bus or Santa's sleigh, hold on. There may be some information and exercises that can help in this rather lengthy chapter of ours.

Best Practice-- Do not implement all of the processes within the PMBOK or any another project management methodology all at once. Ease in the introduction and gain excellence through successful repetition.

Develop Project Management Plan (4.2)

The Develop Project Management Plan process within the Project Integration Knowledge Area is where the plans crafted in each of the Planning processes are collected. It is also where guidance is provided on how the project will unfold or proceed.

The Organizational Process Assets that serve as an input here include change control procedures.

> Configuration management provides and applies technical and administrative direction and monitoring to validate what the current product, service, or environment is and how your project's outputs and deliverables will change that. It helps to ensure that any change in the state of your organization's environment is understood and known and that the revised state or environment can be validated. It addresses both the organization and project.

> The change control system works within configuration management to control changes during the project itself.

The Project Management Plan is the sole output of Develop Project Management Plan. That output integrates and connects the subsidiary project plans (e.g., Scope, Schedule, Quality, Human Resource, Communications, Risk and Procurement Plans).

Collect Requirements (5.1)

Collect Requirements is a process new to the fourth edition PMBOK®. The requirements being collected are the needs and expectations of the stakeholders. Various techniques, such as interviews and focus groups, are used to elicit these requirements so that they may be documented in detail. The outputs of this process are the Stakeholder Requirements Document, Requirements Management Plan, and the Requirements Traceability Matrix.

Define Scope (5.2)

This process was called Scope Definition in the third edition PMBOK®. This process creates the Project Scope Statement which is a detailed description of the project and product. The Project Scope Statement includes the following:

- ➢ Product scope description
- ➢ Project deliverables
- ➢ Project boundaries
- ➢ Product acceptance criteria
- ➢ Assumptions
- ➢ Constraints

The following scope illustration provides a useful tool to work with stakeholders as well as a template to create the primary output of Define Scope - the Project Scope Statement.

Scope Illustration

This illustration shows scope at the simplest level - what's in/what's out and who's in/who's out of the project.　It was derived from an Object Oriented project management workshop delivered by Lois Zells in 1992.[i] Applying this figure with an example, you can begin to see, on a simple level how this communicates the scope of the project.

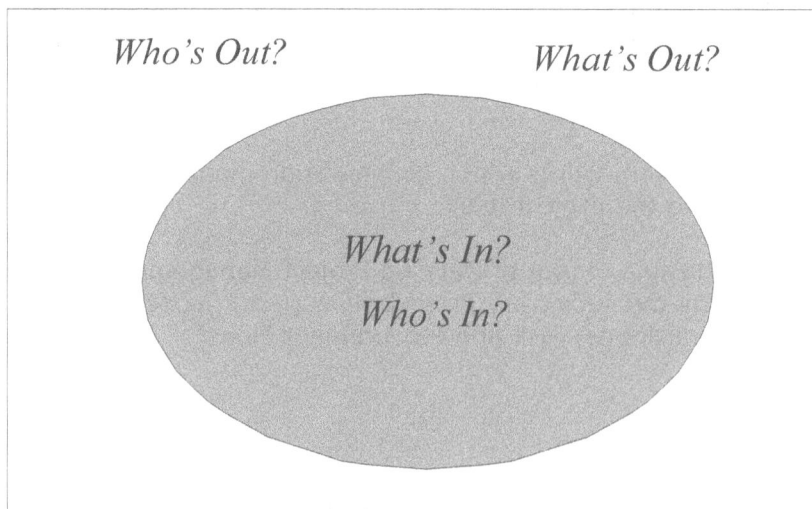

Illustration 5: Scope Statement

Create Work Breakdown Structure (5.3)

This process was called Create WBS in the third edition PMBOK®. The WBS is the fulcrum to modern project management. From it, cost accounts (charter of accounts) can be organized, consistent project updates formed, and schedule activities grouped.

Work Breakdown Structures focus on the deliverable side of a project. Deliverables are tangible objects, products, and artifacts. Examples include reports, software, blueprints, site design, and instruction manuals. Activities are the verbs or actions necessary to create those deliverables. For example, compose a report is the activity; the report is the deliverable.

Best Practice - Reuse and refine previous WBS's and Project Schedules.

The illustration below shows the top–down structure of a WBS. It goes from the project name at the top, down to a task or work package level at the bottom level. By PMBOK® definition the work package is the lowest level of the WBS where work deliverables are assigned. This illustrates decomposition.

The templates a project team uses may be in the form of an organization chart (as shown here) or an indentured, outline list. The key outputs are the WBS itself and the WBS Dictionary. The WBS dictionary is a set of definitions for each WBS element.

```
                          ┌─────────────────┐
                          │    Insurance    │
                          │     Portal      │
                          └────────┬────────┘
          ┌────────────────────────┼────────────────────────┐
  ┌───────┴───────┐        ┌───────┴───────┐        ┌────────┴────────┐
  │    Project    │        │  Requirements │        │ Portal Prototype│
  │ Administration│        │               │        │ (work package)  │
  └───────┬───────┘        └───────┬───────┘        └─────────────────┘
          │                        │
  ┌───────┴───────┐        ┌───────┴───────┐
  │    Weekly     │        │    Gather     │
  │    Status     │        │  Functional   │
  │   Reports     │        │ Requirements  │
  │   (work       │        │               │
  │   package)    │        │               │
  └───────────────┘        └───────┬───────┘
```

	PMP® Exam Tip The work package is the lowest level of the WBS!

```
        ┌───────────┬───────────┬───────────┐
  ┌─────┴─────┐ ┌───┴─────┐ ┌───┴───────┐
  │   User    │ │ Security│ │ Insurance │
  │ Interface │ │ (work   │ │Illustrations│
  │(work      │ │ package)│ │(work package)│
  │ package)  │ │         │ │           │
  └───────────┘ └─────────┘ └───────────┘
```

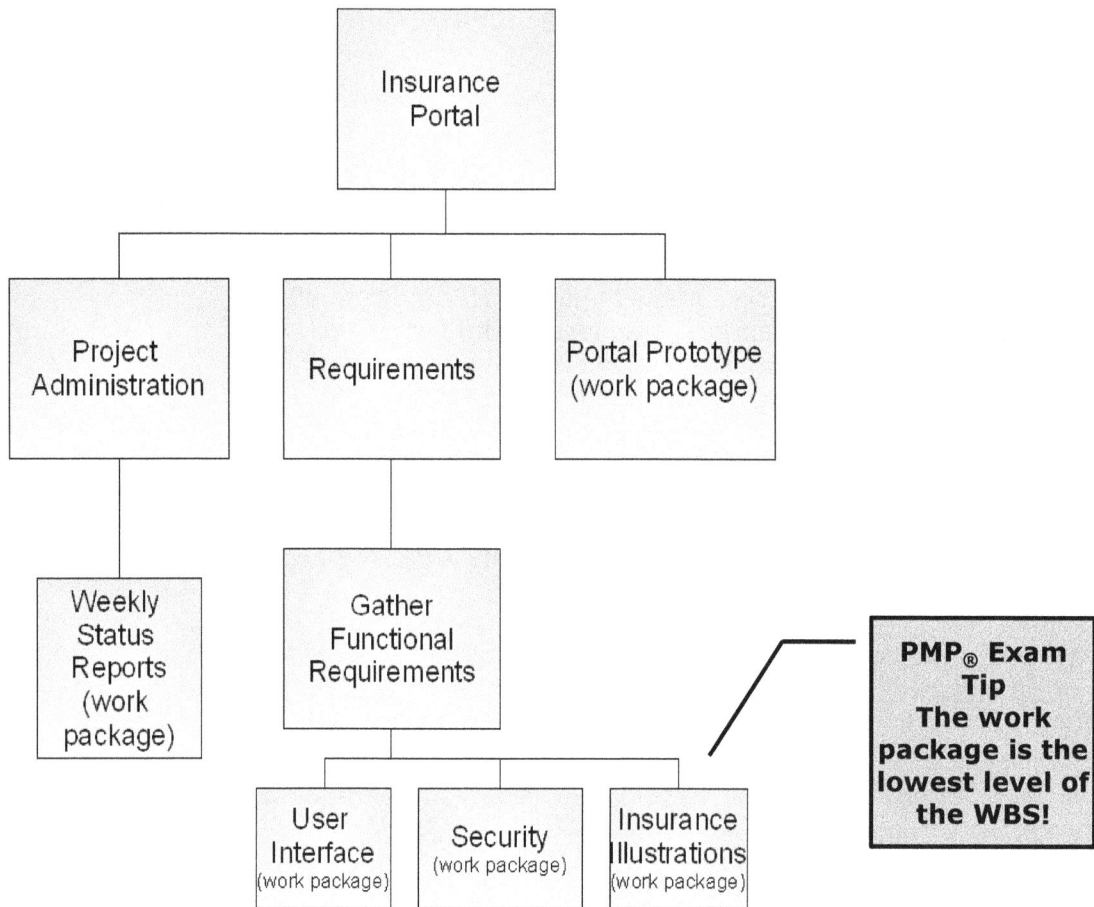

Illustration 6: Insurance Portal WBS

Work not in the WBS is outside the scope of the project!

Time and Schedule Planning (6.1 to 6.5 of the PMBOK®)

There are five processes that occur within Time and Schedule Planning. These are:

1. Define Activities 6.1 (Activity Definition in third edition PMBOK®)
2. Sequence Activities 6.2 (Activity Sequencing in third edition PMBOK®)

3. Estimate Activity Resources 6.3 (Activity Resource Estimating in third edition PMBOK®)
4. Estimate Activity Durations 6.4 (Activity Duration Estimating in third edition PMBOK®)
5. Develop Schedule 6.5 (Schedule Development in third edition PMBOK®)

The WBS establishes the deliverables for your project. As discussed in the previous section, WBS deliverables are tangible artifacts (nouns). Activities are the things that need to happen to create those deliverables. They are the verbs.

The steps involved in specifying those things are Define Activities first, then Sequence Activities, Estimate Activity Resources, and Estimate Activity Durations (which can occur in parallel), then finally Develop Schedule.

Best practice rule of thumb – activities should be between 4 and 40 hours & tied to a single person or resource.

Define Activities (6.1)

Activities should be broken down into the lowest level from which a product can be developed. The general rule is greater than four hours and less than 40 hours. Also as you develop you schedule elements, insert Activities which can be used as milestones.

Examples include:
➢ Project charter document completed
➢ System hardware operational
➢ Software delivered

Sequence Activities (6.2)

Once the activities are defined, then they can be sequenced, estimated, and resources assigned. Sequencing and estimating the duration of activities paves the way to determine the length of a project. Activities need to be sequenced in chronological order. Look for relationships and dependencies among activities while sequencing them. Determine which activities cannot start until another is complete. A good network (or set of dependent, related activities) is key to having a solid project plan to start the project.

Questions to ask yourself when determining the relationships among activities and sequence include:
1. Do two or more activities need to be completed before one can start?
2. What activities depend on other activities?
3. What work can be done in parallel?

There are four accepted forms of activity relationships:

➢ **Finish to Start:** Initiation of the work of the successor depends upon completion of predecessor. Activity B cannot start until Activity A has completed. For instance, you must buy a new computer before the new software can be installed. This is the most common of the four types of relationships.

➢ **Finish to Finish:** Completion of the work of the successor depends on completion of predecessor. Activity A must finish before Activity B can finish. For instance, the turkey must finish cooking before the potatoes finish cooking.

➢ **Start to Start:** Initiation of successor depends upon initiation of predecessor. Activity A must start before Activity B can start. For instance, you must start painting the walls before wallpaper can be hung.

➢ **Start to Finish:** Completion of the successor is dependent upon the initiation of the predecessor. Activity A must start before Activity B can finish (rare). For instance, you must start fertilizing the garden, before I can finish watering the garden.

Once all activities are known (defined) and sequenced the critical path can then be determined. The Critical Path Method (CPM) is the longest series of dependent activities to complete a project. It reveals also the quickest way the project can be done.

Before our extended discussion regarding critical path, let's review two ways of displaying a network diagram (see illustrations below). The first one, activity on the node (AON), is the default for project scheduling software (Clarity, Microsoft, Primavera, and VPMI). The activity name is listed on each node.

The second one, activity on the arrow (AOA), lists the activity name on the arrow then numbers each circle or node. That was used predominantly in the pre-software era of the 1950's to 1960's when schedules were literally hand drawn on butcher paper in project war rooms (e.g. Nimitz submarine and Apollo Moon Mission).

Two Types of Networks: Activity on the Node and Activity on the Arrow.

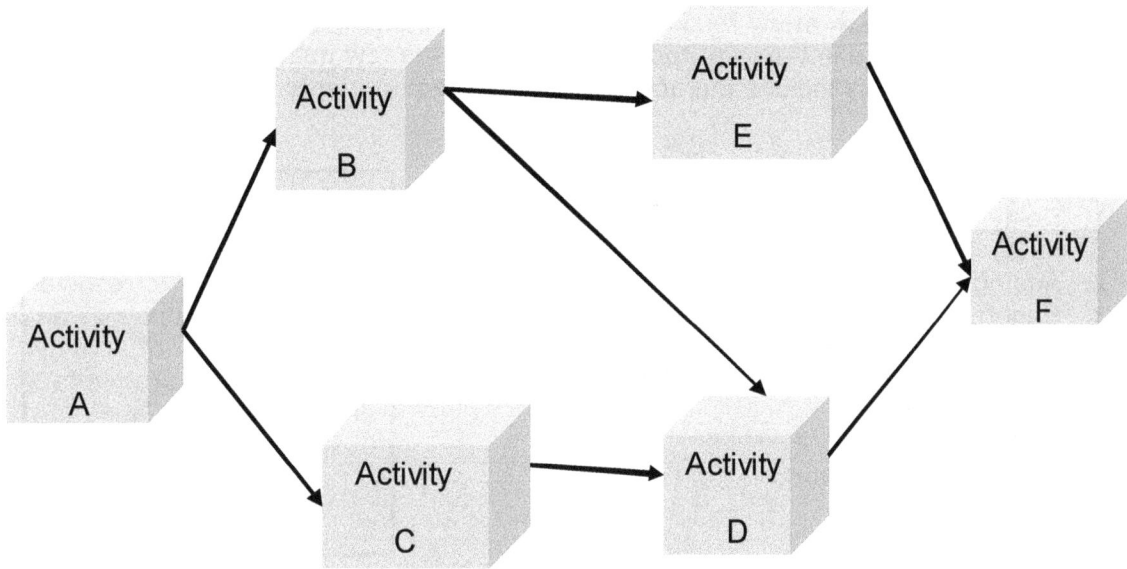

Illustration 7: Activity on Node

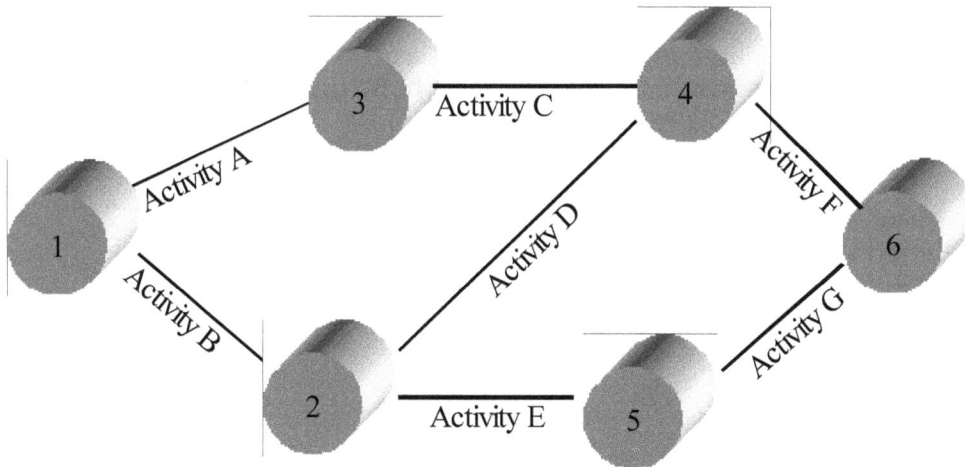

Illustration 8: Activity on Arrow

Estimate Activity Resources (6.3)

Estimate Activity Resources includes people and things. These things are known as equipment, material, and consumables. People include internal employees (full time equivalent – FTE) and external contractors or vendors. The process is tasked with estimating what and how many resources. As resource assignments are requested problems typically arise in terms of too much work for too few qualified resources. Outputs for this process include the activity resource requirements and resource breakdown structure.

You can resolve resource problems by:
1. Delaying selected activities (extend the finish date)
2. Adding additional resources
3. Negotiating for more highly skilled resources
4. Assigning a different resource
5. Re-evaluating task dependencies
6. Reducing Scope
7. Reducing Quality
8. Adding overtime work

PMP® Exam Tip.
Know the ways to resolve resource problems as well as the similarity of Activity Resource Requirements Tools and Techniques to Cost Estimating Tools and Techniques.

Estimate Activity Durations (6.4)

Estimate Activity Durations is one of the most difficult processes in planning a project. It is also the root cause of most project communication breakdowns and failures – the expectation of how long an activity should take versus reality can be a bitter pill to swallow. At the end of a continuum of duration estimating challenges are Parkinson's Law, meaning work expands to fill the time allotted to perform it to not allowing sufficient time to complete the activity.

There are three general problems that result from poor estimates:
1. Under-estimating can cause team to work overtime
2. Over-estimating brings your credibility into question
3. Most accurate estimate – this may cause problems if slippage occurs however there's usually a plausible explanation. This is the best practice and recommended approach.

Develop Schedule (6.5)

With the activities fully defined and sequenced as well as duration and resource load estimated, the all important scheduling development process can proceed. There are two concepts that merit review: lead and lags and imposed date constraints. They are important since they can constrict and impose the scheduled delivery of a project.

Lead and lags are typically outside the performing organization's control. Leads impose a certain duration of time before an activity begins; lags impose a certain length of time after an activity is completed before the next one can begin. Bottom line, they need to be factored into your time estimates.

They are dependent upon a third party in the supply chain or just simple matters of physics. For example, orders within a supply chain require lead time – now the efficiency in a just-in-time production world trims order time – but time for successful fulfillment needs to be factored in. Physical lags include paint or cement drying, establishing a lawn, or cultivating a watershed. They require time to complete – the "watched pot never boils" comes to mind.

Additional schedule constraints include imposed Start-Stop dates that restrict schedule development when key milestones or deliverables must be met. A firm that provides election day balloting equipment cannot miss election day; a supplier delivering the newest Halloween custom or Christmas toys is out of luck if supplying either on November 1 or December 26 respectively; a Tax Software company whose electronic data interchange with the IRS is unavailable on April 10–15 can be out of business.

Imposed Date Constraints can consist of:
1. Start no earlier than (the first day of outdoor swimming)
2. Finish no later than (December 24 for shipping of Christmas gifts)
3. Start no later than (the day after Thanksgiving for delivery of the latest "Tickle me Elmo")
4. Start on (Election Day balloting)

Critical Path

Critical Path Method (CPM) is a tool and technique of Develop Schedule. It uses a bottom up method to estimate the duration of each activity. It allows a project manager to roll up major deliverables and activities needed to produce those deliverables. The critical path of dependent activities is the longest path through the schedule network. That longest path is also the shortest time the project can be completed; which is why it is called "critical" path.

So what happens to those paths not on the critical path? Do we abandon them, neglect them? Absolutely not. Critical path does not convey importance of each activity on the path – just the longest set of dependent activities. It is used for time estimation and for monitoring the schedule's performance. It's important to also determine the slack or float for each non-critical path activity. It's also important to identify that secondary critical path as they often can become the critical path.

Let's work through a graphic example that helps explain the total number of days for each pathway, critical path, secondary critical path, and float. Work through the five steps as presented – the arithmetic is simple but skipping steps often introduces mistakes on the PMP® exam.

The following diagram has Tasks A – P with a separate Start and Finish task.

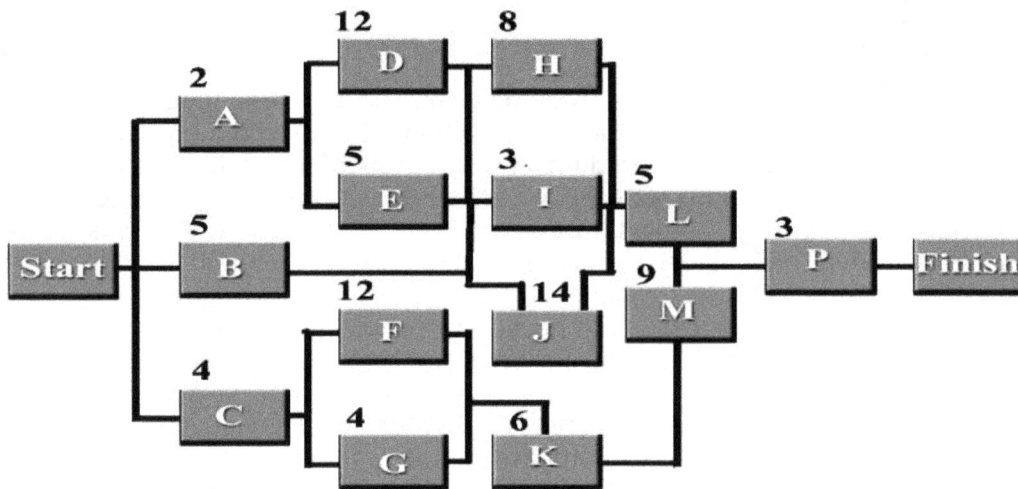

Illustration 9: Critical Path Sample - Beginning

The steps to understand this are as follows.

Step 1 - How many paths are there?

Answer: There are 11
1. A-D-H-L-P
2. A-D-I-L-P
3. A-D-J-L-P
4. A-E-H-L-P
5. A-E-I-L-P
6. A-E-J-L-P
7. B-J-L-P
8. B-I-L-P
9. B-H-L-P
10. C-F-K-M-P
11. C-G-K-M-P

Step 2 – What is the duration of each path?

Path	Duration
1. A-D-H-L-P	30
2. A-D-I-L-P	25

Path	Duration
3. A-D-J-L-P	36
4. A-E-H-L-P	23
5. A-E-I-L-P	18
6. A-E-J-L-P	29
7. B-J-L-P	27
8. B-I-L-P	16
9. B-H-L-P	21
10. C-F-K-M-P	34
11. C-G-K-M-P	26

Step 3 – What is the critical path?

A-D-J-L-P 36

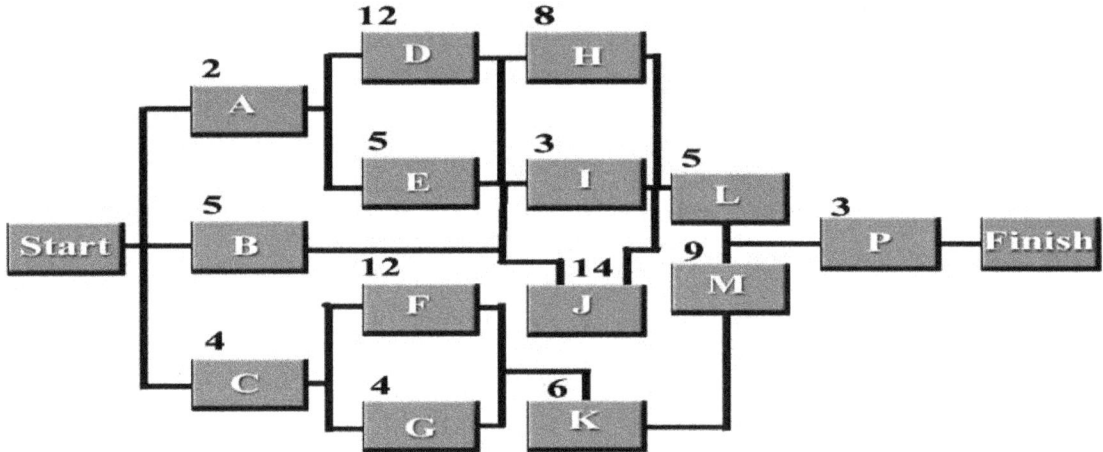

Illustration 10 – The Critical Path

Step 4 – What is the secondary path? C-F-K-M-P = 34 units

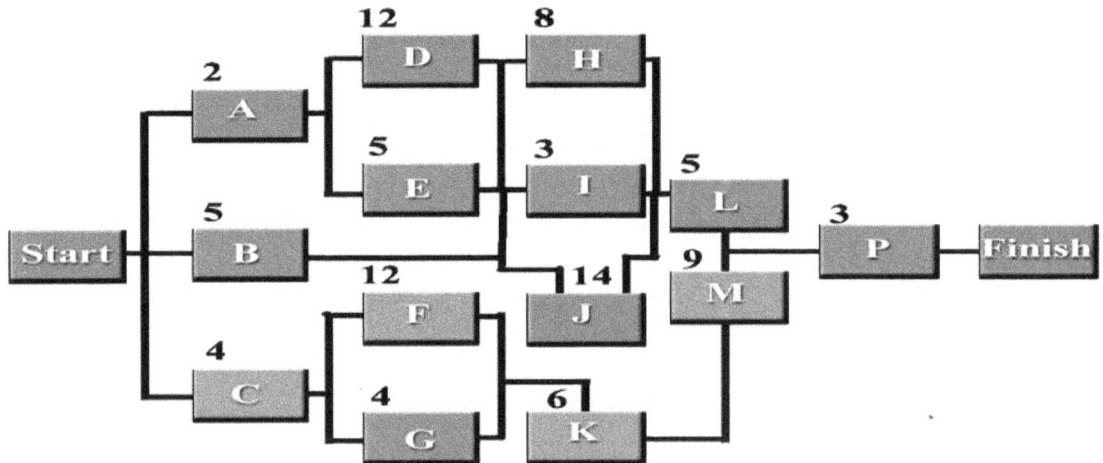

Illustration 11 - Secondary Path

Step 5 – Identify the float and slack.

First here is a legend for how you'll see those numbers arranged on a detailed network diagram. Following this legend will help you determine the total float and slack as well as a completed network diagram.

Early Start	Duration	Early Finish
	TASK NAME	
Late Start	Slack / Float	Late Finish

Path	Duration	Total Float
1. A-D-H-L-P	30	6
2. A-D-I-L-P	27	9
3. A-D-J-L-P	**36**	**0**
4. A-E-I-L-P	23	13
5. A-E-H-L-P	18	18
6. A-E-J-L-P	30	6
7. B-J-L-P	27	9
8. B-I-L-P	18	18
9. B-H-L-P	21	15
10. C-F-K-M-P	*34*	*2*
11. C-G-K-M-P	26	10

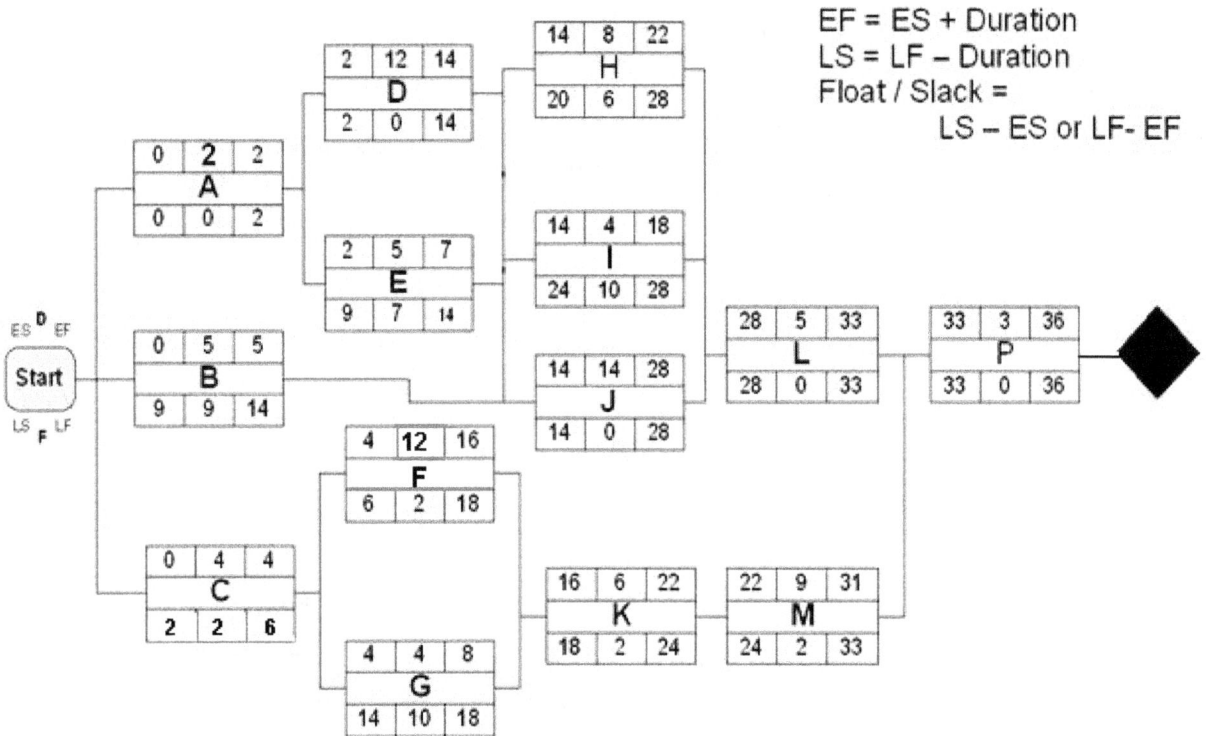

Illustration 12: Float and Slack - Critical Path Analysis is Complete

Duration Compression:

With the scope and deliverables determined (per the WBS), activities defined, estimated and sequenced, you're set. Right? Not always. From the example we shared, what would happen if you needed to compress your schedule from 36 days to 30? How would you do it? You are impacting not just the critical path, but the secondary critical path as well. There are two methods for shortening the duration of the activities on the critical path (and other paths).

Crashing: This means to speed up through additional resources on the critical path activities or

Fast Tracking: Working on activities in parallel that are normally done in sequence.

Now it's time for the cool schedule

One of the challenges of completing the steps we just described is resisting the urge to jump from Scope Statement to the schedule (often thought of as the GANTT Chart). In practice you will likely scribe out a WBS and then work within your project management scheduling tool, or in some cases, create your WBS within it. Regardless of which tools used, it is the thought process that needs some monitoring. Creating a project schedule without activities linked, dependencies noted, and resources loaded only provides a way to mask the lack of project planning, which can be bad.

Illustration 19: GANTT Chart

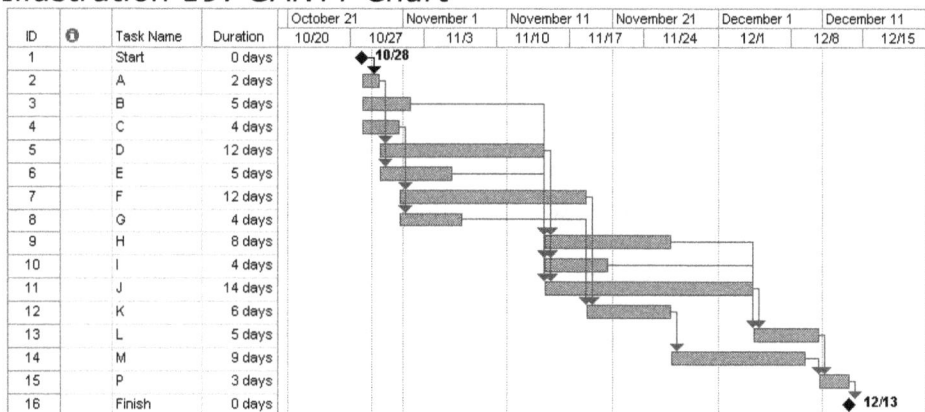

ID	ⓘ	Task Name	Duration
1		Start	0 days
2		A	2 days
3		B	5 days
4		C	4 days
5		D	12 days
6		E	5 days
7		F	12 days
8		G	4 days
9		H	8 days
10		I	4 days
11		J	14 days
12		K	6 days
13		L	5 days
14		M	9 days
15		P	3 days
16		Finish	0 days

Estimate Costs (7.1)

Estimate Costs was called Cost Estimating in the third edition PMBOK®. There are two processes within the Planning Process Group for the Cost Knowledge Area: Estimate Costs and Determine Budget. Cost management is primarily concerned with the cost of resources needed to complete project activities. It also should consider the effect of project decisions on the cost of using the project's product. Lifecycle costing is the total cost to the organization for the acquisition, maintenance, and upgrade of the product over its full useful life.

The result of your cost estimating process is to deliver a bottom line estimate of project cost. Labor costs are derived by duration (hourly, daily, contract total) times rate (per hour, day, contract length) or the formula of $L = D \times R.$

Material costs are derived by amount times unit price. Those costs are then applied to the project activities and presented in a budget. The best practice is to estimate, budget, and monitor cost as well as time. Some organizations do not the have the internal tracking techniques or treat internal resources as "sunk cost." Therefore the project monitoring role focuses almost exclusively on time and scope. In those situations, the power of realizing a true financial return or benefit to cost ratio is lost. Also, the ever strengthening accounting guidelines from Sarbanes Oxley (Section 409) benefit from rigorous project accounting.

Included in your Cost Management Plan should be a contingency reserve whether as a true set aside or possible additional appropriation amount. A contingency reserve is in simplest terms a "rainy day fund" or place to obtain more project funding if things go "bad". This amount is based on the risk identification, analysis, and amortization. It sets aside an amount for the known/unknown risk events.

Determine Budget (7.2)

Determine Budget (called Cost Budgeting in the third edition PMBOK®) involves allocating the overall cost estimate to individual work items in order to establish a cost baseline for measuring project performance. This becomes the Planned Value (PV) for earned value calculations used in Control Costs. The Cost Management Plan sets up the variances and policy. Cost Budget provides additional muscle concerning variances. Example variances include:

> ➢ Your project board may direct the project that any cost/schedule variance in excess of five percent (over or under) should result in a formal change to the baseline of the plan and formal review by the project board.
> ➢ A SOX (Sarbanes Oxley) inspired rule may impact record keeping and recognition of revenue – when received not shipped.

Plan Quality (8.1)

This process was called Quality Planning in the third edition PMBOK®. Within the project management context, quality means carrying out a project with zero deviation from the project specifications and objectives. Zero deviation includes approved changes per an integrated change control process that updates a baselined project plan. There are much deeper and more enriching methods within the quality management movement and project management borrows much of its approach from those movements (e.g., Total Quality Management, Six Sigma, Continuous Process Improvement, Learning Organizations). The ISO 9001 definition for quality is "the totality of features and characteristics of a product or service which bear on its ability to satisfy a given need as well as the conformance to requirements and fitness for use."

A unique slant that project management places on quality is to get stuff done, and make stuff happen. There's agreement to carry out that project with zero deviations, but to do so on time. The balancing act is ensuring that the triple constraints of Scope, Time, and Cost are satisfied. So, while Six Sigma sets a standard of 99.99% of defect free results per million, project management emphasizes quality as well, but to a lower level (95% or 99%) with an emphasis on getting projects done, getting products to market, and limiting scope creep.

This brings up a topic that often provokes some intense discussions – Gold Plating. This is adding extra functionality, higher quality components, expanding scope of work, or looking for better performance than the scope of the project. From a pure project acceleration perspective, gold plating adds no value. Now remembering integrated change control – projects are changeable. It is just that those changes need approval and if you're in the midst of a frequently changing project you need to revisit its objectives and scope.

Within the organizational context, Plan Quality identifies which quality standards are relevant to the project and determining how to satisfy them. This brings the project into proper focus for quality with a hierarchy of standards:
1. organization's standards for quality,
2. department's standards for quality,
3. unit's standards for quality,
4. project standards

Plan Quality needs to be weaved throughout your organization's project lifecycle – not added as an afterthought. There are costs to quality as well, both for conformance and non-conformance. This begins the discussion of the tools and techniques for quality.

Weighing in on the cost side are:

➤ Training
➤ Indoctrination

> ➢ Verification
> ➢ Calibration
> ➢ Testing
> ➢ Maintenance
> ➢ Audits

Weighing in and balancing the other side, cost of non–conformance:

> ➢ Rework
> ➢ Scrap
> ➢ Inventory costs
> ➢ Warranty costs
> ➢ Customer service

If the cost of non-conformance is not enough to compel an organization or project team to think about and implement a plan for quality, here are some additional benefits:

> ➢ Increased Productivity
> ➢ Increased Cost Effectiveness
> ➢ Decreased Risk
> ➢ Satisfied Customers

The results and outputs of Plan Quality include the Quality Management Plan as well as metrics, checklists, baseline, and another plan: process improvement plan. That plan can be updated via the project's integrated change control process.

At the core, the quality management plan addresses how a team will implement quality, what the project quality system will be, and how control, assurance, and improvement will be handled. Goals can be expressed for:

1. Capability
2. Usability
3. Performance
4. Reliability
5. Install-ability
6. Serviceability

The Process Improvement Plan details steps for analyzing processes that facilitate the identification of waste and non-value added activity including:

1. Process boundaries
2. Process configuration
3. Process metrics
4. Targets for improvement

The Process Improvement Plan can be supported effectively by adhering to the Six Sigma DMAIC process of:

1. Define
2. Measure
3. Analyze
4. Improve
5. Control

Develop Human Resource Plan (9.1)

This process was called Human Resource Planning in the third edition PMBOK®. Getting all of the right team members on the right boat paddling in the right cadence - that sums up the Human Resource Planning process. It sounds simple but in practice this can be more difficult to achieve than the more mechanical and engineering oriented processes (scope, activity, and budgeting).

A common frustration faced by project managers is the imbalance between responsibility for a project and amount of specified authority. A project manager is responsible for executing a team's work often without the direct report authority for the team and for customers with whom they did not negotiate the project. They need to operate in a world of ambiguity and flesh that ambiguity out, in a positive manner to fully define all the details of a project. These opposing demands (responsibility/authority and tolerance of ambiguity) can introduce conflict within the team and within the project manager.

Organizational Charts

The Responsibility Assignment Matrix (RAM) is the classic project manager's tool for clarifying roles and responsibilities. The idea is to express, as clearly as possible, what some common roles are for a project and who is responsible. The most often used role definitions form the acronym RACI (responsible, accountable, consulted, and informed). The following example highlights a RAM for creating a fish pond. You'll also have an opportunity to put that into action and create one on your own.

RACI Chart	*Team Member*		
Activity	*Rachael*	*Joshua*	*Annaliese*
Survey the ground	C	A	R
Dig the hole	A	R	C
Purchase materials	R	I	A
Install materials	A	R	I
Purchase fish	R	C	A

RACI Chart	Team Member		
Acclimate fish	C	R	A
Fill the pond	A	C	R
Celebrate	A	R	I

Table 2: RACI Chart

R = responsible A = accountable C = consult   I = informed

The position descriptions and networking enable the project manager to produce a critical output from Human Resource Planning – resource leveling.   Leveling the resource demand with availability is a common challenge on any project. It becomes a balancing act to determine which resources are over or under allocated. An important part of that balancing act is determining not just the demands of your project on a team member but also the competing demands from other projects and operations. A best practice note to remember is that day-to-day production or operations will generally beat out a project for dually assigned team members.

Best Practice - For multi-tasked team members: Operations trumps Project activity

Pointing those available resources to the precise task is essential once those scarce resources have been acquired. The outputs from Human Resource Planning are the roles and responsibilities and project organization chart as well as staffing management plans. The staffing management plans needs to articulate peak levels of activity and team member load. Another important component is to alert team members to when they actually plug in their contribution as shown in the illustration below.

Staff Demand – Numbers of FTE's

ID	Resource Name	Work	September				October				November	
			8	15	22	29	6	13	20	27	3	10
1	Interior Designer	96h					1	1	1			
2	Architect	96h					1	1	1			
3	Project Manager	0h										
4	Owner	68h				1	1	1	2	1		
5	General Laborer	248h								3	2	2
6	Carpenter	160h								2	2	2
7	Plumber	48h									2	2
8	Electrician	48h									2	2
9	Flooring Specialist	16h										1
10	Superintendent	112h						1	1	1		

Illustration 13: HR FTE Demand Grid

Organizational Theory

Networking organizational theory emphasizes the emotional intelligence (EI) needed to succeed as a project manager. Mastering the triple constraints (scope, time, and cost), risk, and quality as well as the requirements of your business or organization are just minimal expectations for a project manager. It may help you gain your first project manager opportunity. To succeed and thrive, project managers need the "softer side" or emotional intelligence. That ensures you continue and advance into senior level management.

Locus of Control and Tolerance of Ambiguity are concepts that will help you understand how your project stakeholders perceive their environment and your project. Project managers need to become masters of fleshing out ambiguous situations, providing structure around them, articulating that structure to others, and then transforming all of that "stuff" into tangible results.

Locus of Control (no it is not a bug)

Locus of control is a helpful measure of whether you perceive that you control events or that events control you. It shapes your view of the world and how you work in a team and organization: do you believe you shape your day's work and destiny or is that destiny forced upon you. An internal locus of control means you believe you're in charge. An external locus means you believe the world is in charge.

A key transition skill from subject matter expert to manager is enhancing your internal locus of control. Project managers need to invoke their will and advance change – whereas a subject matter expert is typically rewarded for performing their role or function according to what has been handed them.

You can sharpen your internal locus of control skills through practice, such as taking risks. Stretch yourself into something new. For example, managing meetings may seem beyond your control and this lack of control may feel stronger when managing a meeting with people at a higher level than you. There are methods for improving meeting management: send out an agenda prior to the meeting, establish guidelines, save the most important topic for the next to last item, etc. Also, distribute results within one hour of meeting close. This demonstrates follow-through and timeliness.

Tolerance of Ambiguity and Risk Management

Tolerance of ambiguity helps to understand how a person approaches new situations and processes new information. Picture a bell curve in your mind. On the left, someone with a low tolerance of ambiguity feels comfortable with established routines and repeat patterns—they view the world in terms of black and white, and right and wrong. On the right, someone with a high tolerance of ambiguity feels comfortable with new endeavors and the unfamiliar, and they view the world in shades of gray. Most people are somewhere in between. Risk management requires the ability to live in both environments. Risk concerns known and unknowns, and at times unknown and unknowns (uncertainty).

A possible risk event resembles something similar to what has been seen before it appears less ambiguous. For example, imagine a loss of electrical power. It's routine to include uninterruptible power supplies and redundant power sources for server rooms in 2007. In 1985, outside cloister mainframe environments, this was new and novel. In the central United States, tornadoes are a powerful reminder that weather is beyond our control. Buildings rated F4 and F5 are normal and routine for records storage and computer equipment protection. Preparing for tornadoes may appear more unnerving than loss of electricity - even though the mitigation steps are much the same (redundant power, safe sites, etc.).

So what?

If you're in a role that requires risk management, then what you bring to the table, your own tolerance of ambiguity, will impact how you perceive risk. High tolerance translates into more risk taking. Entrepreneurs and executives tend to have a higher tolerance. Low tolerance translates into risk aversion. Many project managers fall into this category. However, this is not completely hard-wired. You can shape and stretch it.

Plan Communications (10.2)

The purpose of Plan Communications (called Communication Planning in the third edition PMBOK®) is to determine who the project stakeholders are and what their communication needs are. There are two cornerstones to Plan Communications: (1) the sender – receiver model and (2) the communication paths formula. Each one reinforces the point that communication is important to project success and project managers have the primary responsibility for ensuring that communication is transmitted, received, and understood.

The key parts of Organizational Process Assets are assumptions and constraints. Those are the two elements often overlooked and forgotten in the heat of delivering a project. Constraints can impact any aspect of the project in addition to Plan Communications and Distribute Information itself. For example, while a newer web portal has emerged to update project status, not all team members may be able to access it with the proper computer configuration and thus a fall-back strategy of sharing reports via email is needed.

The formula in the illustration below is the foundation for one of two tools and techniques - those pursuing the PMP exam will need to have this memorized **(N X (N-1)/2).** This formula determines how many communication paths can happen with the number of people in your communication plan.

> ### When planning for how many people you need to communicate with use the formula (n X (n-1) / 2). That lets you know how many messages can happen

Illustration 14: Communication Formula

For example, a project team of six members has 15 communication paths to juggle (6X(6-1)/2). Adding or subtracting team members is not a simple arithmetic progression - it's geometric. Add six more team members to your six member team and it's not 15 paths added 6X5/2 – rather it's 51. ((12 x 11)/2 *or* 66 minus the 15 communication paths you started with). Your team size doubled, but your communication paths more than quadrupled.

The primary output from Plan Communications is the Communication Management Plan. The Communication Management Plan should include the following elements:

> ➢ Filing structure for access
> ➢ Distribution structure (what, to whom)
> ➢ Information, level of detail
> ➢ Production schedules
> ➢ Methods for update

Risk Planning (11.1 – 11.5 of the PMBOK®)

Risk concerns uncertain events that have a probability of occurring. Herbert Simon is considered the father of modern risk management through his work in heuristics, decision making, and semi-structured decisions.[vi] A simple summary of his work and subsequent authors follow. If a risk is 100% certain to occur, then it is an issue. It's known and it's not a risk.

At the opposite end or zero percent is a complete unknown or "unknown, unknown." There does need to be a degree of certainty in order to manage risk. Developing risk responses to positive or negative "unknown, unknowns" completely chokes initiative and progress since teams often chase windmills in a Don Quixote fantasy land (i.e., "It may snow in mid-May, we better postpone testing.") A Risk has a cause and, if it occurs, a consequence.

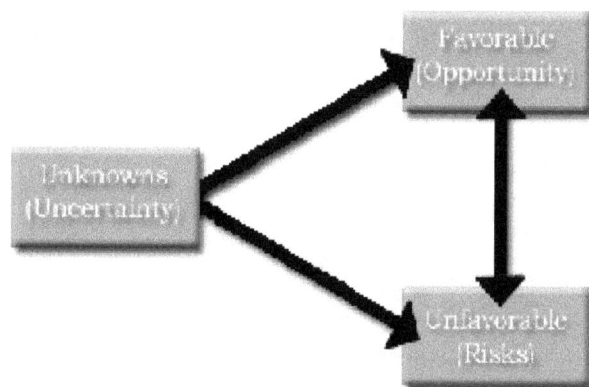

Illustration 23: Risk Spectrum

Plan Risk Management (11.1)

Plan Risk Management (called Risk Management Planning in the third edition PMBOK®) is the process of determining how to approach and plan your risk management activities. This brings your project's risk management approach into alignment with your organization's risk management practices and tolerances.

The Risk Management Plan is the output of Plan Risk Management. The key is to craft one that is readily and easily updatable and helps set the stage to focus on the most probable risks with either the greatest negative or positive impact. Types of risk that may be referenced in the Risk Management Plan include the following:

Types of Risk:

1. Known to Unknown

   OR Discrete-Continuous

2. External to Unpredictable

   AND External Predictable

3. Internal Non-Technical

   OR Technical

4. Legal and Contract/Procurement

Example Risk Events

1. Contractor Insolvency

2. Claims or litigation

3. Risk Conditions

4. Unenforceable clauses

5. Incompetent contractors

6. Inadequate risk assignment

7. Conflict Management

Identify Risks (11.2)

This process was called Risk Identification in the third edition PMBOK®. The output of this process is the Risk Register. That register needs to include the list of risks, potential responses, root cause, and updated risk categories as the project progresses. Additional triggers, warning signs, or measures to determine if risk has or is about to occur should be embedded within the Risk Register. Regardless of how that register is stored (within a project management scheduling software program such as Clarity, VPMI, Primavera, or MS Project or a spreadsheet or a web portal) the Risk Register needs to be dynamic.

A sample risk description follows in this illustration.

Illustration 15: Risk List Sample

Risk Name	Risk Description	Trigger Point
Scope Creep	People adding features and functions outside of the scope	Requests from outside of project team.
Budget Overrun	Spending exceeds budgeted forecast.	When budget variation is greater than 5 percent.

Perform Qualitative Risk Analysis (11.3)

This process was called Qualitative Risk Analysis in the third edition PMBOK®. The Risk Register developed at Identify Risks is now being pruned and shaped into a list that can be effectively managed.

Here are two tables that help illustrate the impact scales used during this process. The type of scale used for impact or priority can vary. What should not vary is changing the values for each data point while you're in midstream of completing the assessment (i.e., you don't change the yard markers during the football game).

Impact Scale

Rating	**Description**	**Impact**
0.9	Very High	Failure to meet major deliverable
0.7	High	Major delay or cost >20%
.5	Moderate	Moderate delay or added cost 10-20%
0.4	Low	Slight delay or cost <5%
0.1	Very Low	Slight inefficiency Insignificant delay

Table 3: Qualitative Risk Impact Scale

Probability Scale

Rating	Description	Definition
1.0	Certainty	Risk inevitable 100% Probability
0.9	Very High	Almost Certain 90% Probability
0.8	Very High	Very High 80% Probability
0.7	High	High 70% Probability
0.6	Moderate	Moderate 60% Probability
0.5	Even Change	50/50 50% Probability
0.4	Low	Low 40% Probability
0.3	Very Low	Very Low 30% Probability
0.2	Slight	Slight 20% Probability
0.1	Unlikely	Unlikely <10% Probability

Table 4: Qualitative Risk Analysis Probability Table

Table 5: Sample Risk Register: PI Matrix

Risk Name	Impact Rating	Probability Rating	RPI Rating
Scope Creep	0.5	0.7	0.35
Budget Overrun	0.9	0.2	0.18

Perform Quantitative Risk Analysis (11.4)

This process was called Quantitative Risk Analysis in the third edition PMBOK®. Perform Quantitative Risk Analysis extends (or in some areas replaces) Perform Qualitative Risk Analysis. The distinction in quantitative versus qualitative is that it considers all possible outcomes within a probability distribution. The decision tree tool provides the best example of this type of tool.

The risk register provides the collection point for the risks identified and prioritized. To accomplish a valid Quantitative Analysis you need to have some concrete data – a good sense of what the probabilities and impact for each course of action really are.

The Tool and Technique of Expected Monetary Value (EMV) is a type of decision tree that calculates the expected monetary value of a decision based on its risk event probability and monetary value.

TECHNOLOGY
AS PROMISED

The output from Perform Quantitative Risk Analysis is the update to the Risk Registers that includes changes to the probabilistic analysis of the project, probability of achieving the project's objectives, revised list of quantified risks, and any trends.

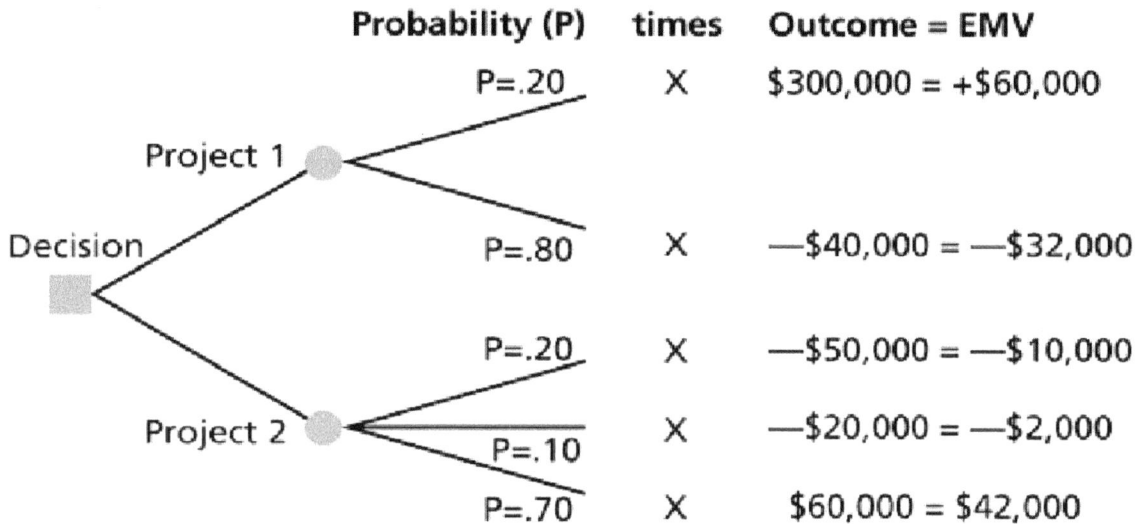

Probability (P)	times	Outcome = EMV
P=.20	X	$300,000 = +$60,000
P=.80	X	—$40,000 = —$32,000
P=.20	X	—$50,000 = —$10,000
P=.10	X	—$20,000 = —$2,000
P=.70	X	$60,000 = $42,000

Project 1's EMV = $60,000 —32,000 = $28,000
Project 2's EMV = —$10,000 —2,000 + 42,000 = $30,000

Illustration 16: Quantitative Risk Analysis Decision Tree

Plan Risk Responses (11.5)

This process was called Risk Response Planning in the third edition PMBOK®. The final process within the Risk Planning group of knowledge areas is Plan Risk Responses. The objective is to manage the planning and implementation of risk strategies. Another objective is to establish risk contingency reserves that allow for estimating inaccuracy in the project budget which then allows for future events which are difficult or impossible to predict.

There are different ways of responding to both negative and positive risk. Those strategies concerning negative risk are what most people assume risk response planning addresses.

#1 Negative – **Threat** classic concept of risk
  ➤ Avoid – go around a thunderstorm while you're flying

> Transfer – reinsure your risk or hire a subcontractor
> Mitigate – reduce the probability of the risk event occurring. Or if that risk event does occur, reduce the impact it – fire is dealt with via halon.
> Accept - acknowledge it exists and move forward – many marketing decisions are made in light of uncertainty with the decision to let the market decide.

#2 Positive – AKA **Opportunity**

> Exploit – take advantage of a demand forecast error that was too low and leverage capital funding to buy 15 more assembly lines ASAP to make more Cabbage Patch dolls.
> Share - take advantage of a demand forecast error that was too low and leverage a partnership with another company off shore to make more Cabbage Patch dolls.
> Enhance - take advantage of a demand forecast error that was too low and leverage improvements in your assembly line to produce more Cabbage Patch dolls for the next holiday season.
> Accept – just be happy you met the Wall Street expectations from your sales of Cabbage Patch dolls.

Plan Procurements (12.1)

In the third edition PMBOK®, there were two procurement planning processes—Plan Purchases and Acquisitions and Plan Contracting. Now there is just Plan Procurements. Procurement planning and management is no longer an afterthought or an occasional event. It has become an area of increasing activity and focus for project managers due to the increase of outsourcing and off shoring since the early 1990's. Outsourcing and off shoring force that to the forefront in two ways:

> Project team members more likely will come from contracted resources or a mix of contracted and internal employees (FTE) than just internal employees alone.

> Project solutions are often brought in from the outside rather than built up from within due to smaller organizations, head-counts, and challenges to "ramp up" an internal term to meet a temporary objective.

Make-or-buy analysis pulls together the organizational needs, competencies, and project opportunity to determine an appropriate course of action (build it in-house, build it with outside expertise, or buy it).   Other considerations in make-or-buy analysis include:

> Direct and indirect costs
> Purchase price
> Maintenance fees
> Cost of purchase and contract management
> Cost of modification
> Cost of technology

The conventional wisdom with make-or-buy-analysis is that buying a solution decreases risks but making the solution helps the organization maintain control. There are three general contract forms with derivatives of each one. It's best to think of those along a continuum from paying as you go along with payments that vary per time consumed (time and material) at one end to a paying when the job is done with one set amount (fixed) at the other end. The first step is to determine the general contract type among time and material, cost reimbursable and fixed (see the following illustration).

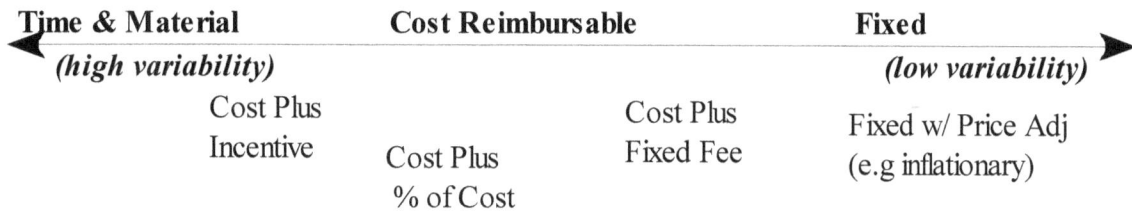

Time & Material	Cost Reimbursable	Fixed
(high variability)		*(low variability)*
Cost Plus Incentive	Cost Plus Fixed Fee	Fixed w/ Price Adj (e.g inflationary)
	Cost Plus % of Cost	

Illustration 17: Contract Type Continuum

Time and Materials Contract – These contracts have a fixed component in the price per hour or unit; the variability comes in through how many hours are applied to a contract. Here are two examples:

1. Bill Rate — a consultant charging a set fee per hour, (but variable depending how may hours it takes to fill the contract).
2. Unit Price — an organization pays amount per unit of service for time of contract total value as a function of quantities supplied.

Fixed price or lump sum

The organization pays a fixed total price for a product (e.g., purchase three industrial electrical turbines for power plant generation). In a fixed price procurement both the buyer and seller have negative financial risk but it is the seller who bears the greatest amount of risk. That risk is typically priced into the fixed price quotation. Fixed priced contracts may contain incentives for meeting deadlines (fixed plus incentives) or they may include a price adjustment (e.g., inflation or depreciation on long term contracts). Here are two examples:

- **Fixed Price Incentive fee**- for each (week, day, month) of early finish a premium is paid. Contract $10,000,000 incentive $10,000/month early finish
- **Fixed Price Adjustment** - Contract may allow for price adjustment(s) based on CPI or material cost inflation.

Cost reimbursable contracts – These may include direct and indirect costs plus a markup for profit (i.e., charge for salary of programmer plus 7% for overhead of the company). It blends in elements of fixed and time and material contracts. Cost reimbursable contracts are frequently found in governmental contracts for construction or national defense.

- ➤ **Cost Plus Fixed Fee** - Buyer pays costs plus a fee for profit. Keeps buyer's cost down since cost overrun does not generate any profit for the seller.
- ➤ **Cost Plus Percentage** - Seller pays all costs plus a percentage of the costs as a fee. Sellers are motivated to spend more money in cost to increase profit.
- ➤ **Cost Plus Incentive Fee**- Buyer pays all cost plus an agreed upon fee and a bonus for bringing in below incentive (e.g., road work, there is often an incentive for completing the project early and a penalty for late work).

Let's compare and contrast the three primary contract types.

Cost Plus	T&M (Time and Material)	Fixed Price
Advantages	**Advantages**	**Advantages**
Lower cost than fixed price	Need people quickly and may use a staff augmentation firm (i.e., "head hunters")	Lower management
Smaller SOW	Easy contract to start up	Total price is known
Protects cost		Most companies have procurement policies

Table 6: Contract Type Advantages

Cost Plus	T&M	Fixed Price
Disadvantages	**Disadvantages**	**Disadvantages**
Requires tracking	No incentive to control costs	Extra charges on changes
Higher management requirements	Profit is built into hourly rate	Seller may try to reduce scope
Buyer takes risk; Seller gets extra money		SOW (statement of work) is more detailed
Total price is unknown		Seller adds cost for increased risk

Table 7: Contract Type Disadvantages

The Procurement Management Plan addresses the following questions:

1. Do we need independent estimates?
2. Project management actions with the procurement team?
3. Are there standardized templates?
4. How do we handle multiple vendors?
5. How do we schedule procurement in the WBS?

Once the make-or-buy decision is to buy then the documents used to select who to buy from are prepared. Which documents are assembled depends on the type of contract and the procurement selection process. Collecting documents for a purchase order or contractor selection may be quick (measured in days) whereas generating documents to select a seller through a competitive bid process for a fixed cost reimbursable contract may take much longer (measured in weeks or months).

At this point of a project, the die is cast in terms of which type of purchase is desired. That can change, but if it does it should be done via a change request. Why such rigidity early on? Selecting sellers via a purchase order versus a request for proposal are two different processes and plans.

> Statement of Work (SOW) – Lays out requirements in enough detail so the vendor knows whether they can perform the task. It is a document providing enough detail to adequately determine the cost of the product.
> Request for Information (RFI) – May be used as the lead in for a request for proposal (RFP) selection and gathers initial, comparison information from competing sellers.
> Statement of Objectives (SOO) – Expresses the problem or opportunity in enough detail so the vendor knows whether they can perform the task.
> Invitation for Bid (IFB) – Procurement document to understand the price of the product or service.
> Request for Proposal (RFP) – Procurement document to understand the ability of the vendor to meet the requirements or objectives as well as understand cost. RFP's express what's needed and allows sellers to determine how to get it done.
> Request for Quotation (RFQ) – Procurement document to get a price quote for the product or services. This is less formal than a bid. RFQ's specify what and how; sellers provide the services or materials.
> Invitation for Negotiation (IFN) – Procurement document that invites the seller into negotiation for a product or service. This can occur when the seller has been selected.
> Contractor Initial Response (CIR) – Procurement document received from the contractor in response to one of the above.

Chapter 4 Exercises

Exercise 22. Major Project Documents.

Although there are commonalities among the major project documents, while identifying which component belongs to which document, notice the different purposes of the documents and the progressive elaboration that occurs with additional documentation.

	Project Charter	Project Management Plan	Scope Statement
Project purpose or justification			
Name and responsibility of person authorizing project charter			
Assigned project manager with responsibility and authority level			
High-level project description			
High-level product characteristics			
Product scope description			
Project deliverables			
High-level requirements			
Project boundaries			
Project management processes chosen by project management team			
Selected project life cycle			
Summary budget			
Cost baseline			
Cost management plan and quality management plan			
Summary milestone schedule			
Schedule baseline			
Quality baseline			
Description of how work will be executed			
Description of how configuration management will be performed			
Description of how changes will be monitored and controlled			
Need and techniques for stakeholder communication			
How integrity of performance measurement baselines maintained			
Project assumptions			
Project constraints			
Information on key management reviews			
Product acceptance criteria			
Project approval requirements			
Measurable project objectives and related success criteria			

Exercise 23. Collect Requirements – Group Decision Making Techniques

Group Decision Making Techniques are a tool and technique of the Collect Requirements process. However, they can be applied anytime a group decision needs to be made. The larger the group, the less likely it is that all will agree on something. For this reason, rules may be put into place to determine the group's course of action. For example, if the group will agree to do whatever most of the people want to do, then it is a majority decision. Read the following description of a small town trying to make a decision, and describe what each of the group decision making techniques would look like. The Majority technique is given as an example.

Littleton is a town of exactly 1000 people. They have a mayor that is trying to help the town reach a decision on whether to allow a weapons research facility that wants to develop radioactive snakes north of their town. Four hundred people live in what is considered "North Littleton," 300 live in "South Littleton," and 300 live in "The Old Mill Area."

1. Unanimity

2. Majority

If 501 or more townspeople agree, that will be the course of action for the town.

3. Consensus

4. Plurality

5. Dictatorship

Exercise 24. Collect Requirements – Questionnaire

Questionnaires are a tool and technique of the Collect Requirements process. Questionnaires are often made, but rarely made well. Critically examine the following questionnaire and mark as many errors as you can find. Check your answers to see how you did.

Opossum Fancier Questionnaire

1. Exactly how much is your income?

2. Are you in favor of the annual agenda proposed by the president of the Opossum Fanciers Association?

3. Should one never not stop to help an injured opossum on the road?

4. How many pet opossums do you own?
    a. Do you own pet opossums?

5. Have you ever taken a substantial amount of time to seriously consider either in the distant or recent past whether opossums may have several distinct and valuable advantages over other common domestic pets such as dogs, cats, and hamsters?

6. What makes the best pet? A. Reptiles B. Marsupials C. Insects D. Mammals

7. How propitious are you towards opossums?

8. Have you ever done something as disgusting and repulsive as eat an opossum?

9. Do you support the promotion of opossums as pets and specialized training for veterinarians in their treatment?

Exercise 25. Collect Requirements – Traceability Matrix

The Traceability Matrix is one of the outputs of the Collect Requirements process. Requirements could be traced to a number of things, including business objectives, product design, and test strategies. The example below shows a Traceability Matrix for a new vehicle being designed by Major Motors. Finish the Traceability Matrix by filling in the "x's" to denote which high-level description is being met by each requirement. Next, examine the matrix. Are there areas of requirements missing or incompatible with the product description?

<table>
<tr><td colspan="2" rowspan="2"></td><td colspan="6" align="center">Requirements</td></tr>
<tr><td>20 air bags</td><td>45 mpg highway</td><td>Can go 250 mph</td><td>Luggage rack on roof</td><td>Emissions in bottom 10% of all vehicles</td><td>1 foot high rear spoiler</td></tr>
<tr><td rowspan="5">High-Level Product Description</td><td>Fast</td><td></td><td></td><td>X</td><td></td><td></td><td></td></tr>
<tr><td>Sporty Design</td><td></td><td></td><td></td><td></td><td></td><td></td></tr>
<tr><td>Environmentally Friendly</td><td></td><td></td><td></td><td></td><td></td><td></td></tr>
<tr><td>Safe</td><td></td><td></td><td></td><td></td><td></td><td></td></tr>
<tr><td>Comfortable</td><td></td><td></td><td></td><td></td><td></td><td></td></tr>
</table>

TECHNOLOGY
AS PROMISED

Exercise 26. Project Charter Sample Internet Portal

The PMBOK® 4th Edition provides and advances the distinction of what should be in a Project Charter and what should be in a Scope Statement. The two were combined in the 1996 edition. The 2000 (2nd) and 2004 (3rd) separated the two but muddied the waters just a bit. The 4th Edition clearly defines what should be in what – though in practice the two are typically combined.

There are three exercises that help you identify what content should be in which deliverable – one of those will have you identify the separate pieces from a project charter that embeds the scope (the sample one provided in the Appendix).

Project Charter Checklist

Read the sample below, and then complete your own project charter checklist.

The mission of the project charter is to authorize or validate the existence of a project and identify the project manager / management function.	
Define the Project Goal(s)	Internet portal to support exchange of customer information to internal staff – sales force in particular.
What is the significance of the project to the corporation/unit?	High significance for continued competitive advantage.
When are the products required?	Q3 2009
What is the maximum cost?	2.5 to 3 million
Define the deliverables	✓ Illustrative values for projections of cash value depending on the product. Current state is via 800 phone number and fax transmission or mail ✓ Delivery channels for new products (direct purchase ala "GEICO") ✓ Contact information (CORM) sent to field reps for inquiries via web
Define the quality metrics	✓ Portal that allows the same access as is

	available today via direct call ✓ Triple constraints
Define assumptions	✓ Current application will be used through Q3 2009 ✓ Portal will exchange data with existing databases; no new back-end databases are required as part of this effort ✓ Compliance projects (HIPAA and SOX) will be completed in time for this project's completion (scheduled for Q1, 2009 delivery)

Project Charter Checklist

My Project's Charter	
Define the Project Goal(s)	
What is the significance of the project to the corporation/unit?	
When are the products required?	
What is the maximum cost?	
Define the deliverables	
Define the quality metrics	
Define assumptions	

Exercise 27. Scope Development Checklist – Sample Internet Portal

Read the sample below, and then complete your own project charter checklist.

Once the project charter is developed a checklist is helpful to determine the scope. The following is a sample scope statement for our Internet Portal project. We do restate the project goals and deliverables from the Charter for Context.

Define the Project Goal(s)	*Internet portal to support exchange of customer information to internal staff – sales force in particular.*
Define the deliverables	✓ *Illustrative values for projections of cash value depending on the product. Current state is via toll free telephone number and fax transmission or mail* ✓ *Delivery channels for new products (direct purchase ala "GEICO")* ✓ *Contact information (CORM) sent to field reps for inquiries via web*
Define constraints	*No interruption of operational databases*
What's in scope?	✓ *Deliverables identified above* ✓ *Interaction with other projects within the Portal Program* ✓ *Interaction with other programs and projects (release and configuration management)* ✓ *Server Hardware* ✓ *Integration with new, emerging field compensation functionality* ✓ *Integration with legacy software and systems* ✓ *Exploration of process improvement* ✓ *Training* ✓ *Release management - transition to operations*

What's out of scope?	✓ Hardware other than server (laptops for field agents) ✓ Work activities directly associated with related projects within the program (no duplication of effort) ✓ Field compensation functionality ✓ Legacy software/system replacement ✓ Though the primary purpose is not process improvement in aka six sigma approach – should the need arise this, will become a separate project)
If this project results from a Request for Proposal Response (RFP), what would you post to a bidder's conference before completing the RFP? **OR** If this project is internal to your organization, what questions, if any, would you want clarification on before you begin?	*RFQ for contract resources is anticipated for web design – due to accelerated timeline we may need to select from three vendors (snap, crackle, or pop) that we have existing relationships with. An RFI and RFP need to be planned as well.*

Your own project scope statement checklist.

My Project's Scope Statement Checklist	
Define the Project Goal(s)	
Define the deliverables	
Define the constraints	
What's in scope?	
What's out of scope?	
If this project results from a Request for Proposal Response (RFP), what would you post to a bidder's conference before completing the RFP? **OR** If this project is internal to your organization, what questions, if any, would you want clarification on before you begin?	

Exercise 28. Scope / Charter

Go to the Appendix and fill in the Box – Scope / Charter for the sample Project Charter. For an in-depth discussion which elements do you typically see combined in your organization?

Exercise 29. Vacation WBS

Take a trial run at creating WBS for a vacation. Using post-it notes   (recommended when working in groups) or just writing out on a piece of paper, create a first and second level WBS. Number your WBS with an indentured outline (i.e., 1.0 Plan Vacation — 1.1, Call, 1.2 Research). An example list oriented WBS for a vacation is provided below.

Sample WBS Solution – Pikes Peak Vacation

1　Plan
   1.1　　　　Pre-plan activities and logistics: Lodging, Airfare, destination
      1.1.1　　　Travel
      1.1.2　　　Hotels
      1.1.3　　　Airfare
   1.2　　　Cost
2　Travel to destination
   2.1　　　Pack luggage
   2.2　　　Flight
3　Pikes Peak
   3.1　　　Lodging
      3.1.1　　　Reservation
      3.1.2　　　Hotel Stay
   3.2　　　Activities
      3.2.1　　　Cog Railway
      3.2.2　　　Garden of the Gods
      3.2.3　　　Focus on the Family Tour
      3.2.4　　　 Pikes Peak Ascent Run
   3.3　　　Meals
      3.3.1　　　Continental breakfast is included within hotel
      3.3.2　　　Restaurants within walking distance
         3.3.2.1　　　Pizza
      3.3.3　　　Bread and Breakfast Inn Breakfast
   3.4　　　Local Transportation
4　Travel from
   4.1　　　Return Flight

Now it's your turn. Write a WBS for a vacation you want to take (If you're a project manager you deserve one every once in a while).

Exercise 30. *Create a WBS (First, Second, and Third level only).*

Now for a second pass at creating a WBS. This time we leave the fun of a vacation for your project. A sample is included for an Investment Portal. Review it and then using post-it-notes or the next page, develop a WBS down to the third level.

Investment – Insurance portal for agents.

1   Charter
    1.1   Compose
       1.1.1   Field productivity definition
       1.1.2   New products definition boundaries established
       1.1.3   Contact information
       1.1.4   Scope statement
       1.1.5   Charter elements – constraints, boundaries, risks...
    1.2   Review
       1.2.1   Steering committee review
       1.2.2   Project team review
       1.2.3   President review
    1.3   Approve
       1.3.1   Steering committee approval
       1.3.2   Project team approval – support – buy in - acknowledgment
       1.3.3   President's approval
2   Plan
    2.1   Compose
       2.1.1   Field productivity definition
       2.1.2   New products definition boundaries established
       2.1.3   Contact information
       2.1.4   Project charter cycled incorporated
       2.1.5   Project sub plans (scope management through communication) completed
    2.2   Review
       2.2.1   Steering committee review
       2.2.2   Project team review
       2.2.3   President review
    2.3   Approve
       2.3.1   Steering committee approval
       2.3.2   Project team approval – support – buy in - acknowledgment
       2.3.3   President's approval

3   Define, Design and Build Illustrations
    3.1   Analysis & Design
       3.1.1   Business requirements specification
       3.1.2   Systems requirements specification
          3.1.2.1   Applications architecture
          3.1.2.2   Infrastructure architecture
    3.2   Training for developers
    3.3   Welcome in the communication's division – web programmers
       3.3.1   Massage and physical therapy for project manager
    3.4   Hardware / Server configuration
       3.4.1.1   Define server needs
       3.4.1.2   Develop RFI/RFQ

	3.4.1.3	Select vendor
	3.4.1.4	Purchase
	3.4.1.5	Install
	3.4.1.6	Harden
	3.4.1.7	Load balance
3.5	Develop	
	3.5.1	Illustrations user interface
	3.5.1.1	Testing (or see 3.6)
	3.5.1.1.1	Unit
	3.5.1.1.2	User
	3.5.1.1.3	Integration
	3.5.1.1.4	System
	3.5.2	Illustrations data access – legacy systems
3.6	Test	
	3.6.1.1	Testing (or see 3.5)
	3.6.1.1.1	Unit
	3.6.1.1.2	User
	3.6.1.1.3	Integration
	3.6.1.1.4	System
3.7	Deploy	
3.8	Transition to operations	

4 Deliver
  4.1 Validate Testing
  4.2 Validate Operational Readiness
  4.3 Launch the "Illustrations Product - 2020"

Exercise 30. WBS

Now it's your turn. Write a WBS for your own project.

Exercise 31. WBS Dictionary

The WBS Dictionary is an output of the Create Work Breakdown Structure process. The WBS Dictionary is the companion document to the Work Breakdown Structure, which is the primary output of the Create Work Breakdown Structure process. Using the WBS below created to plan a family reunion, choose one the work packages and make a WBS Dictionary for that work package. There is an example and space for your WBS Dictionary on the next page.

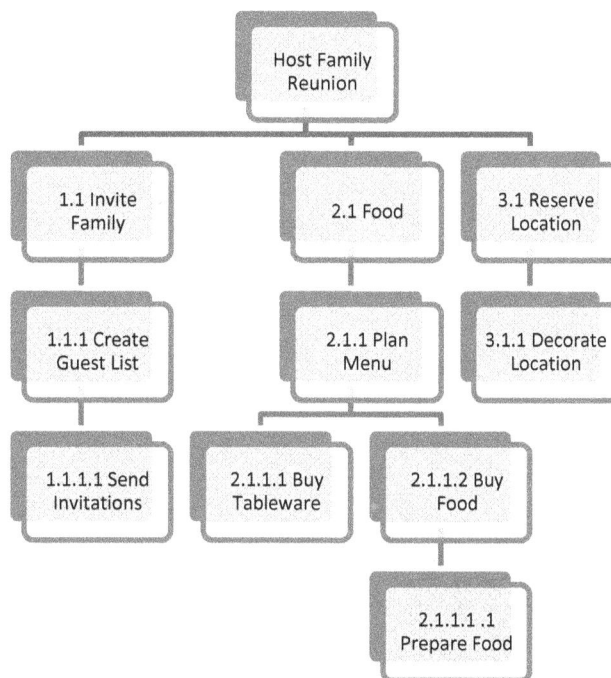

WBS Dictionary		
	Example	Work Package of your Choice
Code of Account Identifier	*1.1.1.1 Send Invitations*	
Statement of Work	*Send invitations to all family members telling the time and place of the annual family reunion*	
Responsible Organization	*The Brian Schmoll family*	
List of Schedule Milestones	*Design invitations, Mail invitations*	
Associated Schedule Activities	*Obtain all addresses, Obtain stamps, Design invitations, Print invitations, Stuff envelopes, Address envelopes, Put on return label, Stamp envelopes, Mail invitations*	
Resources Required	*Address list, stamps, envelopes, paper, computer, software to design invitations, printer, ink, return labels, pen*	
Cost Estimates	*$25 (mostly for stamps)*	
Quality Requirements	*Check addressed envelopes against address list. Count final envelopes to assure right number.*	
Technical References	*User manual for software used to design invitation*	
Contract Information	*No contracts involved*	

Exercise 32. Define Activities – Activity List

Creating the Activity List for the Define Activities process involves looking at your WBS and making a to-do list by breaking down the Work Packages. Create an Activity List by studying the WBS below. Give each activity an identifier (Activity Name) and a brief description of the scope.

Activity List	
Activity Name	**Scope of Work**

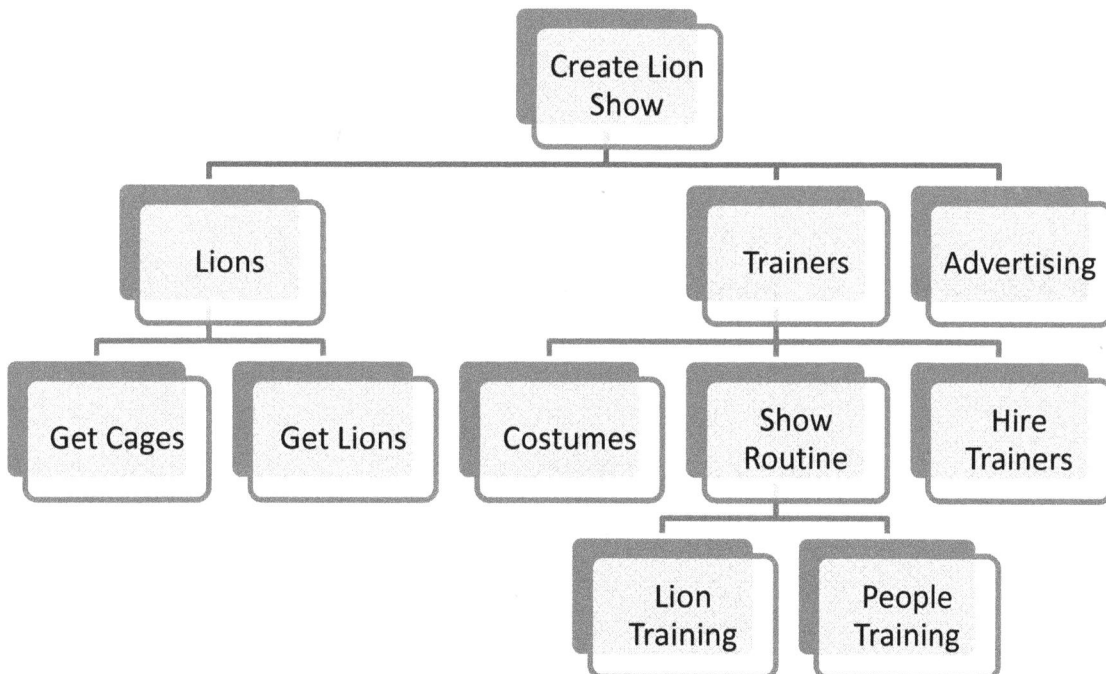

```
                        ┌──────────────┐
                        │  Create Lion │
                        │     Show     │
                        └──────────────┘
        ┌──────────────────────┼──────────────────┐
   ┌─────────┐            ┌──────────┐       ┌─────────────┐
   │  Lions  │            │ Trainers │       │ Advertising │
   └─────────┘            └──────────┘       └─────────────┘
    ┌────┴────┐      ┌──────────┼──────────┐
┌──────────┐ ┌──────────┐ ┌──────────┐ ┌──────────┐ ┌──────────┐
│Get Cages │ │Get Lions │ │ Costumes │ │  Show    │ │  Hire    │
└──────────┘ └──────────┘ └──────────┘ │ Routine  │ │ Trainers │
                                       └──────────┘ └──────────┘
                                    ┌──────┴──────┐
                               ┌──────────┐ ┌──────────┐
                               │   Lion   │ │  People  │
                               │ Training │ │ Training │
                               └──────────┘ └──────────┘
```

Exercise 33. Define Activities – Milestone List

The Milestone List is an output of the Define Activities process. This is a simple list of the project's major milestones with each milestone being described as either mandatory or optional based on the requirements of the project. Choose either a project you have worked on or a common project such as building as house, and list about five major milestones. For each milestone, check whether it is mandatory or optional.

Milestone 1   Mandatory ☐   Optional ☐

Milestone 2   Mandatory ☐   Optional ☐

Milestone 3   Mandatory ☐   Optional ☐

Milestone 4   Mandatory ☐   Optional ☐

Milestone 5   Mandatory ☐   Optional ☐

Exercise 34. Sequence Activities

A. Determine which activity relationship is being described (Finish to Start; Finish to Finish; Start to Start; or Start to Finish).

> ➤ Becky's mother tells her to start getting up and getting ready for the day so she can finish making all the beds.

> ➤ Becky's mother is waiting for her to pick out a book so she can read it to her.

> ➤ Becky's father is waiting for her mother to finish baking her cake so he can finish cleaning up the kitchen.

> ➤ Becky and her mother are in the kitchen doing the dishes. Becky is drying the dishes after her mother washes each one.

B. Think up an example from everyday life of each of the four activity relationships.

> ➤ **Finish to Start**

> ➤ **Finish to Finish**

> ➤ **Start to Start**

> ➤ **Start to Finish**

Exercise 35. Sequence Activities - Dependencies

The relationship between the sequence of two activities may be described as Mandatory (must be done in that order), Discretionary (order is preferred but not required), and External (relationship with non-project activities).

A. Identify which of these three dependencies is being described.

	Mandatory	Discretionary	External
1. The project team is waiting for the city to issue them a building permit so they can start digging the foundation of their new office building.			
2. After the team has dug a hole for the foundation, they will pour the cement for the foundation.			
3. The team plans on choosing the siding color after choosing the interior paint color.			
4. The roofing team is waiting for the hardware store to deliver the shingles so they can start nailing shingles to the roof.			
5. The painting crew plans on applying a coat of primer before applying the Robin's Egg Blue interior paint.			

B. Alternate Terms

What are other terms for Discretionary Dependencies? What are other terms for Mandatory Dependencies?

Exercise 36. Estimate Activity Resources – Activity Resource Requirements

The Estimate Activity Resources process estimates the type and quantity of materials, people, equipment, and supplies required to perform each schedule activity. The activities are found in the Activity List created in the Define Activities process. For each of these activities, practice estimating the resources that you will need.

Activity Resource Requirements	
Activity Name	**Resources**
Make Cookies	1 person with some cooking experience; 1 kitchen with an oven, cookie sheets, measuring cups, spoon, and bowl; Groceries including flour, butter, oatmeal, raisins, brown sugar, egg, and cinnamon.
Change Flat Tire	
Paint the Living Room	
Make Toast	
Make a Snowman	
Give a Dog a Bath	

PMP Scrimmage® Curriculum, Edition 3.01   *Page 113*
www.tapuniversity.com
TECHNOLOGY
AS PROMISED

Exercise 37. Estimate Activity Resources – RBS

The Resource Breakdown Structure (RBS) is a hierarchical graph showing the resources needed by resource category and resource type. Here is an example RBS for making cookies. Make your own RBS below for any activity that you would like.

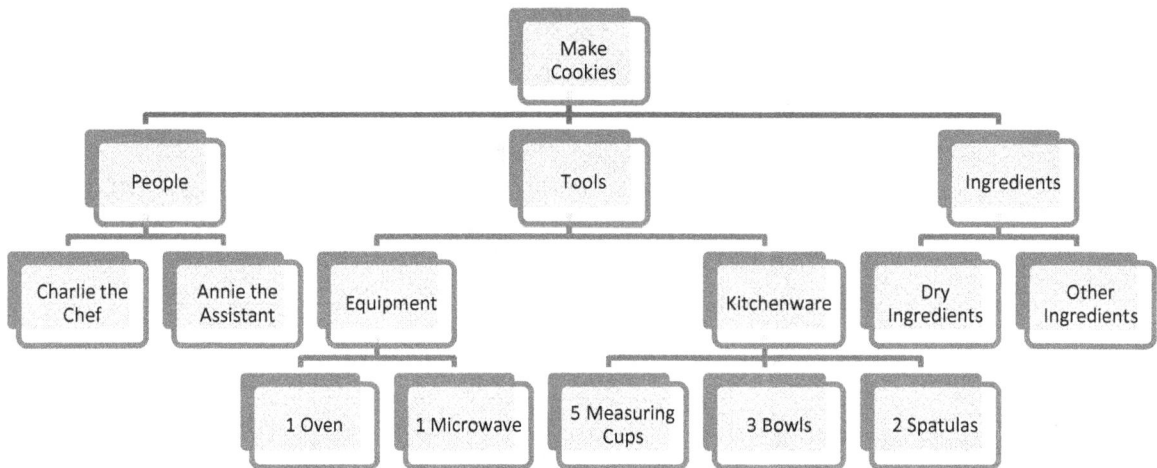

Your RBS:

Exercise 38. PERT and 3-Point Estimate

Murphy has gathered estimates on how many days individual activities will take for his project on reintroducing Jackalopes to South Dakota. PERT is calculated (P+(4xML)+O)/6. Three-point estimates are calculated (P+ML+O)/3. Calculate both PERT and 3-Point Estimate for each activity.

Project Activity	Pessimistic	Most Likely	Optimistic	PERT	3-Point
1. Acquire Breeding Stock	300	100	20		
2. Raise 100 young Jackalopes	200	150	50		
3. Obtain landowners' permission for their release	90	60	3		
4. Release Jackalopes	50	14	5		
5. Monitor Jackalopes in wild	300	100	90		

Exercise 39. Critical Path - "A Scrimmage"

PROJECT: Assemble a $19.50 bookshelf purchased at Shopko for your daughter (Rachael) to hang Barbie accessories and books. Your daughter is the executive sponsor. *Create a network diagram using the suggested Table below. Determine the activities on the critical path - the series of activities, which determines the earliest completion of the project. Identify the critical path in your diagram by listing the path (i.e. A-B-D-F-G).*

ID	Activity	Duration (minutes)	Predecessor	Critical Path?
A	Read instructions	3	--	
B	Group "like" parts together	6	--	
C	Verify drawer assembly	3	A	
D	Assemble right shelve to bottom shelf	2	B	
E	Screw in four screws	3	C,D	
F	Place left shelf on bottom shelf	2	E	
G	Screw in four more screws	4	F	
H	Place in top shelf	2	G	
I	Find new screw driver in garage	6	H	
J	Screw in four more screws	8	I	
K	Put middle shelf in	8	J	
L	Place hanging brackets on back	4	I	
M	Screw in hanging brackets	6	K	
N	Verify fit	5	M, L	
O	Take upstairs to Rachael's room	2	N	

Exercise 40. Branding Iron Activity Sequencing and Critical Path

The head wrangler is planning for his team to brand and vaccinate the calves. Fill in all the boxes using his time estimates for getting the first calf branded. Which is the critical path? What is the fastest possible time to brand the first calf? If the wrangler wants to start now, but only one cowhand is available and the rest won't be back for half an hour, which task should this cowhand start? Will the others be back in time to avoid delays to the critical path?

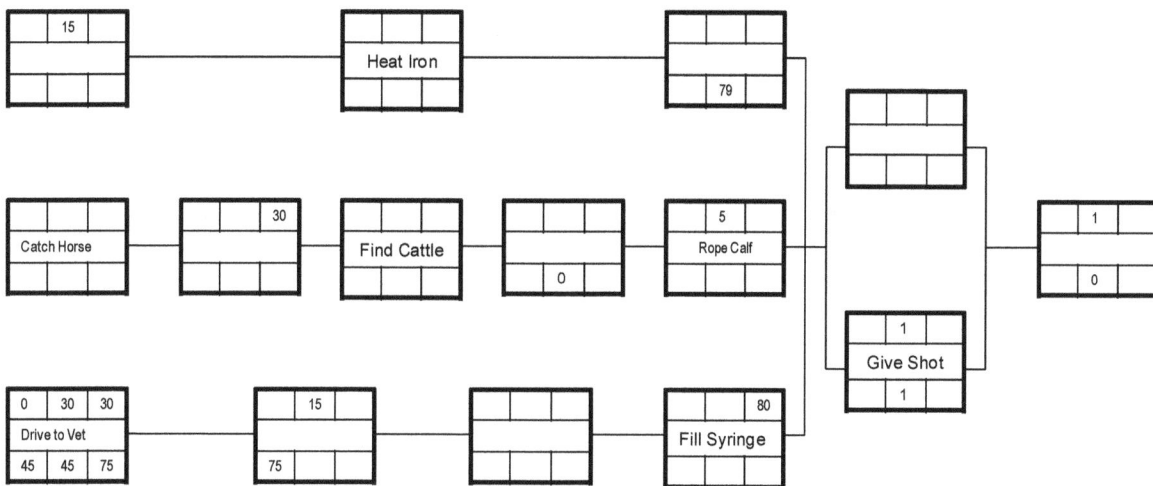

Activities

Find Branding Iron (15 minutes)
Remove Iron from Fire (1 minute)
Give Calf Shot (1 minute)
Catch Horse (15 minutes)
Round up Cattle into Corral (60 minutes)
Drive to Veterinarian Office (30 minutes)
Drive Back from Veterinarian Office (30 minutes)
Buy Vaccination Bottle from Veterinarian Office (15 minutes)

Heat Iron (30 minutes)
Rope Calf (5 minutes)
Saddle Horse (15 minutes)
Find Cattle in Pasture (30 minutes)
Brand Calf (2 minutes)
Let Calf Go (1 minute)
Fill Syringe with Medication (5 minutes)

Exercise 41. Construct a project schedule in MS Project, CA Clarity, Primavera, or VPMI

Using the WBS from your earlier exercise as your guide for the first and second level tasks, construct a draft schedule.

You will do this in two steps.

1. Transform the WBS into a simple 15 - 25 task project.
Embed second level tasks within each first level task. For example, buy materials is a second level task to planning.

2. Once the simple transformation occurs complete the following tasks:
    a. Enter all of your known resources first in the resource tab of MS Project. Type in their first and last name as well as their overall bill rate. Use a formula of average hourly rate times 1.4 to 1.5. This provides a rough measure for benefits, employee cost, space usage, supplies etc. Benefits and taxes needed to hire and pay a person are in the 30 - 35% range above hourly rate. So, for a person who makes $40 per hour use $60 per hour.
    b. Enter all tasks so that a single resource is tied to a single task -- no multiple resources.
    c. Tasks need to follow the 4/40 rule (more than four hours and less than 40 hours).
    d. Enter the predecessor tasks for each task. You can do this at the first level task level first.
    e. Predecessor tasks are based on dependencies. Dependencies exist both for tasks and resources.
    f. For significant events insert a milestone tasks (zero) duration.
    g. Enter a repeating task for weekly meetings.

Exercise 42. Schedule Bar Chart

A bar chart is a clear way to communicate a project schedule. For this exercise, draw the four horizontal bars representing the activities in the Project Time Frame Area.

Activity	Activity Description	Start Date	Calendar Time	Project Time Frame				
				Year 1	Year 2	Year 3	Year 4	Year 5
1.1	Develop Blueprints	Middle of Year 1	Six months					
1.2	Choose Contractors	After Activity 1.1	Nine months					
1.3	Building Construction	After Activity 1.2	Two years					
1.4	Hiring Employees	Start of Year 4	Fourteen months					

Exercise 43. Estimate Costs

1.   Analogous Estimating, Parametric Estimating, and Bottom-Up Estimating are three techniques used to estimate costs. Decide which is being used in each scenario.

	Analogous Estimating	Parametric Estimating	Bottom-Up Estimating
Major Motors is building a new car. They think it will cost $20 Million to develop, as that is what the last car cost to develop.			
Major Motors has begun a project to specially paint 10 special edition cars with a colorful landscape design. A painting company will supply the workers for $10,000. The black paint will cost $1000, the blue paint will cost $500, the green paint will cost $200, and the white paint will cost $100. The project is estimated to cost $11,800.			
Major Motors is building a road at its testing facility. The contractor will bill them $50,000 per mile of road. They want a 4-mile round track, so they estimate that this project will cost them $200,000.			
Rat-Free Apartments, Inc. is building a new apartment building. They are told that the flooring they chose will be $1 per square foot. The apartment building floors will be 20,000 square feet, so they estimate that the flooring will cost $20,000.			
Rat-Free Apartments, Inc. is remodeling a particular unit. The flooring will cost $500, the painting will cost $200, and the stove will cost $300. They estimate this project will cost $1000.			

2. Using one of your current or past projects as an example, how could have you used each of the following estimation techniques?

Analogous Estimating

Parametric Estimating

Bottom-Up Estimating

TECHNOLOGY
AS PROMISED

Exercise 44. Activity Cost Estimates and Basis of Estimates

Activity Cost Estimates and Basis of Estimates are two outputs of the Estimate Costs process. For each of the five activities, write an estimate of how much you think it will cost in the Activity Cost Estimates column. Then, write how you came to that estimate in the Basis of Estimates column. The Basis of your Estimates can include how you arrived at your estimate, any assumptions, any constraints, how confident you are in the estimate, and the range of the estimate ($20-$30; within $100, etc).

Activity	Activity Cost Estimates	Basis of Estimates
1. Buy candy bar		
2. Buy a dog		
3. Buy dinner for two at restaurant		
4. Build a garage		
5. Write a software user manual		

TECHNOLOGY
AS PROMISED

Exercise 45. Sample Resource and Staffing Plan for Internet Portal

What are the resources needed for this project?

One full time project manager for one year; two business analysts for one year at 20 hours per week (half time or one FTE); two programmers for one year at 20 hours per week (half time or one FTE); one contract specialist for three month at full time load (one fourth FTE); and one QC senior tester for one year at half time (half FTE). Total FTE's: two and three quarters.

What is their availability in number of hours per week?

Availability is high and certain due to priority – may need to back fill one business analyst due to anticipated maternity leave for 10 weeks.

What is the annualized FTE (full-time equivalent)?

Two and three quarters FTE's

For example, a project that requires five people at 30 hours per week for 10 weeks is equal to one FTE (1,500 hours). One year ranges anywhere from 1,400 hours to 2,200 hours. If a person works 40 hours a week for 52 weeks, they work 2,080 hours. This is rarely achieved. Why? Vacation, sick leave, holiday, etc. A more realistic expectation is in the 1,600 - 1,780 hour range.

Exercise 45. Resource and staffing plan

What are the resources needed for this project?

What is their availability in number of hours per week?

What is the annualized FTE (full-time equivalent)?

PMP Scrimmage® Curriculum, Edition 3.01   *Page 123*
www.tapuniversity.com
TECHNOLOGY
AS PROMISED

Exercise 46. Sample budget overview for Internet Portal

What items within the budget need to be tracked? (Go ahead and type over the sample cost categories provided for your reference).

Item	Cost
1. Travel – training for Insurance Portal Max	$10,000
2. Software Licensing – Apache, Oracle and Insurance Portal MAX Solution 2020	$1,250,000
3. Hardware – IBM Z series	$150,000
4. People – one year (how many team members) 2.75 FTEs at 125,000 per year loaded rate (salary plus benefits and office space)	$343,750
5. Testing Fees – server balancing and stress tests	$10,000
6. Consulting Fees	$920,000
Total	$2,683,750

Exercise 46. Create a budget overview

What items within the budget need to be tracked?

Item	Cost
1.	
2.	
3.	
4.	
5.	
6.	
Total	

Exercise 47. Determine Budget – Cost Performance Baseline

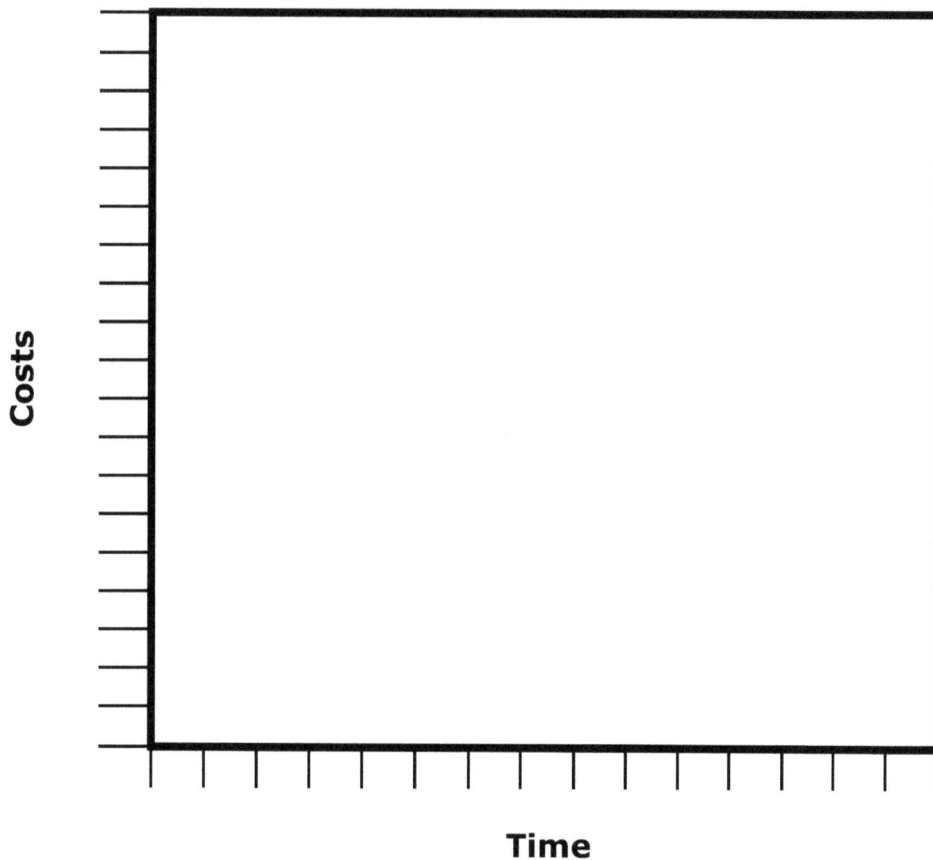

The Cost Performance Baseline is an output of the Determine Budget process. It shows project costs over time, and is typically an S-shaped curve, denoting that costs tend to be lower at the beginning and end of a project.

Draw the Cost Performance Baseline in the graph below of a project you've worked on, or an imaginary project. First label the x-axis with the appropriate time interval markers (days, months, years, etc.) and then label the y-axis with the appropriate cost interval ($100s, $1000s, $100,000s, etc.). Lastly, draw the line that represents the project costs throughout the length of the project.

Cost Performance Baseline

Costs

Time

Exercise 48. Quality Plan for Internet Portal

Quality planning for a project involves –

Ensuring the product(s) developed functions properly and as specified – this is akin to quality control.
Ensuring that the project objectives are met – this is akin to quality assurance.

Step 1. Review and feedback of various project activities including
   ✓ **Project Charter and Plan Verification by the Portal Steering Committee**
   ✓ **Best practice review of Insurance Portals**
   ✓ **Test results shared on daily basis with project team during beta testing and final acceptance testing**

Step 2. Milestone reviews by the project team each Friday morning and by the Steering Committee every other Tuesday.

   ✓ **Weekly performance reports that note SPI or CPI of less than .95 for escalation to the company president**

Step 3. Open communication with all project team members, sales force, and operations.
   ✓ **Post analysis and design proposal with invitation for everyone to comment (and incentives to do so)**
   ✓ **Daily build and test sessions with the combined project and user committees**
   ✓ **Use of Big Insurance's weekly ezine to push information to appropriate groups as defined in the Communications Planning section of the Plan**

Exercise 48. Quality Plan

Quality planning for a project involves –

Ensuring the product(s) developed functions properly and as specified – this is akin to quality control

Ensuring that the project objectives are met – this is akin to quality assurance

Step 1. Review and feedback of various project activities including (ensure objectives are met)

Step 2. Product of the project review (product develop functions as specified)

Step 3. Open communication with all project team members, sales force, and operations.

Exercise 49. Plan Quality – Cost of Quality

Cost of Quality is a tool and technique of the Plan Quality process. It includes both the costs of conformance and non-conformance. Look at the example below of the Cost of Quality for the Quack Factory. Then, using a project of your own or an imaginary project, list examples of Cost of Quality for each of the four categories.

Quack Factory Cost of Quality Example

1. Cost of Conformance - Prevention Costs

   Training session for employees on how to use rubber duck painting machine

   Develop manual on how to melt rubber and pour it into molds

2. Cost of Conformance - Appraisal Costs

   Inspection of each box of finished rubber ducks

3. Cost of Non-Conformance - Internal Failure Costs

   Scrapping of all rubber ducks that have melted parts or poor painting

4. Cost of Non-Conformance - External Failure Costs

   Taking customer complaint calls

   Refund money to customers for defective ducks

Your Project Cost of Quality

1. Cost of Conformance - Prevention Costs

2. Cost of Conformance - Appraisal Costs

3. Cost of Non-Conformance - Internal Failure Costs

4. Cost of Non-Conformance - External Failure Costs

Exercise 50. Plan Quality – Quality Checklists

Quality Checklists are an output of the Plan Quality process. They are a simple tool, yet they can be quite useful in ensuring that steps in a process are not missed due to human memory. Look at the example below of a Quality Checklist for addressing formal invitations. Then make your own Quality Checklist using a process in one of your own projects or an imaginary project that would benefit from using a quality checklist.

	Formal Invitation Checklist
√	Examine list to make sure each name has formal title (Mr., Mrs., Ms., Dr., etc.)
√	Examine list to make sure each name is the given first name (no nicknames)
√	Examine list to make sure each name is current (update names to married/divorced names)
	Examine list to make sure each family includes all family members (add any new spouse or children, exclude any former family member from divorce or deceased)
	Examine list to make sure each address includes zip code
	Compare addressed envelopes with final address list

Exercise 51. Sample responsibility assignment matrix (RAM) for the Internet Portal.

Using the PMBOK® as a guide, complete the RAM Responsibility Assignment Matrix (RAM). The first page is an example.

Work Breakdown Structure element (high level) **People**	Project Charter	Project Plan	Define and Build the Solution	Deliver the Solution
Exec. Sponsor	A	A	A	
Project Manager	R	R	R	A
Business Analysts	C	C	C	C
Sales management	I	C	C	C
Sales force	I	C	C	C
Quotation team	I	C	C	C
Testing	I	I	C	R
Corporate Contracting	I	C	C	I

RAM Legend

Responsibility	Time Involved	Update frequency	Information needed from others for review	Information produced for others	Inherited responsibility
I = Informed	_____ hours per week	Daily - weekly	Project reports	Status Updates	
C = Consulted	_____ hours per week	Daily -- weekly	Design and test results	Deliverables	I
A = Accountable	_____ hours per week	Daily - weekly	Deliverables	Approvals	I, C
R = Responsible	_____ hours per week	Daily - weekly	Activities	Project summaries	I, C, A

Exercise 51. Construct a responsibility assignment matrix (RAM).

Work Breakdown Structure element (high level) People	Project Initiation and Planning			
Exec. Sponsor				
PM				
*				
*				
*				
*				
*				
*				

RAM Legend

Responsibility	Time Involved	Update frequency	Information needed from others for review	Information produced for others	Inherited responsibility
I = Informed	_____ hours per week	Daily - weekly			
C = Consulted	_____ hours per week	Daily - weekly			I
A = Accountable	_____ hours per week	Daily - weekly			I, C
R = Responsible	_____ hours per week	Daily - weekly			I, C, A

Exercise 52. *Sample Responsibility / Authority Balance for Internet Portal*

Please list where you think your organization is on the following scale. Where does the responsibility / authority relationship lie — heavy on responsibility without authority, vice versa, or at equilibrium.

What would you share as the best way to manage responsibility / authority and ambiguity / clarity to someone just hired into a PM role?

Within the "Big" insurance company the balance is tilted toward more responsibility and a
lack of authority. That is changing as we implemented a Project Management Office
and, as in this project, there is high level visibility for strategic projects. In the past we
have been little more than schedule stewards – little or no authority but all of the
responsibility.

Exercise 52. Responsibility / Authority Balance

Please list where you think your organization is on the following scale. Where does the responsibility / authority relationship lie - heavy on responsibility without authority, vice versa, or at equilibrium.

What would you share as the best way to manage responsibility / authority and ambiguity / clarity to someone just hired into a PM role?

TECHNOLOGY
AS PROMISED

Exercise 53. Develop Human Resource Plan – Maslow's Hierarchy

Organizational Theory is a tool and technique of the Develop Human Resource Plan process. There are numerous organizational theories which attempt to explain human behavior. A well-known organizational theory is Maslow's Hierarchy of Needs. Maslow proposed that humans are always in a state of need. When a lower-level need is satisfied, humans try to satisfy the need on the next level. This is useful to understand because those with whom we are working have different motivations. Here are five different Project Managers' descriptions of why they want a particular project management job. Write their names next to the level on the pyramid below indicating their level on Maslow's Hierarchy of Needs.

Hope Parsons: *"The requirements of this job mesh perfectly with my natural skills and personality. I truly enjoy managing projects in this industry, and I feel that the completed projects are making the world a better place."*

Katherine Goodwill: *"I really need this job. I'm a single mom who has been unemployed for 8 months now. I haven't been able to pay the rent or electric bill, and I'm barely able to get enough groceries to put meals on the table."*

Jack Thompson: *"I want to work with the project managers and executives at this company. They're the kind of people I want as mentors and friends. I want to be known by others as a project manager at this company."*

Oliver Horents: *"I've been a team member on similar projects, but what I really want to be is the actual project manager. I want people to look at me and know I'm their leader who will get this thing accomplished."*

Michael Woodson: *"I'm interested in this job largely because I know once I'm hired, I'll be able to stay as long as I want. It's a solid industry and the company has never had lay-offs. Also, they have a great retirement plan!"*

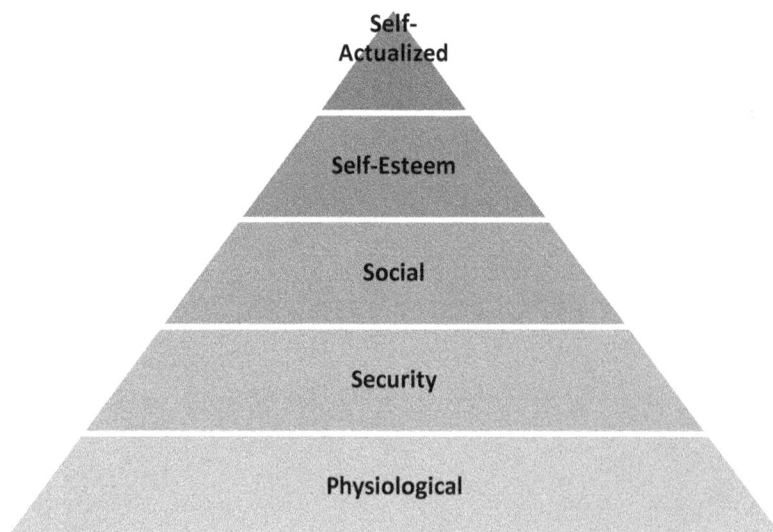

Self-
Actualized

Self-Esteem

Social

Security

Physiological

Exercise 54. Develop Human Resource Plan – Profiling

Organizational Theory is a tool and technique of the Develop Human Resource Plan process. This exercise applies Achievement Theory, Theory X and Y, Locus of Control, and Tolerance of Ambiguity, which are all organizational theories. After obtaining some understanding of these theories, practice writing some profiles. Here is the situation: the FBI has given you descriptions of a rogue Project Managers that might be in your area. Using the FBI's description, create a profile of the person to use in describing the wanted person to your team.

1. Project Manager "X" has a very low tolerance of ambiguity and ascribes to Theory "X."

Project Manager "X" assumes his team is a bunch of lazy bums, so he micromanages and punishes them. He needs exact figures—if a team member says a task is about half done, he will become unglued and demand to know whether that means 49%, 50%, or 51%.

2. Project Manager "Y" is very highly motivated by affiliation. She ascribes to Theory "Y."

3. Project Manager "Sweet Potato Sam" has a low locus of control and a high tolerance of ambiguity.

4. Project Manager "The Yellow Yam" has a high locus of control and is motivated by power.

5. Project Manager "Yukon Gold" is motivated by achievement and has a low tolerance of ambiguity.

Exercise 55. Communication Formula

Using the Communication Formula, calculate the paths of communication. Try to do it with the formula memorized.

1. There are 5 people on the team. How many communication paths are there?

2. There were 10 people on the team, but 3 left. How many communication paths are there now?

3. There were 20 people on the team, but now 10 more have been added. How many more communication paths are there now?

4. There were 8 people on the team, but then 13 communication paths were removed. How many people are on the team now?

5. There are 3 people on team A, 5 people on team B, and 4 people on team C. Everyone on team A and B can communicate with each other and everyone on team B and C can communicate with each other. However, team A and team C are not allowed to communicate with other. How many communication paths are there?

Exercise 56. Plan Communication – Communication Methods

Identify which of the three communication methods each example represents.

	Interactive	Push	Pull
1. Intranet Site			
2. Meetings			
3. Letter			
4. Memo			
5. Phone Calls			
6. Knowledge Repository			
7. Report			
8. Fax			
9. Video Conferencing			
10. Hallway Conversation			

Exercise 57. Sample Communication Plan for Internet Portal
Audience

The RAM identifies audiences by their role. This section provides some additional explanation and a communication plan which should include all of these elements.

Who are the stakeholders? **Insurance sales force, internal operations, IT, and project team.** Describe each one and whether they are in the RAM? For example, who is your:

Executive Sponsor (SOS)? **Company president has personally intervened; the profile is helpful though her time is a challenge.**
Project manager? **Veteran Sam Snead**
Key team members? **Best developers and top sales people**
Outside Department members you need to interact with? **Contracting**
Primary customer? **Sales force, operations and policy holders**
Primary suppliers? **One of three contracting agencies**

Meetings

How are they scheduled? **Outlook**
How are results shared and validated?   **Via Project Intranet**
Who is included, for what? **Open to all employees for reports and team members / steering committees for meetings**
How is notice provided? **Email invite seven days before**

Exercise 58. Project Updates

Updates

What project information is restricted? Financial to whom? **Steering Committee and PM only**

What project information is public? **Summary report and Feature Illustrations**

How often are project reports that summarize progress completed? **Each Friday**

How often do team members need to report their progress? **Daily**

What is the essential project status information? **RYG reports.** Is Red, Yellow, Green reporting used? **YES.** Is earned value? **YES**

Exercise 57.　*Create a Communication Plan*

Audience

The RAM identifies audiences by their role. This section provides some additional explanation and a communication plan which should include all of these elements.

Who are the stakeholders? Describe each one and whether they are in the RAM?
For example who is your: **Executive Sponsor?** **Project manager?** **Key team members?** **Outside Department members you need to interact with?** **Primary customer?** **Primary suppliers?**

Meetings

How are they scheduled?
How are results shared and validated?
Who is included, for what?
How is notice provided?

Exercise 58. Project Updates

Updates

What project information is restricted?   To whom?
What project information is public?
How often are project reports that summarize progress completed?
How often do team members need to report their progress?
What is the essential project status information?
Is Red, Yellow, Green reporting used?
Is Earned Value Used, Expected, or Accepted (EV)? If not, what could be done to introduce it?

Exercise 59. Sample Escalation Plan for Internet Portal

A special form of communication is known as escalation. This is what and to whom you need to communicate with if a problem arises that can not be solved by the immediate project team or first or second level above that team.

It is helpful for you to identify this within your communication plan. Go ahead and extend your communication plan you just completed with an outline of how issues will be escalated.

In order to ensure that an issue (or risk event or action item) does not hamper forward progress, the following are some escalation guidelines. **Resolution is defined as either a solution or plan of action. The following contain three guidelines. What's missing from this list? What is not necessary in your opinion?**

1. Issues not resolved by the immediate project team are escalated to the project sponsor within **eight** hours.

    Issue name, date, time, and person who identified the issue are noted. **Due to project importance, the company president wants e-mail and voice mail left for any issues that block forward progress within eight hours.**

2. Issues not resolved by the project sponsor within 24 hours are escalated to the next level higher. **No higher level**

3. Resolution is defined as one of two things:
    1. **Actual resolution of the problem or issue.**
    2. **Plan to solve the problem or issue that is agreed to by the project team and impacted stakeholders. The plan needs to specify a follow up date, initial course of action, and acceptance criteria.**

Exercise 59. Escalation Plan

A special form of communication is known as escalation. This is what and to whom you need to communicate with if a problem arises that can not be solved by the immediate project team or first or second level above that team.

In order to ensure that an issue (or risk event or action item) does not hamper forward progress, the following are some escalation guidelines. **Resolution is defined as either a solution or plan of action. The following bullets contain three guidelines. What's missing from this list? What is not necessary in your opinion?**

- Issues not resolved by the immediate project team are escalated to the project sponsor within _____ hours. Issue name, date, time and person who identified the issue are noted.

- Issues not resolved by the project sponsor within _____ hours are escalated to _____

- Resolution is defined as:

Exercise 60. Plan Risk Responses – Strategies

Strategies for Negative Risks or Threats and Strategies for Positive Risks or Opportunities are two tools and techniques of the Plan Risk Responses process. The strategies for Negative Risks are: Avoid, Transfer, Mitigate, and Acceptance. The strategies for Positive Risks are: Exploit, Share, Enhance, and Accept.

Which strategy is being used in each of the situations below?

1. Angie wants to get a house cat, but she's worried about the risk of having cat hair all over her furniture. So, she decides that she will get a hairless cat.

2. Angie is worried about the risk of vet bills that could occur if her hairless cat becomes injured, so she buys pet health insurance.

3. Angie's husband says the risk of his friends teasing him is too great if they get a hairless cat. They decide they will get the cat, but try not to tell anyone about it, so it'll be less likely that he gets teased.

4. When Angie's husband discovers how much he can sell hairless kittens for, he teams up with another hairless cat owner and they develop a scheme to start breeding the two cats, and then raising and selling the hairless kittens.

Exercise 61. Risk Management Plan Sample

Definition

Risk involves uncertain events that have not occurred yet. The result of those events may be positive or negative. In general, the result is perceived to be negative. Risk management is the art and science of managing those future, unknown events.

Risk Management Approach. Effective risk management occurs when relevant project risks are identified, analyzed, and prioritized. The art is in identifying enough risks to ensure reliability and validity without overwhelming the process and stalling action.

What is your team's Risk Management approach and how does it contrast with the PMBOK®? Is there a separation of positive (opportunity) and negative (threats) risks?

List three to five risks (negative or positive) in the table on the following page.

Columns in gray are optional for this exercise.

Short Name	Risk Description	Charter Risk Assessment (High, Med, Low)	Size of Loss	Prob-ability of Loss	Risk Exposure (Prob-ability X Size)	Priority	Mgmt Strategy (avoid, transfer, mitigate, accept)	Person responsible
Silver Bullet	An IT group is advocating for new portal technology that has great reviews and claims for no testing	Medium	100,000	Med (30%)	30,000	Medium	Mitigate	Use proven technologies only and confront unproven claims
HIPAA 2 rules	HIPAA additional rules may alter design	High	70,000	High (50%	35,000	High	Transfer	Include in consulting contract
Vendor goes Bankrupt	2 of the 3 proven contracting firms are financially stressed	High	150,000	25%	37,500	High	Transfer	Secure two consulting firms for parts of the contract

Exercise 61. Risk Management Plan

Definition

Risk involves uncertain events that have not occurred yet. The result of those events may be positive or negative. In general, the result is perceived to be negative. Risk management is the art and science of managing those future, unknown events.

Risk Management Approach. Effective risk management occurs when relevant project risks are identified, analyzed, and prioritized. The art is in identifying enough risks to ensure reliability and validity without overwhelming the process and stalling action.

What is your team's Risk Management approach and how does it contrast with the PMBOK®? Is there a separation of positive (opportunity) and negative (threats) risks?

List three to five risks (negative or positive) in the following table.

Columns in gray are optional for this exercise.

Short Name	Risk Description	Charter Risk Assessment (High, Med, Low)	Size of Loss	Probability of Loss	Risk Exp. (Probability X Size)	Priority	Mgmt Strategy (avoid, transfer, mitigate, accept)	Person responsible

TECHNOLOGY
AS PROMISED

Exercise 62. The Risk Processes

1. Form a team of 2 or 3 people and select a hypothetical project. Your project might be building a castle, developing lunar real estate, planning a local sports tournament or family reunion, or any other project your team would like.

   My project is:_____

2. The Plan Risk Management process. This process creates the Risk Management Plan. Fill in the following details or your plan...

a. Decide how you will be defining the impact of your risks by selecting an Impact Scales in one of your texts, or creating your own.

b. Decide how much to budget for risk management: $_____

c. Describe the tolerance your stakeholders have for risk:_____

d. What are a few of the general categories of risks for your project? (See PMBOK p.244 for example of Risk Breakdown Structure with general categories on top).

   _____

3. The Identify Risks process. Identify 8 risks for your project. There should be both negative risks (threats) and positive risks (opportunities).

Risk Name	Threat or Opportunity?
	T O
	T O
	T O
	T O
	T O
	T O
	T O
	T O

4. The Perform Qualitative Risk Analysis process. For each risk, determine the Impact rating and the Probability rating. Then multiply these to obtain your overall RPI rating. Use the Impact Scale you decided upon in the Risk Management Planning process.

Risk Name	Impact	Probability	RPI Rating

5. The Perform Quantitative Risk Analysis process. Select one of your risks and choose two potential response strategies or two sets of circumstances. For each strategy/circumstance, choose two potential outcomes and estimate the probability of each outcome. For example, if the risk is being sued by Castle Construction Company who believes you copied their work, Response Strategy 1 could be to hire an expensive legal firm and Response Strategy 2 could be to hire a more affordable, less-experienced firm. The potential outcome for each strategy is to either win or lose the case. There may be a higher probability of winning with the expensive firm. (Note that you do not have to restrict the use of this tool to risk responses—you may examine potential outcomes of any decision within your project.)

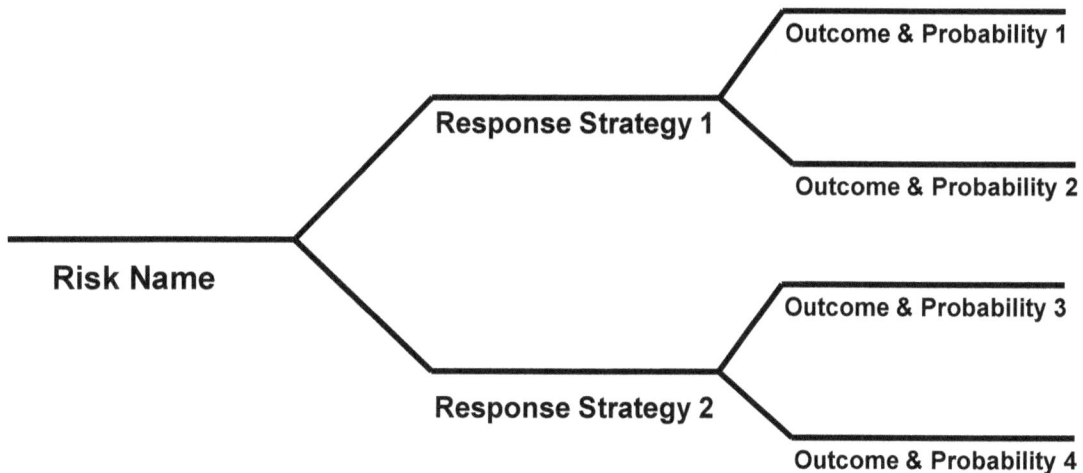

```
                                              ┌ Outcome & Probability 1
                          Response Strategy 1 ┤
                                              └ Outcome & Probability 2

       Risk Name
                                              ┌ Outcome & Probability 3
                          Response Strategy 2 ┤
                                              └ Outcome & Probability 4
```

6. The Plan Risk Responses process. For 5 of your risks, decide among the seven strategies which are: Avoid, Transfer, Mitigate, Accept, Exploit, Share, and Enhance. Then write a brief description of your specific response. For example, you may be concerned about water damage to your castle from the moat, so your strategy is to Transfer, and the description is to buy a homeowner's insurance policy.

Risk Name	Strategy	Description of Response

7. The Monitor and Control Risks process. Throughout your project, be aware of new risks and risk events, and respond to them. Also, you may wish to perform risk audits to assure your responses were effective.

Exercise 63. Plan Procurements – Make or Buy Analysis

Make or Buy Analysis is a tool and technique of the Plan Procurements process. Make or Buy Analysis is the process of analyzing all the needed factors to determine whether a good or service is better done in-house, or if it should be bought from another organization or individual.

Edward is beginning to manage a project that includes the development of security footstep identification software. He belongs to an organization of about 200 employees. His organization employs 18 programmers, and although the organization is somewhat under-staffed, because the project is important, Edward is allowed to have whichever programmers he wants. Edward is now trying to decide whether he should have the footstep software developed internally, or whether he should hire another organization to develop it. In performing this Make or Buy Analysis, there are many things to consider. Think of several things you would suggest that Edward consider and write them below.

Exercise 64. Sample Specific Contract Requirements for Internet Portal

With your Scope Statement and review completed, discuss the final steps your selected project takes in contract negotiation. Use the following questions to guide your discussion and record your notes below.

1. What type of contract is typically used in your current or former organization: Fixed, Cost Plus, Time and Material? **All contracts are used and both fixed and time and material may be used for this project.**

2. Based on contract type, how much risk does your organization typically assume? **Lesser risk due to nature of our business – heavily regulated.**

3. What parts of the contract, in addition to administrative broiler plate and company introduction, seem to be the same from client to client? **Administrative and preferred seller list.** Have those been captured in a shared repository somewhere (intranet site, shared folder)? **More informal but accessible via legal.**

4. What are the expectations for a project manager in managing the customer relationship? **Fulfills the role of contract administrator.** What is the norm for communication (e.g. weekly phone calls, email updates, when do in-person visits occur)? **Daily contact is needed during this project.** What does the project manager own in terms of responsibility? **All** End to end (client to project) or project functions only?

Exercise 64. Identify Specific Contract Requirements

With scope statement and review completed, discuss the final steps your selected project takes in contract negotiation. Use the following questions to guide your discussion, record the notes below and prepare a poster for reporting to the larger group.

1. What type of contract is typically used in your current or former organization: Fixed, cost plus, Time and Material?

2. Based on contract type, how much risk does your organization typically assume?

3. What parts of the contract, in addition to administrative broiler plate and company introduction, seem to be the same from client to client?

   Have those been captured in a shared repository somewhere (intranet site, shared folder)?

4. What are the expectations for a project manager in managing the customer relationship? What is the norm for communication (e.g. weekly phone calls, e-mail updates, when do in-person visits occur)? What does the project manager own in terms of responsibility? End to end (client to project) or project functions only?

| |
| |
| |
| |
| |
| |
| |
| |
| |
| |
| |
| |

Exercise 65. Identify Contract Type

Mark the box that best describes the type of agreement—Time and Materials (T&M), Cost Plus Fixed Fee (CPFF), Cost Plus Percentage of Cost (CPF) (CPPC), Cost Plus Incentive (CPIF) or Fixed Price.

	T&M	CPFF	CPF	CPIF	Fixed
1. Andrea said that she would clean Andy's hamster cage for a year, but Andy has to reimburse her for the shavings plus pay her $50.					
2. Andrea's mother is paying her 2 cents a minute to pick "bouquets" of dandelions from the yard.					
3. Antonio is reimbursing his daughter for a weekly planner and set of pens in return for her reminding him 3 days in advance of his wife's birthday and their anniversary. Additionally, if his daughter goes above and beyond the contract and finds out what his wife actually wants, Antonio pays his daughter ten dollars. This contract has a strict confidentiality clause.					
4. Antonio pays his niece twice the cost of her gas in return for driving his daughter to her weekly electric guitar lessons.					
5. Andy offered his sister five dollars to take the blame for teaching the family dog to retrieve the neighbors' newspapers.					
6. Antonio told his daughter he would pay her 5 cents each time she played "Jingle Bells" repeatedly on her electric guitar while his in-laws stopped by.					
7. Andy's mother needed a cake mix, frosting, butter, pork rinds, and eggs to make her locally-famous Piggy Cake, so she sent Andy to the grocery store. She agreed to pay him 3 times whatever the total cost of the groceries was.					
8. Antonio paid his daughter five dollars to teach him how to attach photos to his emails.					
9. Tired of hearing his co-workers brag about the fish they catch, Antonio tells his children to go buy themselves fishing poles, cell phones, and a camera and he'll pay them back. If they catch a fish larger than 20 pounds, he'll give them $100 if they call him so he can drive down to the river and get his picture taken with the fish.					
10. Antonio's wife, Ashley, is tired of hearing him complain about the gas mileage he gets with his van. She pays their son for the cost of gas plus $20 for buying cans of gasoline and sneaking gas into the van daily for three months while it's in the garage at night.					

Exercise 66. Plan Procurements - Contract Types

The different types of contracts each have advantages and disadvantages that make some more suitable for certain situations. Contract Types are a tool and technique of the Plan Procurements process. For each situation, circle the type of contract (Fixed Price, Cost Reimbursable, or Time & Materials) you would suggest.

1. Mary is a project manager working on procuring some needed services. Her budget is very tight, and she needs to know what the exact cost will be.

Fixed Price	Cost Reimbursable	Time & Materials

2. Ryan needs a subject matter expert for the skyscraper project he is working on. One of his team members found a professor at a local university who teaches a course on skyscraper construction, and he does consulting at the rate of $150/hour. Ryan isn't sure how many hours of consultation he'll need during the duration of the project.

Fixed Price	Cost Reimbursable	Time & Materials

3. Crystal is leading a software development project. They've run into a difficult part in the programming that no one on her team has the expertise to do. One of the programmers mentions that his friend has the needed expertise. Crystal talks to the expert programmer who states that he is unsure how long the work would take, but he's willing to be paid a set price per line of code.

Fixed Price	Cost Reimbursable	Time & Materials

4. Paul has a very precise description of the machine he wants developed for his project. The scope statement is detailed, and even the exact brand of materials that he wants used for the project are specified. In the past, he has ordered similar machines from Custom Machines for You, so he knows what this one should cost.

Fixed Price	Cost Reimbursable	Time & Materials

5. Janet has found a contractor that she believes will do an excellent job. However, neither she nor they have a very good idea of the scope of the project. As they work on the project, there will be plenty of progressive elaboration.

Fixed Price	Cost Reimbursable	Time & Materials

Exercise 67. Plan Procurements - Specific Contract Types

Read the PMBOK®'s description of Contract Types under the Plan Procurements process. For each of the three types of Fixed Price contracts, and for each of the three types of Cost Reimbursable contracts, write an example. Examples may include actual contracts you've worked with, or contracts that you could have used on your projects.

1. Firm Fixed Price (FFP)

2. Fixed Price Incentive Fee (FPIF)

3. Fixed Price with Economic Price Adjustment (FP-EPA)

4. Cost Plus Fixed Fee (CPFF)

5. Cost Plus Incentive Fee (CPIF)

6. Cost Plus Award Fee (CPAF)

Chapter 5 - Now Make That Project Happen (Execution)

"Get 'R Done!" Larry the "Cable Guy" was born and raised in Nebraska (Pawnee City in the southeast corner of the state). He's remained pretty attached to the state although he now lives in Florida. He still frequents University of Nebraska football games (a skybox does wonders for attendance) and we can assure you that his accent is not a "southern Nebraskan" one, though many of his mannerisms are at home here.

Larry's signature catch phrase is "Get 'R Done." That is also perfect for project management and the processes within Execution. It's all about making stuff happen and getting it done. Project management succeeds when a well formed plan is executed effectively. That execution can be sabotaged by inept planning and missing what the stakeholders want, confusing the business objectives, or launching out on a non-sanctioned effort just to name a few. It can also be sabotaged by too much overhead and processes or methodologies that can choke progress.

A good rule of thumb for project management time and process overhead is between 7% and 15% of an overall project's time and budget. For example in a 100,000 hour project or a $1,000,000 project the time and budget spent to manage the project, coordinate team activities, update reports, etc., should be between 7,000 to 15,000 hours or $70,000 to $150,000 respectively. Trim that down too thin and the risk of missing project objectives increases considerably. Consume over 20% and the project infrastructure becomes bloated, unwieldy, and visible progress ends.

The processes presented in the PMBOK® fit within the "Get 'R Done" motto. The pivotal process is to Direct and Manage Project Activities. Similar to the Planning Processes, Develop Project Management Plan process, Direct and Manage Project Execution serves as the center point to execute project actions. Those actions include allocating funds, developing designs, creating and controlling project deliverables, and updating the project with approved changes. As the project manager and team are making stuff happen, they should check the project's progress with planned objectives and quality (Perform Quality Assurance), get team members from internal resources or through contractors (Acquire Project Team), validate and, if needed, enhance the skills of those team members (Develop Project Team), share information and request project status updates (Distribute Information), and finally request and select sellers.

Direct and Manage Project Execution (4.4)

The first process in the Executing Process group is Direct and Manage Project Execution. That process is within the Integration Knowledge Area. The Project Management Plan serves as the primary input. The board is set, the die is cast, now it's time to execute.

TECHNOLOGY
AS PROMISED

Remember that the project plan may have been developed in one setting by a primary author or may be a collection of several documents penned by a dozen team members. Some parts of the project plan may still be in development (Procurement Plans) even as the project work begins (recall also the iterative loops among Planning–Executing–Monitoring/Controlling).

Direct and Manage Project Execution is the process most impacted by the application area. Requirements and design activities for architecture, engineering, and information technology organizations or departments fit within this process. Focus groups, market research, medical research, and branding for product development, pharmaceutical, and health care organizations fit within this process as well. It is this process where stakeholders and project sponsors perceive the project work is done. Planning, while appreciated, is often seen as little more than overhead. This process also receives and responds to changes to the project (Integrated Change Control organizes those changes). Ultimately this process produces the "stuff" from your project (tangible and intangible deliverables).

Perform Quality Assurance (8.2)

Perform Quality Assurance is done during the execution phase of the project and uses all of the planned and systematic activities implemented within the quality system to provide confidence that the project will satisfy the relevant quality standards that are required. It has a twofold focus:

1. The quality of the project management processes.
2. The quality of the results or product of the project.

The quality audit is an external review of the project to see how it complies with the organizational and project governance. The focus then is on the project management process not the product or output of the project.

There are two kinds of outputs that result from the Perform Quality Assurance process – requests and updates. The requested changes should be to improve the organization's process which should not only assist the current project but future ones as well.

Acquire Project Team (9.2)

Acquiring project team members comes from one of two general sources:
internal employees (FTE's) or contractors. The project manager and project team work on several different, sequential projects together or are recruited together for a specific project.

The real world application from the outputs is to ensure you have adequate resources to meet the scope of the project within the given time frame or, in the event you do not, adjust the scope and time of the project to match the resources. Again in the real world, you often have to deliver it all on time and with the scope expressed with less than necessary resources. Figuring out how you balance all of that is what makes the profession of project management challenging and far from boring.

Develop Project Team (9.3)

Whether you have sufficient or less than ideal resource levels, maximizing the productivity of your team is well within your span of control and influence. This leads to the second Human Resource process within the Executing Process Group – Develop Project Team. The purpose of team development is optimizing the competencies of your team members and maximizing the effectiveness of teamwork.

A gap analysis can be helpful to identify areas for which team members could use additional training. The goal is to ensure that money is wisely spent to leverage existing skills and acquire new skills. Applied over time and with consistency, knowledge, skills, and abilities (KSA) become competencies. Combine competencies with a person who has the innate talent for a project role and you have a winning combination.

After all the team building, recognition, and competency building, the primary output from Develop Project Team is the Team Performance Assessment. Often the best recognition is a meaningful, positive, and constructive performance assessment for the team and each team member.

Manage Project Team (9.4)

Managing the project team involves keeping the project team together, moving them forward, and finishing tasks together. Together works. Now, together does not mean in the same office, cubicle, or one mind. A project team is likely to have some virtual team members, people working on at least six other projects and activities other than your project. Together means keeping focused on the activities at hand and supporting its mission.

As your project team performs and goes through various stage left/right entry and exits, the following five stages occur.

1. **Forming** - What is important at this stage is that purpose and mission are established. A lack of purpose will leave a group in the storming stage.

2. **Storming** - This occurs as the group wrestles with their purpose and task(s) they must do. The storming occurs as people get to know each other and get to know what must be done. Everything about management is simple, except for people. Bold statement? No, rather it is recognition that people and groups of people bring all sorts of wonderfully challenging perspectives and opinions. Management moves from science to art as a manager learns to understand differences in people and how to leverage

those differences. Some storming is necessary. Lack of storming indicates a group of people who may have gone stale or do not care or begin to have group think (where everyone just agrees).

3. **Norming** – This occurs as a new group establishes their boundaries, turf, and informal expectations. At this point, a group has a discernible identity to those outside of it. It also has a rite of passage for new members.

4. **Performing** – This occurs when the group executes its work efficiently and effectively. Conflict is openly addressed. Objectives are met. The group becomes a team. The mission of that team supersedes the ego of each person in it. Addition of a new member to the team is a test of its level of performance. Sometimes a new member can take the team to a higher level. Other times adding a new member to get a job done introduces inertia and conflict to the team. You have to start back at the forming stage. Whether the team accepts or rejects new members is not a measure of its performance. It is more a measure of the broader organizational culture. Earlier in my career, I felt all high performance teams should embrace new members. No clicks or enclaves should be allowed.

5. **Reforming or adjourning -** Some group process overviews omit this stage. Reforming is the reconstitution of a group after its work has been accomplished.

Observation and conversations are among the oldest techniques in management and unfortunately, ones that are too often ignored. If team members are virtual, substitute phone calls and instant messages for what would typically take place via in-person conversations. Observation of work produced or team interactions can also be done virtually.

Distribute Information (10.3)

This was called Information Distribution in the third edition PMBOK®. In this process, the Communications Management Plan is being executed and relevant information being made available. Distribute Information also helps assess whether you are doing what you said you would do in the planning phase. You need a good sense of your organizational culture in order to determine whether your project environment supports reporting of good and bad news. Unfortunately, as in ages past, the messenger, or rather their career, is still all too often punished today.

Manage Stakeholders Expectations (10.4)

This was called Manage Stakeholders in the third edition PMBOK®. We have shared that perceived project success is determined by how stakeholders think, feel, and believe the project has succeeded.

Sample stakeholder issues include:

> Resource conflict resolution for a key team member from another team
> Sharing equipment
> Customer sign off on a new design
> Governmental regulatory approval for power grid

Conduct Procurements (12.2)

In the third edition PMBOK®, there were two execution processes in the procurement knowledge area—Request Seller Responses and Select Sellers. Now there is only Conduct Procurements.

> Qualified Seller Lists – Most companies have lists of approved sellers or even a short list of sellers with whom they have previous experience.
> Procurement may have to research candidates. In this case, you need to manage not only your own project team, but the efforts of procurement personal (buyer or attorneys or both).
> Bidder Conferences are also referred to as a pre-proposal, pre-bid, or vendor conference. It is typically a meeting with sellers prior to each prospective seller submitting their proposal to the buyer. These can be done in person or virtually. The goal is to provide a clearer view of your organization's procurement practice, ensure a level playing field from which to choose the most appropriate vendor, and remove as much ambiguity as possible to ensure the most accurate and comprehensive responses are available from each vendor.

With seller proposal(s) safely nestled into the hands (or virtual connection) of your project team, the next step is to select a seller. The only new input to this process is the Proposals developed by each seller. You'll see that the other inputs have been used previously.

Methods to evaluate and then select a seller include best practices for procurement selection from weighting systems (pre-assigned) to seller rating systems and proposal evaluation techniques. A generally accepted best practice is to separate the technical or content portion of the seller response from the budget or pricing information. The goal is to select the most compliant and lowest total cost of ownership (TCO) seller. The lowest priced seller may not prove to be the best fit or overall lowest TCO seller.

Contact negotiation comes into play at the end – once all prospective sellers have been compared via consistent screening systems, independent estimates, expert judgment, preferred seller rankings, evaluation techniques, and weighting systems.

Why would contract negotiation be last? The answer is to find one or two preferred sellers and negotiate with the preferred or highest ranked one. The second place seller, if adequate, can be kept as a possible replacement should negotiations not go forward with the first seller. In Fixed Contracts and in some public sector organizations, it may be difficult to negotiate price. For those in private sector settings, the goal is not just constraining price at this stage; rather it is confirmation of fit, detail clarification, and terms.

Some contract basics are:
1. A contract is a legal relationship subject to remedy in the courts.
2. Boilerplate - the boilerplate version will be altered depending on the specific requirements of the project.
3. By definition, contracts have terms and conditions (T&C) that must be adhered to. Most organizations have a standard contract template which covers corporate T&Cs regardless of with whom they are entering into a contract.

Whatever form the contract takes, it is generally the key document in procurement management. It shapes the way you, as the buyer's project manager, plan, implement the plan, and control the contractor. Once the contract is consummated, the following roles and responsibilities need to be fulfilled. Project team and contract team friction can occur due to a lack of role confirmation.

Chapter 5 Exercises

Exercise 68. Direct and Manage Project Execution – Change Requests

One of the inputs to the Direct and Manage Project Execution process is Approved Change Requests. In the course of implementing these change requests, new Change Requests may arise. These Change Requests are categorized into four types—Corrective Actions, Preventive Actions, Defects, and Updates. Identify the type of Change Request listed below.

	Corrective Actions	Preventive Actions	Defects	Updates
1. The Quack Factory has not been meeting its daily quota for making a batch of special rubber ducks. A request has been submitted to speed up one of the major steps of the process by reducing time allowed for the paint to dry.				
2. Most of the ducks coming off of the line had the orange paint from their bills smeared all over their wings. A request has been submitted to increase the drying time between colors to fix this problem.				
3. The paint drying time for the ducks is now so long that they are overheating and some of their heads are melting off. Because of this, a request has been submitted to lower the temperature of the dryer.				
4. Now that they are almost ready to ship some ducks, the shipping process activities are better understood, so they have been added to the WBS.				
5. Individuals have been assigned as responsible for specific shipping process activities, so the WBS Dictionary can be revised to include these names.				
6. Rumors have been flying that the cost of raw rubber will be doubling within the next three months. So a request has been submitted to buy as much rubber as possible now.				
7. The cost of this special batch of ducks is starting to exceed budget. To save on materials cost, a request has been submitted to decrease their size to about the size of a dime.				

Exercise 69. Perform Quality Assurance – Spaghetti Diagram

Process Analysis is a tool and technique of the Perform Quality Assurance process. The Process Improvement Plan is put into action to identify ways to better the processes in place. A number of Six Sigma and Lean tools may be used to facilitate this.

The Lean Six Sigma tool called Spaghetti Diagram is also called a transportation or workplace diagram. It's called a Spaghetti Diagram because the lines often cross like a plate of spaghetti. The numbers indicate the route. It can show the route of information, people, or material. Organizations are often shocked to see how many miles a file or paper can travel within their company. Study the Spaghetti Diagram below showing how a file traveled around an office. In the box at the bottom, quickly sketch an example of how much some type of information, file, person, or material travels around your office or home.

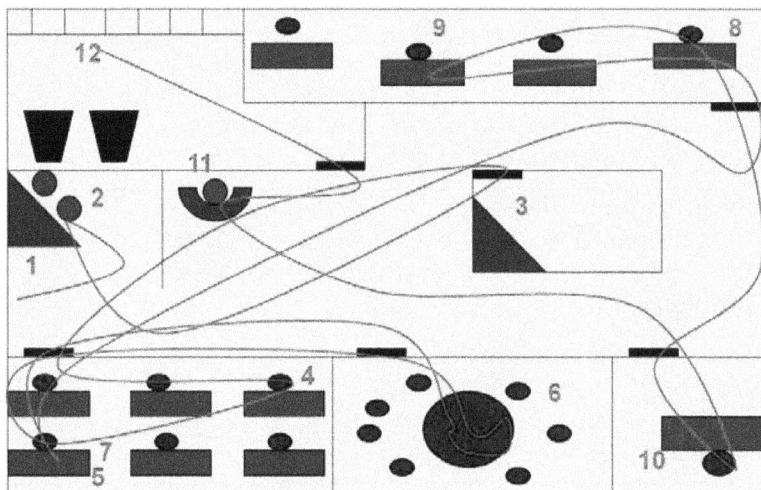

Exercise 70. Perform Quality Assurance – SIPOC Analysis

Process Analysis is a tool and technique of the Perform Quality Assurance process. A SIPOC Analysis is a Lean Six Sigma tool that may be used to facilitate this. Study the example, and the use the next sheet to perform a SIPOC Analysis of a process in your workplace.

Supplier(s)	Inputs	Process	Outputs	Customer(s)
MedOffice Supply Co.	Health insurance forms, envelopes, stationery, postage machine, paper Should be received within two weeks of ordering	Review patient sheet Look up each charge on Medicare list Type charges on insurance form	Completed health insurance forms with charges mailed to patient's insurance company and patient Mailed within 1 week Amount of charges correct	Patient's health insurance company
Medicare	List of current allowable charges Notice of changes should be 1 month in advance	Make two photocopies Address envelopes Health insurance form in mail to insurance company		Patient
Nursing Department	Patient sheet with sticky labels from materials Should be received within 24 hours of patient discharge	Mail copy to patient File 1 copy in office	Updated patient billing file Notation of date bill set to insurance company	

SIPOC Diagram Exercise

Supplier(s)	Inputs	Process	Outputs	Customers

Exercise 71. Sample - Keep everyone in the loop – Internet Portal

Prepare a 10 - 15 minute overview of the complete project plan. Address the high points of scope, schedule, and resources. Also mention your communications, quality, risk, and change control strategies. Do this in a manner that supports your current organization's structure and culture. To complete this exercise write it out on the next page after you review this example one from our Internet Portal.

The Internet Portal Project Plan addresses "Big Insurance" companies most critical need for supporting its distributed sales force of over 4,000 licensed life and health care insurance agents. It also provides the tools for an enhanced direct search by online customers.

Our agents are at a competitive disadvantage today compared by "Eastern Insurance Corp" and "Cable Guy Insurance Properties." They deliver illustrative insurance values on the fly.

The project plan is direct and connects all of the pieces together.

- **Deliverables**
  - ✓ **Illustrative values for life insurance – projections of cash value depending on the product. Current state is toll free telephone number and fax transmission or mail.**
  - ✓ **Delivery channels for new products**
  - ✓ **Contact information (CORM) sent to field representatives for inquiries via web.**
- **Success Criteria**
  - ✓ **Increased sales by 10%**
  - ✓ **Increased net margin (EBITA)**
  - ✓ **Increased membership (customers)**
  - ✓ **Reduced employee time/labor to process illustrative values**
- **Work Estimate**
  - ✓ **18 months for foundation for content managers**
  - ✓ **20 people peaking (45,000 - 60,000 hour project $2.25 to 3 million)**
- **Project Mission**
  - ✓ **The mission of this project is to improve the productivity of the sales force while also supporting the overall program mission of enhanced portal delivery.**
- **Commitment of the Organization**
  - ✓ **President is the sponsor. Budget has been established (one million external) plus that much authorized for internal hours consumed. Steering Committee and Project Manager identified.**
- **What's in scope/what's out of scope**
  - ✓ **In scope**

- ✓ **Deliverables identified above**
- ✓ **Interaction with other projects within the Portal Program**
- ✓ **Interaction with other programs and projects (release and configuration management)**
- ✓ **Server Hardware**
- ✓ **Integration with new, emerging field compensation functionality**
- ✓ **Integration with legacy software and systems**
- ✓ **Exploration of process improvement training**
- ✓ **Release management - transition to operations**
- ✓ **Out of scope**
  - ✓ **Hardware other than server (laptops for field agents)**
  - ✓ **Work activities directly associated with related projects within the program (no duplication of effort)**
  - ✓ **Field compensation functionality**
  - ✓ **Legacy software/system replacement**
  - ✓ **Though the primary purpose is not process improvement in aka six sigma approach – should the need arise this will become a separate project)**
- ✓ **Initial Risks: negative or positive**
  - ✓ **Duplication of effort with other projects – associated in days lost**
  - ✓ **Alienation of the sales force**
  - ✓ **Gold plating**
  - ✓ **Transition to the new system – are any sales people left behind – disruptive technology.**

o **Delivery date: September 5, 2009**

We have listed the delivery time in extra bold font to represent the commitment of the project team to deliver this on time. While we will hold the line on expenditures and have iron clad control of scope – the team realizes that above all else – September 5, 2009 must be met!

Exercise 71. Keep Everyone in the Loop

Prepare a 10 - 15 minute overview of the complete project plan. Address the high points of scope, schedule, and resources. Also mention your communications, quality, risk, and change control strategies. Do this in a manner that supports your current organization's structure and culture. To complete this exercise write it in the space provided below.

Deliverables:
In-Scope & Out-of-Scope:
Risks:
Most significant project highlight:

Exercise 72. Sample Status Reports Process for Internet Portal

Your project has begun and plans are completed. Consider now what you do to report status for the following stakeholders:
1. Team Members
2. Managers (above)
3. Managers (across)
4. Customer (State or County)

Go ahead and write your response in this workbook after reviewing this example for the Internet Portal.

Number one "project management" process is Direct and Manage Project Activities for the Internet Portal team – we know our game plan – we need to execute it.

1. Team Members:
   a. Meetings (meaningful) — status
   b. Issues log (AIR — action items, issues, and risks)
   c. Create a mid-stream schedule in MS Project
   d. How far are you into implementation? How many tasks are completed per day? What's the spreadsheet 'tick list' and what do completed action items look like for the 10 sites? 100 agents, 200 agents, all agents?
   e. Electronic access / manual access
2. Managers (above):
   a. President — daily / weekly
   b. Board of directors (director, legal, deputy) — status report with one page cover memo (dash board with red/yellow/green status)
3. Managers (across): status report with one page cover memo (dash board with red/yellow/green status)
   a. Agent Sales Force
   b. Operations
4. Customer: email update and public website: two page brochure, dog and pony show, updates, incentives.
   a. Current Policy Holders
   b. Users
5. Vendor: Ted and Wally's Consulting Solutions -
   a. Project manager
   b. Installation tea

Exercise 72. Status Reports

Now it's your turn - what you do to report status for the following stakeholders:
1. Team Members
2. Managers (above)
3. Managers (across)
4. Customer (State or County)

Go ahead and write your response below:

Team members:

Managers (above)

Managers (across)

Customers

Others

Exercise 73. Acquire Project Team - Resource Calendars

For this group exercise, assume that everyone in your group is on a project team. Write their names in the first column. Your team is starting a new project of moderate importance that should last about a year. Determine the availability of each team member for this new project. When done, you have made a resource calendar which enables you to make a more accurate project schedule.

Resource Calendar	
Project Team Member Name	**Project Availability**
Mr. Example	*He is able to contribute every Wednesday afternoon to the project, except during the month of December as he has a higher priority project finishing then, and except during the first two weeks of June when he will be on vacation.*

Exercise 74. Develop Project Team – Team Building Activities

Team Building Activities is one of the tools and techniques of the Develop Project Team process. The purpose of these activities is to help individual team members work more effectively together. Write down your responses to each of the following questions, and if you are working in a group, discuss your answers with each other.

A. In the past, what type of Team Building Activities have you participated in?

B. In your opinion, what is the best type of Team Building Activity, and why?

C. Teams go through five stages of development—forming, storming, norming, performing, and adjourning. Have you ever been on a team that reached the performing stage? If so, what do you attribute this to?

D. Have you ever been on a team that people worked so badly with each other the project goals could not be met? If so, what do you attribute this to?

E. What would be your best advice to a rookie Project Manager who wants to assure as much as possible that their new team will work well together?

Exercise 75. Develop Project Team – Recognition and Rewards

Recognition and Rewards is a tool and technique of the Develop Project Team process. People are more likely to behave in ways that they know will lead to rewards. Keep in mind that what may be a reward to one person, may not be desirable to another person. The person being rewarded should have had some control over the situation that led to the reward. The Develop Human Resources plan outlines the reward system for a project. What, if anything, would you suggest as appropriate rewards in these situations? It could range from a positive mention in their employee file, a simple "thank-you" or a large bonus.

Situation	Recognition/Reward
1. When a team member became ill, Jamie worked a week of 16-hour days to keep the project on schedule.	
2. A five-member project team was able to complete their project two months ahead of schedule and slightly under-budget.	
3. James volunteered to coordinate the office holiday party.	
4. Jake noticed that someone had spilled a drink on the conference table earlier, so he cleaned up the mess.	
5. The entire year Julie has worked on a certain project, she has always sent out her status reports on time.	
6. When a visiting client expressed concerns about driving a rental car in a large city, John volunteered to drive the client where they wanted to go with his own car.	

Exercise 76. Manage Project Team – Resolving Conflict

Conflict can be resolved by forcing, smoothing, compromise, confrontation and withdrawal. Which method is being described in the following scenarios?

	Forcing	Smoothing	Compromise	Confrontation	Withdrawal
1. Samantha and Hal are arguing why the project has fallen behind schedule. They decide they better gather data on the possible reasons since neither is certain they really know what the problem is.					
2. Margie is fighting with her mother about her poor grades. Margie's father tells them that grades aren't important and they calm down a little.					
3. We'll switch to neon-colored paper clips for all our reports. Why? Because I'm the boss and I say so.					
4. Paul and Mary disagree on whether or not to buy a new car. Every time Mary wants to discuss it, Paul runs out of the room.					
5. Paul wants to buy a black truck and Mary thinks they should get a white car. They decide to get a white truck.					
6. Which only leads to a temporary solution?					
7. Which never results in resolution?					
8. Which is considered the best method to resolve conflict?					

Exercise 77. Manage Project Team – Tools and Techniques

The Manage Project Team process lists five tools and techniques—Observation and Conversation; Project Performance Appraisals; Conflict Management; Issue Log; and Interpersonal Skills. Spend some time thinking about the questions on these tools and techniques and write your answers below. If you're working in a group, use them as discussion questions.

1. **Observation and Conversation.** How often do you observe your team members working? How often do you have one-on-one conversations with your team members?

2. **Project Performance Appraisals.** Have you filled out/written project performance appraisals for your team members? If so, did you find it useful?

3. **Conflict Management.** How does your current team resolve conflict? Which of the conflict resolution strategies are used most often?

4. **Issue Log.** Do you use an Issue Log? If not, how do you track and manage issues?

5. **Interpersonal Skills.** The PMBOK® lists Leadership, Influencing, and Effective Decision Making as the three most important interpersonal skills. Do you agree? What skills would you add?

Exercise 78. Manage Stakeholders Expectations – Issue Log

The Issue Log is an input to the Manage Stakeholders Expectations process, and updates to the Issue Log is an output. You're the Project Manager for the construction and opening of a new ice cream store. On your team, you have Suzie (responsible for building the exterior of the building), Edward (responsible for the interior of the building), Harvey (responsible for hiring ice cream store employees), Sally (part of project management team), and Sam (responsible for marketing).

The following four emails are in your inbox. How would you record them in your Issue Log? The first one is done for you.

1. To: Me ProjectM   From: Mr. Sponsor   Re: Papaya Flavor
Hey ProjectM--my wife said last night that nobody eats chocolate ice cream anymore. Let's replace it with papaya instead. I know the executive team will disagree, so let's not tell them.

2. To: Me ProjectM   From: Local City Official   Re: Bad Permit
Dear Sir: the person who issued you your building permit is not actually a city employee; he is a disgruntled former employee. Therefore, you have no permit. Please re-apply as soon as possible or we will disallow further construction.

3. To: Me ProjectM   From: Sam Teemember   Re: Suzie is Mean
I don't wanna work on this project anymore! You can't make me! Suzie laughed at my Mr. Ed tie, so I never want to see her again. So I can't be on the same project that she's on. Don't give her a bonus, she doesn't deserve anything.

4. To: Me ProjectM   From: Functional Manager   Re: Suzie Needed
Hi ProjectM, sorry to do this to you after I promised that you could have Suzie full-time for the next six months, but I'm going to need her back in two months for a top priority project. I regret the inconvenience.

Issue Log				
Issue Name	**Responsible**	**Urgency**	**Potential Impact**	**Resolve By**
Papaya Flavor	*Sam*	*Low*	*Low*	*3 weeks*

Exercise 79. Procurement

The purpose of this exercise is to understand source selection criteria, which is an output of the Plan Procurements process, and to understand proposal evaluation techniques, which is a tool and technique of the Conduct Procurements process.

You will be soliciting and then evaluating proposals for your current project. The purpose of your project is to build a unique, but not too expensive, zoo in your metropolitan area. You will make your decision based on five key attributes (your source selection criteria) that you will use to rate the proposals.

1. The first attribute is Cost—decide what you want the other four attributes to be and write them in the shaded boxes to the left of Cost. You may choose among: Years the company has been in business; Uniqueness of idea; Length of time to complete; Technical capability; Project Manager ability; Warranty; Business size; and References.

	Source Selection Criteria					Total Score
	Cost					
Proposal A	2					
Proposal B	1					
Proposal C	4					
Proposal D	3					

2. Four companies submitted proposals after reading about your source selection criteria. Read each proposal on the next page and rank them 1-4 on each criterion. So "1" would be given to the best proposal for that attribute and "4" would be given to the worst proposal. After ranking them all, add up the score for each proposal to determine the best one. *Bonus points: if you wish, weight your criteria so that some attributes are worth more than others.*

Proposals for Zoo

Proposal A
Our company has 100 employees, has been in business for 5 years and can complete this zoo for 3 million dollars in 4 years. We suggest a zoo that is entirely underground with low lighting and is shaped like a sewer. There will be plenty of domesticated rats and alligators that are allowed to roam free. We don't have the technical capability now, but will hire experts if we are selected. The Project Manager will be Jerry, who has just graduated from high school with honors. We will warranty the product for 6 months. We don't have any references we can provide you at this time.

Proposal B
Our company has 20 employees, been in business for 1 year and can complete this zoo for 2 million dollars in 2 years. We suggest a zoo of domesticated animals. It will include every breed of cat, dog, cow, and horse. There will be a dedicated breeding program so that visitors can visit the Pet Shop & Barn and buy their own pet cow (or cat, dog, or horse) to take home as a souvenir. We have done two similar zoos and have all the technical capability in-house. The Project Manager will be Alyssa, who has her PMP and is also a veterinarian. We will warranty the product for 3 years. We have five references that we can provide you from CEOs of zoos that we have constructed in Europe.

Proposal C
Our company has 200 employees, has been in business for 50 years and can complete this zoo for 4 million dollars in 7 years. We suggest a zoo of all the standard animals—zebras, elephants, tigers, bears, etc. The sidewalks and cages will all glow in the dark so that we can have visitors pay to enter the zoo at night, too. We have a sub-contractor that has helped in the past in order to meet the technical capabilities. The Project Manager will be Adam who has had ten years of experience in managing projects which construct exhibits and has earned his BA in physics. We will partially warranty the product for 3 months. We have thirty references we can provide you from happy patrons of other zoos we have constructed who said they will be returning to the zoo again.

Proposal D
Our company has 45 employees, has been in business for 27 years and can complete this zoo for 3.5 million dollars in 5 years. We suggest a zoo of diseased an unwanted animals. For example, we will have an exhibit of chimps who have been infected with lethal human diseases in the course of research, as well as vicious animals who have either severely maimed or killed a human, such as a bull who has gored someone. There will also be a Mosquito house, where different enclosures will have mosquitoes infected with different diseases, such a Malaria and West Nile Virus. We do not have the technical capabilities, but we're certain we can figure it out as we have a smart team. The Project Manager will be Jamie who has 7 years experience managing IT projects, has her masters in Philosophy, and has her PMP. We will not offer a warranty. We have two references from the parents of one of our board members.

Chapter 6　- Make Sure that Stuff is Really Happening – (Monitor & Controlling)

The monitoring and controlling processes ensures adequate insight and measurement into how a project is to be executed. The plans have been set, the die has been cast and project activities are underway – inspecting what you expect is critical for success.

Inspect what you expect

Remember a project gets one year behind one day at a time. **Plans do not have to be perfect to succeed; but they do need to be controlled and perfectly open to review.** Teams do not overtly sabotage project performance; however it is all too human to pull back and withhold information when tasks are not completed and problems arise.

Monitor and Control Project Work (4.4)

Monitor and Control Project Work is the umbrella process to all monitoring and controlling processes. It establishes minimal and best practices for project metrics and reporting. This process oversees that all other processes are being performed as they should be— from the beginning to the end of the project.

Perform Integrated Change Control (4.5)

This was called Integrated Change Control in the third edition PMBOK®. Whereas Monitor and Control Project Work guides the overall control processes – Perform Integrated Change Control shapes change requests, configuration management, and the detail level.

The goal is to ensure that only authorized changes are made. That does not prevent change altogether or the introduction of unwieldy change control processes.   It only prevents unauthorized changes. There is a bit of a balancing act between ensuring project control that scrutinizes each change and ensuring timely delivery and nimbleness in amending the project.

Change Control does not have to be the "naughty project management" phrase that wastes time and resources. If implemented well, 1 to 2 hours spent each week ensuring changes are understood and then approved keeps your project on track, one day at a time.

Change Requests (an input to this process) introduce the formal change request. By formal we do not mean it has to be signed in triplicate form and routed through 12 layers of management. In a few cases it does, but we have also seen effective help ticket, e-mail, web portal, and one page change requests. Sometimes the change request amounts to little more then a project manager composing an email to a project stakeholder that incorporates the desired change from a conversation they had.

What do unauthorized changes look or sound like? Here are some examples:

> ➢ "While you're completing the design for the new sub-division, let's slip in a new water retention technique." That new water retention is not bad in itself. The concern is the "slipping in" part.
> ➢ "Go ahead and produce 28 extra PDF reports for Spacely International. Since we're not printing them there's no need to track a change. We can just produce those at the end of the day." There may indeed not be a cost – the concern is if you're delivering future projects for Spacely, how do you know what's expected in terms of report delivery?
> ➢ "While I was in scoping your knee and repairing the ACL tear, I thought I would go ahead and clean those heart arteries and do a little lipo for you". That sounds absurd and would be rejected outright – however if we treated surgery like some stakeholders treat projects, then we would end up with that very scenario.

The Change Request Status Update output represents the completed Perform Integrated Change Control process - in simplest terms these are the decisions whether to accept or reject a change request.

Verify Scope (5.4)

This process was called Scope Verification in the third edition PMBOK®. The ultimate result of scope verification is whether your project sponsor and stakeholder(s) accept the end result of your project. In practice, this often involves "perceived project completion" as much as "paper project completion." What do we mean by that? Perceived project completion is assessed or measured by the stakeholders' view (not the project teams'). If communication has been consistent, changes or interruptions to the project shared, and progress reports forwarded on a timely basis, the stakeholders' perspective will align with the project team. If, however, a project team has received a project charter and then gone into "witness protection" to get their project done and, by the way, ignored stakeholder requests for updates – regardless of whether the project is successful, the perception is likely it is not.

There is one tool and technique for Verify Scope: Inspection. This tool should not be applied only at project completion. While Verify Scope is performed at project completion, it also is wise to begin reviews of the project's scope at each step or stage gate of your project – even as you complete significant milestones. Some organizations may call these walk-throughs, reviews, milestone reviews, stage gate reviews, or project performance meetings.

The outputs are the Accepted Deliverables and Change Requests. The Change Requests arise as the multiple reviews occur prior to project completion. Changes at project completion and closure typically keep the project open or set the stage for an ensuing new project.

Control Scope (5.5)

This process was called Scope Control in the third edition PMBOK®. Do you remember the triple constraint: Scope, Time, and Cost? Perform Integrated Change Control is important for each of the processes – tamper and mess around too much with scope, time, or cost and project failure is at your door step. Scope addresses the "what" part of the "what, when, how much" question.

Scope control addresses change over the course of a project; some of these are due to progressive elaboration. However, a scope change request a week or worse yet, each day, are a sign that the project sponsor, stakeholders, and even team do not buy into the project's mission.

Control Schedule (6.6)

This process was called Schedule Control in the third edition PMBOK®. Control Schedule addresses the "when" question of the triple constraint. It uses the schedule management plan and schedule baseline as the reference inputs and applies the performance reports and approved change request as the change oriented inputs.

A key question to address is "what method will you use to track performance?" Possible selections are percentage complete or tracking actual hours worked on a task against the baseline. Just knowing what is finished is not enough. Many programmers will get to the 85 percent mark on day two of a 30 day project.

Ask how much more time is required to complete the task instead of % of completion.

The remaining 15 percent seems to take a lifetime. Tracking actual completion is a better guide of how well your estimates have been. Record responses and keep a log on who tends to over and under-estimate.

If the project is off schedule, additional planning must be accomplished to determine how to get it back on track or to justify the delay to the Project Sponsor. Use Variance Analysis Comparison of actual performance to dates versus planned performance. In simple terms check how you're doing versus how you thought you would be doing.

Control Costs (7.3)

This was called Cost Control in the third edition PMBOK®. Control Costs is the third leg of the triple constraint. It is probably the most visible yet least understood or applied part of the PMBOK®.

Let's roll up our sleeves and dig into one of the more complicated, yet if applied well, one of the most valuable tools: earned value management (EVM). Earned value is based on the idea that projects earn or generate value as work is completed. So, a project to build a new 68-story office tower generates value while it's being built; not just when it is "topped off" and fully operational. The foundation of EVM is the following formulas.

Acronym	Term	Formula	Definition
PV	Planned Value		What is the estimated value of work planned to be done?
EV	Earned Value		What is the estimated value of the work actually accomplished?
AC	Actual Cost		What is the actual cost incurred?
BAC	Budget at Completion		How much did you budget for the total job?
CV	Cost Variance	EV - AC	Negative number is over budget, positive is under budget
CPI	Cost Performance Index	EV / AC	I am getting $_____ worth out of every dollar I spend
SV	Schedule Variance	EV - PV	Negative number is behind schedule, positive is ahead of schedule
SPI	Schedule Performance Index	EV / PV	I am progressing at _____% of the rate that was planned
EAC	Estimate at Completion	BAC / CPI	As of now, how much do we expect the total project to cost?
ETC	Estimate to Completion	EAC - AC	How much more do we expect the project to cost?
ETC	Estimate to Completion	BAC - EV	How much more do we expect the project to cost (factoring in Earned Value)?
VAC	Variance at Completion	BAC - EAC	How much over/under budget will we be at the end of the project?

PMP Scrimmage® Curriculum, Edition 3.01   *Page 181*
www.tapuniversity.com
TECHNOLOGY
AS PROMISED

Tricks for Memorizing Earned Value Formulas
The Variance Formulas

CV = EV - AC
CPI = EV / AC
SV = EV - PV
SPI = EV / PV

It is helpful to take note of the patterns. For instance:
1. These four formulas are all derived from only 3 terms—EV, AC, and PV.
2. These four formulas all have two terms that are either subtracted or divided.
3. EV is the first term in all these formulas.
4. The two "Cost" formulas have Actual <u>Cost</u> (AC) as the second term, which leaves PV for the second term of the two "Schedule" formulas.
5. The two "Cost" formulas have the same terms, as do the two "Schedule" formulas—the difference is whether they are subtracted or divided.
6. The two formulas with two-letter acronyms are subtracted, whereas the two formulas with three-letter acronyms are divided.

The Completion Formulas

EAC with flawed assumptions =	**AC + ETC**		
EAC with typical variation =	**AC + ((BAC- EV) / CPI)**	*OR*	**BAC / CPI**
EAC with atypical variation =	**AC + BAC - EV**		
ETC with typical variation =	**(BAC – EV) / CPI**	*OR*	**EAC - AC**
ETC with atypical variation =	**BAC - EV**		
VAC =	**BAC - EAC**		

Again, take note of the patterns. For instance:
1. The 3 EAC formulas start with AC (except the shortcut formula).
2. The 2 ETC formulas and VAC start with BAC (except the shortcut formula).
3. The three terms in VAC=BAC-EAC all end in the letters "ac."
4. The only difference between the 2 "typical" formulas from their corresponding "atypical" formulas is that the "typical" formulas are divided by CPI.
5. The only difference between the two EAC variation formulas from their corresponding ETC formulas is that "AC" is first added to the formula for the EAC. You can remember this by the letters <u>EAC</u> ending in AC, whereas ETC does not.
6. **If you are recalling one of the 4 atypical/typical formulas, start with BAC – EV. Next, if it is an _EAC_ formula add "<u>AC</u>" to the front. Lastly, if it is a *typical variation* formula, divide it all by CPI, which is the indication of how your cost variance has typically been.**

Also, think logically about what you are calculating with all these formulas.
1. If you need the estimate at completion and you've been going on flawed assumptions (EAC), the best you do is state how much you've spent (AC) and add an estimate of how much more it will be (ETC).
2. If you're asked how much the total cost will be off (varies) from the budget (VAC), simply find the difference between the budgeted amount (BAC) and what you think the total cost will be (EAC).

Earned Value Example

Let's walk through an earned value scenario with Rachael (it may be about nine years too soon to worry about her college costs, but it's always good to prepare and panic now about rising college costs).

Rachael is currently enrolled in the Fall Semester at Southern Illinois University in Edwardsville (SIUE) as an Industrial Engineering Major in the new Olin Engineering Institute where tuition is $15,000 per year. She's spending a little more than Mom and Dad had planned so they did a little snooping and found out she's $7,500 over budget by the end of the first semester of her sophomore year. They're in and want an explanation (she had always been such a responsible child).

Illustration 18: Earned Value Example

4 year college 15k per year. Today is year 1.5					
RACHAEL'S SPENT 37.5K					
PV %?	37%	AMT?	15000		
		YEAR 1	YEAR 2	YEAR 3	YEAR 4
PLANNED PER YEAR		15,000	15,000	15,000	15,000
PLANNED CUMULATIVE		15,000	30,000	45,000	60,000
PV	22500	CV (COST VAR) = EV - AC			-7500
AC	37500	SV (SCHEDULE VAR) = EV - PV			7500
EV	30000	CPI = EV/AC			0.8
		SPI = EV/PV			1.3333333
		EAC =			75000

We discover upon further review that the reason she's over budget $7,500 is because she's doubled up on classes and has actually completed the end of her sophomore year. If she continues at this pace, she'll be able to graduate at the end of the summer after her junior year. So Mom and Dad decide to run some numbers to confirm costs. We discover a negative cost variance and cost performance index. That makes sense since we're so over budget. Yet the schedule variance (SV) and schedule performance index (SPI) are strong (positive $7,500 and 1.33).

> *In earned value, positive SV and CV are good – it means you're ahead of schedule or under budget respectively. Negative SV and CV are bad — it means you're behind schedule or over budget respectively.*
> *SPI and CPI values greater then 1.0 are also "good" — you're ahead of schedule or under budget. SPI and CPI values less than 1.0 are "bad" — you're behind schedule or over budget.*

That confirms that Rachael is indeed doing what she said she was doing – loading up on all of those extra classes.

The underlying concept behind earned value is that projects generate value as they progress, as work is completed. The value is determined based on percentage of work completed and the prior budgeted amount for that work. The PV does not change. The values that change are AC and EV.

Perform Quality Control (8.3)

Perform Quality Control is the process that ensures your project is meeting its objectives. To do so, specific project results are monitored to check for compliance. Perform Quality Control precedes and works closely with Verify Scope to provide the "proof" that the project has indeed met project scope. In addition to the project artifacts listed frequently as inputs, the quality control plan, checklists, and metrics serve as inputs to all of those wonderful tools.

The tools and techniques used to monitor and control the quality of a project can be separated into:
1. Those that help a project team understand their process connections (Cause and Effect, Flowcharting).
2. Those that attempt to identify trends (Control Charts, Histograms, Pareto, Scatter Diagrams).
3. Those that generate data for review (Statistical Sampling, Inspection, and Approved Change Request Review).

The Normal Distribution Curve

The normal curve is the statistical concept behind populations and groups. The normal curve allows approximation and attribution to a larger population based on a selected sample. The greater the accuracy required (e.g., 99.73 percent) the greater number of standard deviations (SD) from the mean observation required. So you do not have to have a sample of one million test results; rather a sample size of 1,000 with a high confidence interval.

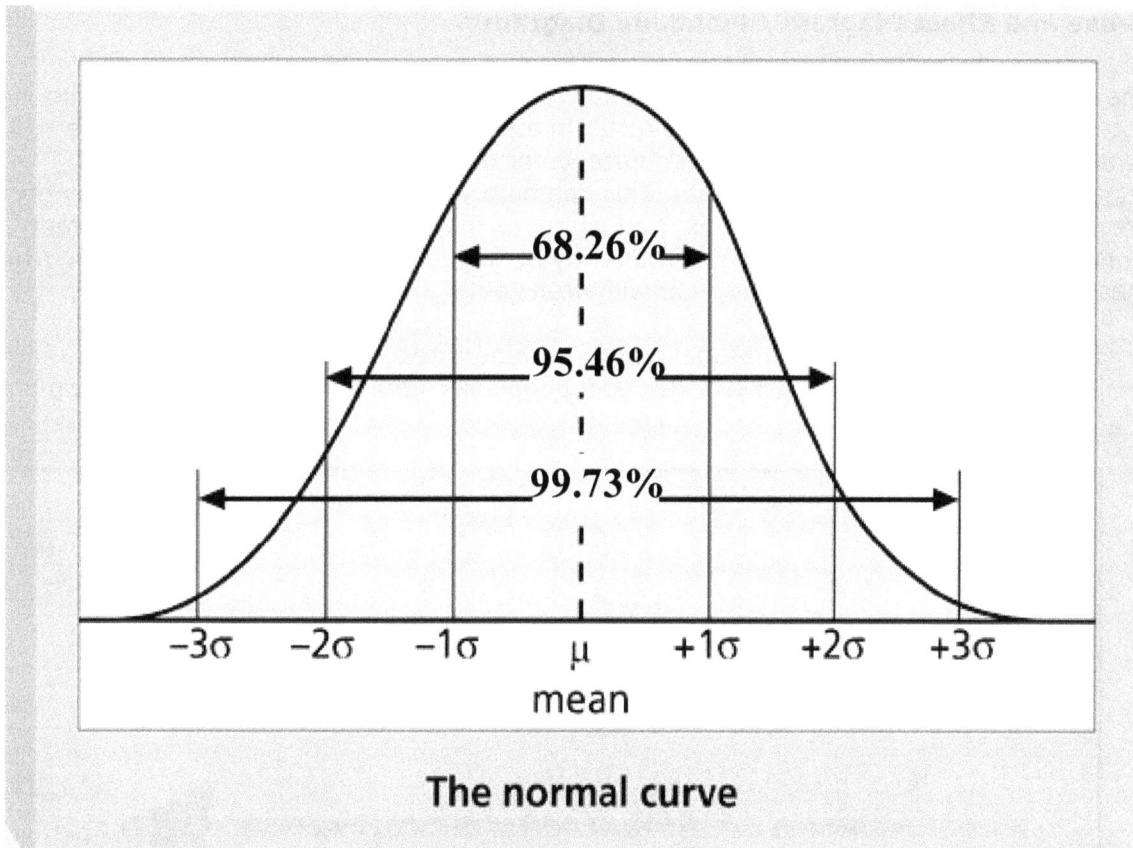

Illustration 19: Normal Distribution Curve

Half of the curve is above the mean and half of the curve is below the mean.

+/- 1 sigma is equal to 68.26%
+/- 2 sigma is equal to 95.46%
+/- 3 sigma is equal to 99.73%
+/- 6 sigma is equal to 99.99%

Cause and Effect Diagram / Fishbone Diagram

The cause and effect diagram (a.k.a. Ishikawa or Fishbone) is used to explore all the potential or real causes or inputs that result in a single effect or output. Causes are arranged according to their level of importance or detail, resulting in a depiction of relationships and hierarchy of events. This can help you search for root causes, identify areas where there may be problems, and compare the relative importance of different causes. In this diagram, causes are frequently arranged into four major categories. While these categories can be anything, you will often see:

1. Manpower, methods, materials, and machinery recommended for manufacturing
2. Equipment, policies, procedures, and people recommended for administration and service.

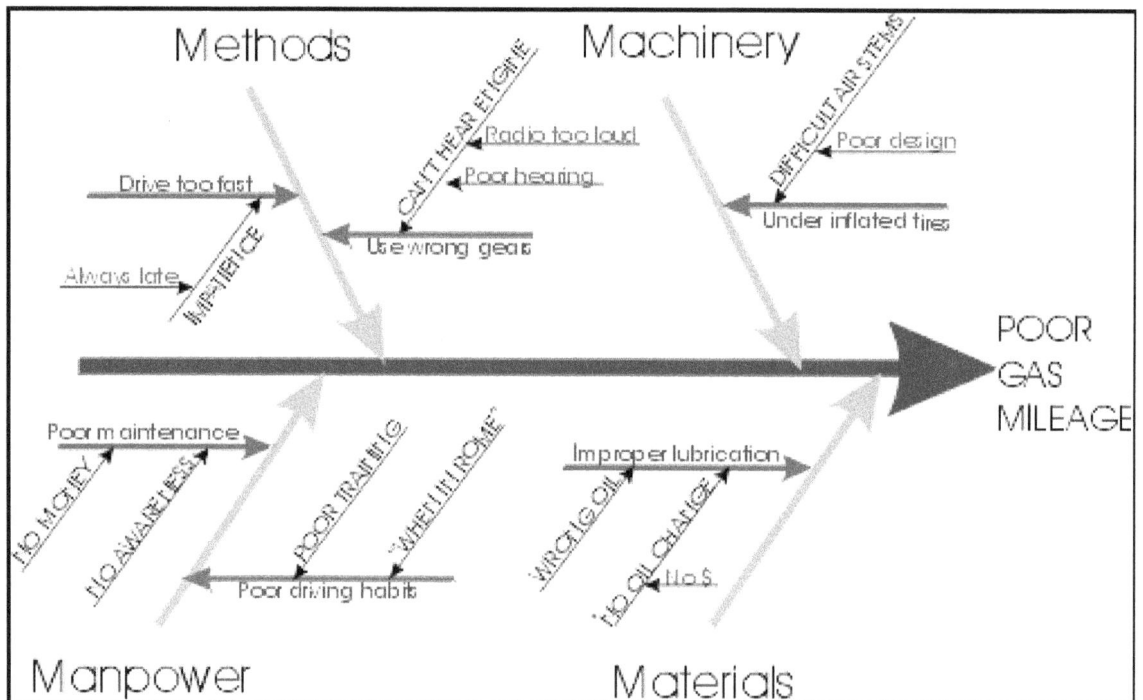

Illustration 20: Fishbone / Cause-Effect Example: Poor Gas Mileage

Run Chart

A run chart is a line graph that shows data points plotted in the order in which they occur. They are used to show trends and shifts in a process over time. Rule of Seven Trend – if there are seven consecutive and consistent points (increasing or decreasing) a trend is established.

Steps to Construct a Run Chart
1. Draw and label the vertical (y) axis using the measurement units you are tracking (e.g., numbers of defectives, number of graduates, percent defective, etc.).
2. Draw and label the horizontal (x) axis to reflect the sequence in which the data points are collected (e.g., week one, week two, or 8AM, 9AM, 10AM, etc.).
3. Plot the data points on the chart in the order in which they became available and connect the points with lines between them.
4. Calculate the average from the data and draw a horizontal line across the chart at the level of the average.
5. Interpret the chart and decide what action to take. Are trends present? Would the chart look different if everything were perfect? The key is to look for trends and not focus on individual points.

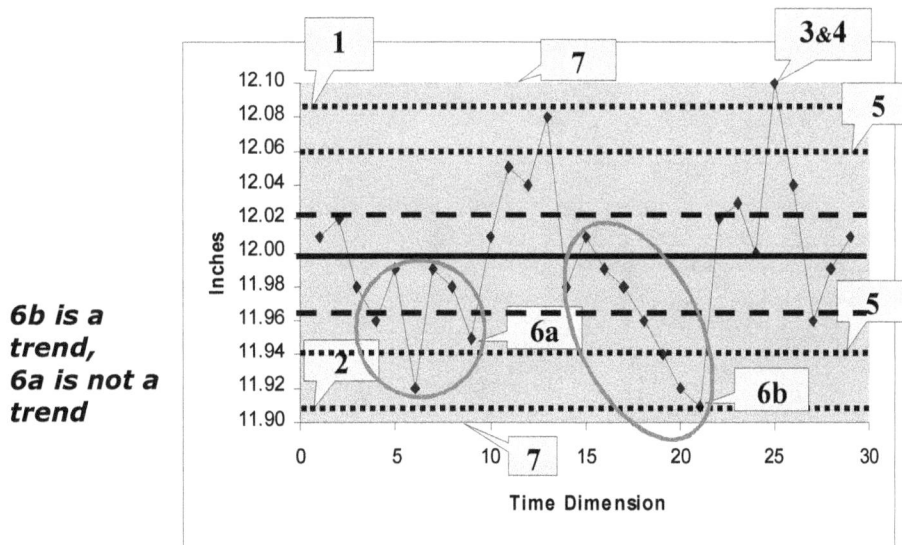

Illustration 21: Run Chart

Pareto Diagram (80/20 rule):

Key Points
1. Ranks defects in order of frequency
2. Uses a bar chart
3. Depicts distribution of 100% of defects

Pareto diagrams are a type of bar chart, ordered by frequency of occurrence, which shows how many results were generated by type or category of identified cause. Rank ordering is used to guide corrective action that the project team should first take to fix the problems that are causing the greatest number of defects. Pareto diagrams are conceptually related to Pareto's Law, which holds that a relatively small number of causes will typically produce a large majority of the problems or defects.

Example:

PARETO DIAGRAM

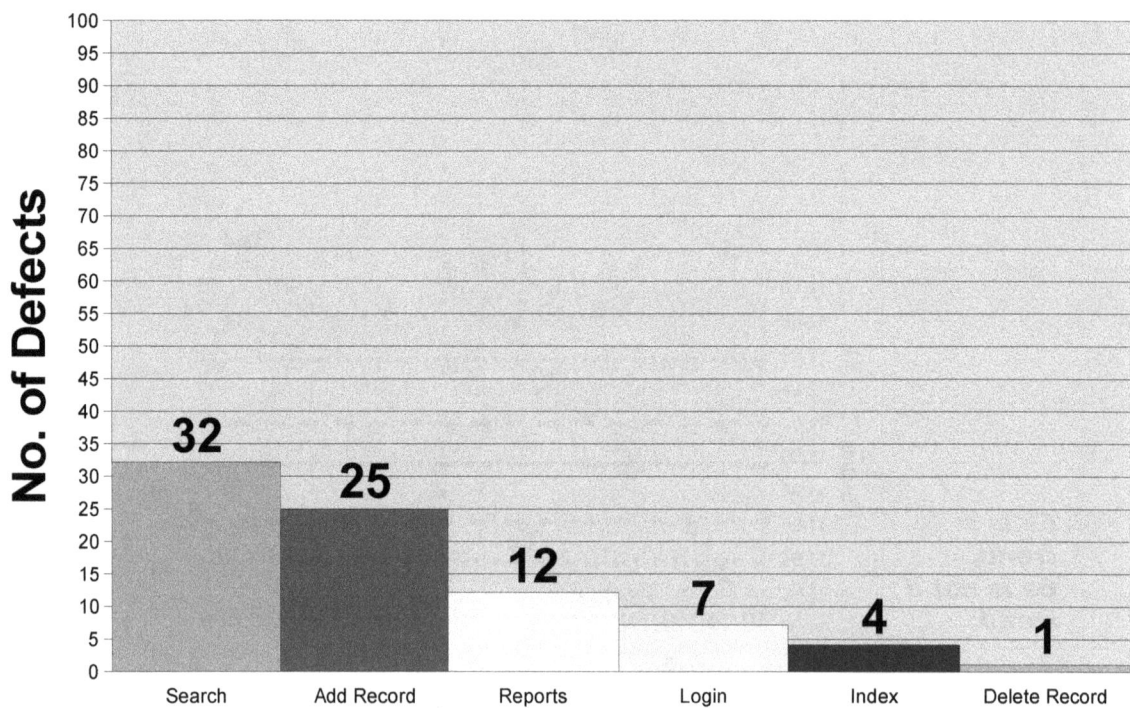

Illustration 22: Pareto Diagram

Report Performance (10.5)

This was called Performance Reporting in the third edition PMBOK®. As mentioned, performance reporting gathers all relevant (and yes, all too often some irrelevant) project performance data and distributes that as meaningful information to the project stakeholders. Data collected on a regular basis include scope, schedule, cost, quality, as well as, risk and procurement.

The performance reporting data can be overwhelming – the art of project management is ensuring accurate and timely data is collected, and then trimmed down to usable information that's shared with stakeholders at the level of detail necessary to perform their review. The premise is there is a distinction between data (observations and facts) and information (data that have been evaluated and assessed).

Monitor and Control Risks (11.6)

This was called Risk Monitoring and Control in the third edition PMBOK®. This process helps the project team detect new risks (positive or negative), detect whether a risk event has occurred, and respond to risks events that have occurred, tapping into contingency reserves as necessary.

Risk Name	Risk Description	Trigger Point
Scope Creep	People adding features and functions outside of the scope	Requests from outside of project team.
Budget Overrun	Spending exceeds budgeted forecast.	When budget variation is greater than 5 percent.

Administer Procurements (12.3)

This was called Contract Administration in the third edition PMBOK®. It serves as a microcosm of the overall project. For procurement intensive projects there are really three projects and teams: the buyer's team and project; the seller's team and project, as well as the combined team. Some organizations have a separate team or department to administer the contract (so in a way that adds a fourth layer).

Success from a procurement focused project requires each of those teams. However, a negative risk of procurement based projects is disconnected and competing teams (us versus them mentality).

Buyer-conducted performance reviews and companion audits need to provide more than just a superficial pass or walk through. The negative risk for both buyer and seller of becoming too close to each other is that formal reviews are skipped over. Again, an adversarial relationship is not desired, but some separation is needed to avoid the Enron – Anderson Consulting ethical lapse and breakdown.

Chapter 6 Exercises

Exercise 80. Monitor and Control Project Work

The Monitor and Control Project Work process concerns assuring that the actual work being performed is consistent with what was described in the Project Management Plan. Write your responses below, and discuss them if you're working in a group.

1. Assuming you use a Project Management Plan, how often throughout a project do you look at it?

2. Do you update your Project Management Plan during a project? If so, how often do you typically update it?

3. What methods do you use to know whether the project is currently on schedule, budget, and scope?

4. How often do you want updates from your team members? Does it differ by team member?

5. In what format do you want your updates from team members (conversation, report, email, etc.)? Does it differ depending on the project and team members?

Exercise 81. Perform Integrated Change Control

You are on the Configuration Control Board for a project that is developing a stuffed white Easter Bunny. The following change requests have been submitted for your review during your Change Control Meeting. How will you as a board member respond to each request? Will you accept the change, reject the change, or ask for more information?

1. We would like to extend the deadline for having the bunnies on the shelves in May to having them on the shelves in July.

2. We would like to use a softer material for the bunny fur which we are able to obtain at a discount so it will not increase the budget.

3. We would like to have an assortment of pink, purple, and green bunnies rather than white bunnies.

4. We would like to make the bunnies without tails in order to cut costs and avoid going over budget.

5. We would like to add a robotic component to the bunnies that allows them to chase the owner's pet cats and dogs.

Exercise 82. Verify Scope

The Verify Scope process only has one tool & technique—inspection. This process inspects completed project deliverables. There can then be one of two outputs—Accepted Deliverables or Change Request. For this exercise, you're inspecting the deliverables from a catering vendor. For each, using the Scope Statement, decide if it's an Accepted Deliverable. It it's not, write a Change Request.

Scope Statement	Deliverable	Is it an Accepted Deliverable?	If Change Request, what is it?
Strawberries with their stem still intact, dipped half-way in white chocolate.		*No*	*Dip strawberries in white chocolate, not dark chocolate.*
Pumpkin pie with one dollop of whipped cream per slice.			
Banana Split with a spoon, 3 scoops of ice cream, 2 pieces of bananas, and 4 cherries.			
Cake with frosting and three candles.			

Exercise 83. Change Control Triple Constraint

There are three general types of change that need management during the life of the project:

1. Changes to the scope of the project
2. Changes to the schedule (time)
3. Changes to the budget

A project manager needs to influence, guide, and ensure project change is accomplished through a structured process called integrated change control. The mission is not to add bureaucracy - this is not about pages of paper or endless loops. The mission is to ensure successful project execution and tracking the changes that impact the project.

Change control steps

What are your recommended change control steps? Let's see an example from our Internet Portal project.

Example Change Control Steps:

Confirm what is really involved with the Internet Portal project — need to have clear, concrete understanding of what's to be accomplished by all parties (Home Office, Ted and Wally's, and Sales Force). What's the "known state," what's the baseline?

Requests received verbally are either typed by the requestor or project manager and submitted for project steering committee approval via email.
   Format for the request is as follows — the Big Insurance Company Change Request Form.

Requestor receives confirmation of request and disposition of request.
All changes are logged and maintained in project files.

Exercise 83. Change Control Triple Constraint

There are three general types of change that need management during the life of the project:

1. Changes to the scope of the project
2. Changes to the schedule (time)
3. Changes to the budget

A project manager needs to influence, guide, and ensure project change is accomplished through a structured process, called integrated change control. The mission is not to added bureaucracy -- this is not about pages of paper or endless loops. The mission is to ensure successful project execution and tracking the changes that impact the project.

Change control steps

What are your recommended change control steps? Write them in the space provided below.

1.
2.
3.
4.
5.

Exercise 84. *Earned Value Scrimmage*

Earned value assignment - Project 4th of July Fireworks

Project Facts:
Total Project Budget - $28,000
Planned Duration - 10 days
Planned Resource usage - four people, four hours per day OR 160 hours total
Resource usage estimate confidence – 98 percent (you have several years experience)
Material cost - $12,000
Resource cost - $16,000 or **$100.00** per hour
Project start date - June 25
Project completion date - July 4, 11:00 pm

Project Status Date - July 3, 5:00pm
Actual Expenditures (AC) as of July 3 - $26,500
Planned Budget (PV) as of July 3 - $26,000
Budget variance - $(500.00)
Number of hours planned for project completion on July 3 at 5:00pm - 140.
Actual hours of project completed – **150, No delays. Everything is on track.**
Material cost has been spent and is sunk **$12,000**

1. Compute the Earned Value Amount

2. Complete the following table.

Planned	Earned	Cost	Variance		Performance Index	
Budget $	**EARNED VALUE $**	**Actual Cost $**	**Cost Variance $**	**Schedule $**	**CPI**	**SPI**
PV	**EV**	**AC**	**(EV-AC)**	**(EV-PV)**	**EV/AC**	**EV/PV**
26,000		$26,500				

3. What's the EAC (estimate at completion)? Use the formula for everything's on track, no need for corrective action.

4. What's the ETC (estimate to completion)?

5. Your Chief Financial Officer has been breathing down your neck because the fireworks are $500.00 over budget. You're feeling good about it based on earned value. Why and what would you share with your CFO so he doesn't explode.

Exercise 85. Earned Value Basics

The first step in mastering Earned Value is memorizing what the acronyms stand for. Next to the acronym, write out what it stands for.

BAC	*Budget at Completion*
AC	
PV	
EV	
CV	
CPI	
SV	
SPI	
EAC	
ETC	
VAC	

Next, write the acronym next to its description.

	Amount budgeted for the work *performed* so far. It can be calculated as BAC * (work completed / total work).
	How close to schedule the project is in terms of cost. A negative number means the project is behind schedule and a positive number means the project is ahead of schedule. It is calculated EV – PV.
	Amount of money budgeted for the entire project.
	How much over or under budget the whole project will be. It is calculated BAC – EAC.
	Amount of money actually spent.
	What will be spent to finish remaining project or activity. It is calculated ETC = (BAC – EV) / CPI. (This is algebraically equivalent to ETC = EAC - AC).
	Amount budgeted for work *scheduled* so far. It can be calculated as BAC * (time passed / total time scheduled).
	What will be spent on the whole project or activity. It is calculated AC + ETC.
	How the actual spending differs from the amount budgeted. A negative number means you are over budget and a positive number means you are under budget. It is calculated EV - AC.
	The percentage of the planned rate you are progressing. A number more than 1 means good performance and a number less than 1 means poor performance. It is calculated EV / PV.
	How much value you are getting from every dollar spent. A number greater than 1 indicates good performance and a number less than 1 indicates poor performance. It is calculated EV / AC.

Exercise 86. Earned Value Practice

Budget at Completion (BAC) is the amount of money budgeted for the entire project.
Actual Cost (AC) is the amount of money actually spent.
Planned Value (PV) is the amount budgeted for work *scheduled* so far.
It can be calculated as PV = BAC * (time passed / total time scheduled).
Earned Value (EV) is the amount budgeted for the work *performed* so far.
It can be calculated as EV = BAC * (work completed / total work).

A. Joshua and Jolene are remodeling three rooms in their home and decided they can spend $15,000 and take three months on this project. They planned to spend the same amount of time and money on each of the three rooms. They have just finished remodeling the first room (the kitchen) which took two months and cost $7,000.

1. What is the BAC?_____
2. What is the AC?_____
3. What is the PV?_____
4. What is the EV?_____

B. Felicia is spending ten days in Hawaii on vacation and decided she can spend $200 a day in her quest to obtain 20 stunning souvenirs that will make all her friends jealous. However, after the first day she spent $500 on 10 souvenirs.

1. What is the BAC?_____
2. What is the AC?_____
3. What is the PV?_____
4. What is the EV?_____

C. Damian needs to drive 1000 miles in 20 hours in order to get to the annual Friends of the Manatees convention. He has $300 he can spend to get there. After 5 hours, he has driven 250 miles and spent $100 on gas and snacks.

1. What is the BAC?_____
2. What is the AC?_____
3. What is the PV?_____
4. What is the EV?_____

More Formulas

Cost Variance (CV) is how the actual spending differs from the amount budgeted. A negative number means you are over budget and a positive number means you are under budget. It is calculated CV = EV - AC.

Cost Performance Index (CPI) is how much value you are getting from every dollar spent. A number greater than 1 indicates good performance and a number less than 1 indicates poor performance. It is calculated CPI = EV / AC.

Schedule Variance (SV) is how close to schedule the project is in terms of cost. A negative number means the project is behind schedule and a positive number means the project is ahead of schedule. It is calculated SV = EV – PV.

Schedule Performance Index (SPI) is the percentage of the planned rate you are progressing. A number more than 1 means good performance and a number less than 1 means poor performance. It is calculated SPI = EV / PV.

A. Meagan has $500 and 5 days to make 1000 party mints. It's the end of the third day and she has used $400 and made 900 mints.

1. What is the BAC?_____
2. What is the AC?_____
3. What is the PV?_____
4. What is the EV?_____
6. What is the CV? _____
7. What is the CPI? _____
8. What is the SV? _____
9. What is the SPI? _____
10. Is she under, over, or exactly on-budget?_____
11. Is she progressing slow, fast, or exactly on-schedule?_____

B. Five-year-old Molly has a neighbor whose yard is full of fireflies at night. The neighbor kid will let her run around and catch as many as she can for a dollar an hour. Molly wants to catch 50 fireflies in a jar and her father gives her two dollars to do so. After one hour, Molly has caught 40 fireflies and gives the neighbor kid the first dollar before starting on her second hour.

1. What is the BAC?_____
2. What is the AC?_____
3. What is the PV?_____
4. What is the EV?_____
6. What is the CV? _____
7. What is the CPI? _____
8. What is the SV? _____
9. What is the SPI? _____
10. Is she under, over, or exactly on-budget?_____
11. Is she progressing slow, fast, or exactly on-schedule?_____

And Yet More Formulas!

Estimate At Completion when assumptions flawed (EAC) is what will be spent on the whole project or activity. It is calculated EAC = AC + ETC.

*Estimate At Completion with typical variation (EAC) is what will be spent on the whole project or activity. It is calculated EAC = AC + ((BAC – EV) / CPI). (This is algebraically equivalent to EAC = BAC / CPI).

Estimate At Completion with atypical variation (EAC) is what will be spent on the whole project or activity. It is calculated EAC = AC + BAC – EV.

*Estimate To Completion with typical variation (ETC) is what will be spent to finish remaining project or activity. It is calculated ETC = (BAC – EV) / CPI. (This is algebraically equivalent to ETC = EAC - AC).

*Estimate To Completion with atypical variation (ETC) is what will be spent to finish remaining project or activity. It is calculated ETC = BAC – EV.

Variance At Completion (VAC) is how much over or under budget the whole project will be. It is calculated VAC = BAC – EAC.

A. April and Andy are building an addition to their home. They have $30,000 to spend on the project and want it completed in 100 days. It is now the end of day 75 and they have spent $25,000. They believe the addition is exactly halfway completed.

    1. What is the BAC?_____

    2. What is the AC?_____

    3. What is the PV?_____

    4. What is the EV?_____

    6. What is the CV? _____

    7. What is the CPI? _____

    8. What is the SV? _____

    9. What is the SPI? _____

    10. Are they under, over, or exactly on-budget?_____

    11. Are they progressing slow, fast, or exactly on-schedule?_____

    12. What is EAC for typical variation?_____

    13. What is ETC for typical variation?_____

PMP Scrimmage® Curriculum, Edition 3.01   *Page 201*
www.tapuniversity.com
TECHNOLOGY
AS PROMISED

Practice

A. PV = 10; AC = 8; EV = 12.
    1. What is CV?_____   Are you over, under, or on Budget?
    2. What is CPI? _____
    3. What is SV? _____   Are you behind, ahead, or on Schedule?
    4. What is SPI? _____

B. PV = 500; AC = 600; EV = 550.
    1. What is CV?_____   Are you over, under, or on Budget?
    2. What is CPI? _____
    3. What is SV? _____   Are you behind, ahead, or on Schedule?
    4. What is SPI? _____

C. PV = 3000; AC = 2000; EV = 8000.
    1. What is CV?_____   Are you over, under, or on Budget?
    2. What is CPI? _____
    3. What is SV? _____   Are you behind, ahead, or on Schedule?
    4. What is SPI? _____

D. PV = 20,000; AC = 50,000; EV = 40,000.
    1. What is CV?_____   Are you over, under, or on Budget?
    2. What is CPI? _____
    3. What is SV? _____   Are you behind, ahead, or on Schedule?
    4. What is SPI? _____

E. PV = 300; AC = 300; EV = 250.
    1. What is CV?_____   Are you over, under, or on Budget?
    2. What is CPI? _____
    3. What is SV? _____   Are you behind, ahead, or on Schedule?
    4. What is SPI? _____

F. PV = 7; AC = 10; EV = 7.
    1. What is CV?_____   Are you over, under, or on Budget?
    2. What is CPI? _____
    3. What is SV? _____   Are you behind, ahead, or on Schedule?
    4. What is SPI? _____

G. PV = 600; AC = 580; EV = 650.
    1. What is CV?_____   Are you over, under, or on Budget?
    2. What is CPI? _____
    3. What is SV? _____   Are you behind, ahead, or on Schedule?
    4. What is SPI? _____

Exercise 87. The Normal Distribution Curve

To find the range of height for a given standard deviation, take the mean then both add and subtract the value of the standard deviation multiplied by the given standard deviation. For example, 2 standard deviations account for 95.46% of the population. If you want to know the range of height for 95.46% of American men, multiply the value of standard deviation in this population (3 inches) by the number of standard deviations you are interested in (2), which is 6. Next add and subtract 6 from the mean to get the range, (5'9" plus 6" is 6'3") and (5'9" minus 6" is 5'3") so 95.46% of American men fall into the range of is 5'3" to 6'3".

Mean Height of American Men: **5'9"**
Standard Deviation: **3"**

Mean Height of American Women: **5'4"**
Standard Deviation: **2.5"**

68.26% of American women are within what height range? _____ to _____

68.26% of American men are within what height range?   _____ to _____

95.46% of American women are within what height range? _____ to _____

99.73% of American men are within what height range?   _____ to _____

Exercise 88. Construct a Fishbone Diagram

Write the problem at the head of the fish, and list major potential causes for the problem on the three large arrows. Draw smaller arrows leading to the major arrows to list the reasons for the main causes.

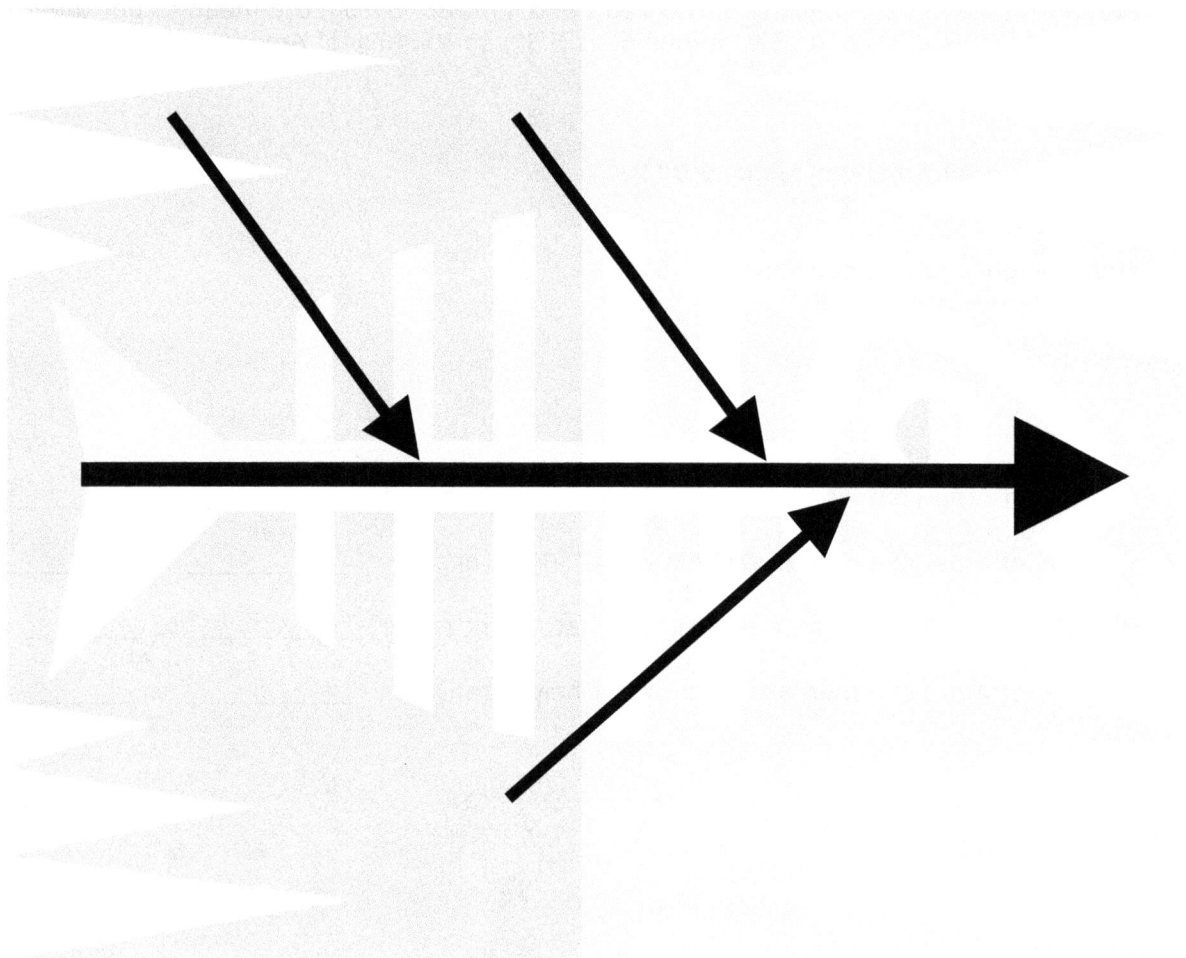

Exercise 89. Control Chart

1. Plot dots representing the clinic's average time to see patients on that day.
2. Draw the mean and lines representing 3 std deviations above and below mean.
3. Inspect chart for trends, patterns, shifts, and out of control processes.

Mean = 34   Standard Deviation = 9

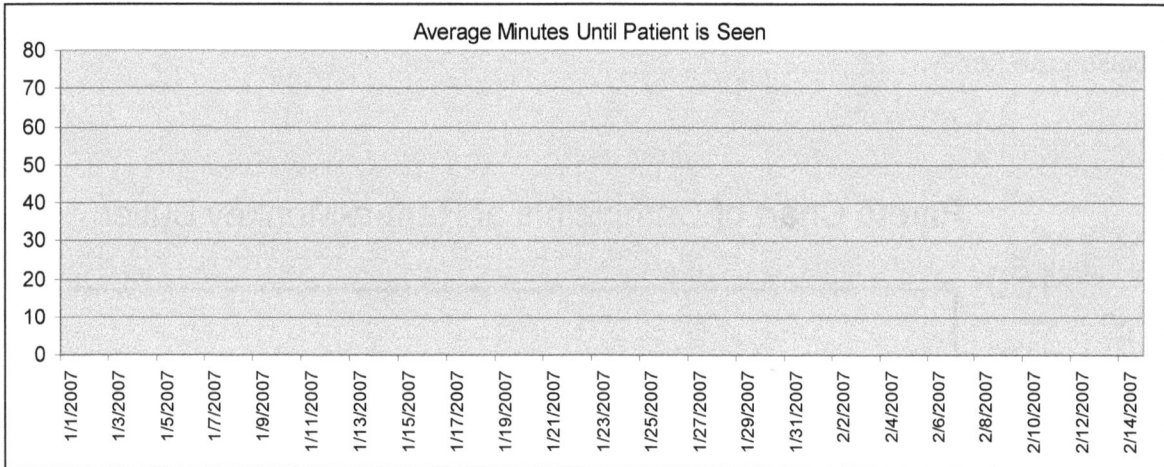

Average Minutes Until Patient is Seen

Day	Mean Min	Day	Mean Min	Day	Mean Min	Day	Mean Min
1-Jan-2007	75	12-Jan-2007	29	23-Jan-2007	30	3-Feb-2007	40
2-Jan-2007	30	13-Jan-2007	32	24-Jan-2007	38	4-Feb-2007	31
3-Jan-2007	33	14-Jan-2007	35	25-Jan-2007	30	5-Feb-2007	40
4-Jan-2007	32	15-Jan-2007	37	26-Jan-2007	38	6-Feb-2007	31
5-Jan-2007	31	16-Jan-2007	42	27-Jan-2007	30	7-Feb-2007	40
6-Jan-2007	32	17-Jan-2007	43	28-Jan-2007	38	8-Feb-2007	30
7-Jan-2007	32	18-Jan-2007	33	29-Jan-2007	30	9-Feb-2007	34
8-Jan-2007	30	19-Jan-2007	32	30-Jan-2007	39	10-Feb-2007	35
9-Jan-2007	31	20-Jan-2007	33	31-Jan-2007	30	11-Feb-2007	33
10-Jan-2007	43	21-Jan-2007	30	1-Feb-2007	39	12-Feb-2007	34
11-Jan-2007	26	22-Jan-2007	25	2-Feb-2007	30	13-Feb-2007	34
						14-Feb-2007	3

Exercise 90. Pareto Diagram

The Rent-a-Monkey Butler Company is reviewing the customer complaints from the last year. There were 8 customers who complained that their monkey was delivered late. The most common problem was that many of the customers, 70 in fact, were unhappy because they believed the monkey was missing some type of important skill, reflecting a lack of complete training. Fifty customers disliked the way the monkey was dressed and 5 customers reported being bitten by their monkey. There were 12 other people who had strange complaints ranging from the monkey gambling away their life savings to trying to poison the family.

Pareto Chart of Complaints at Rent-a-Monkey Butler

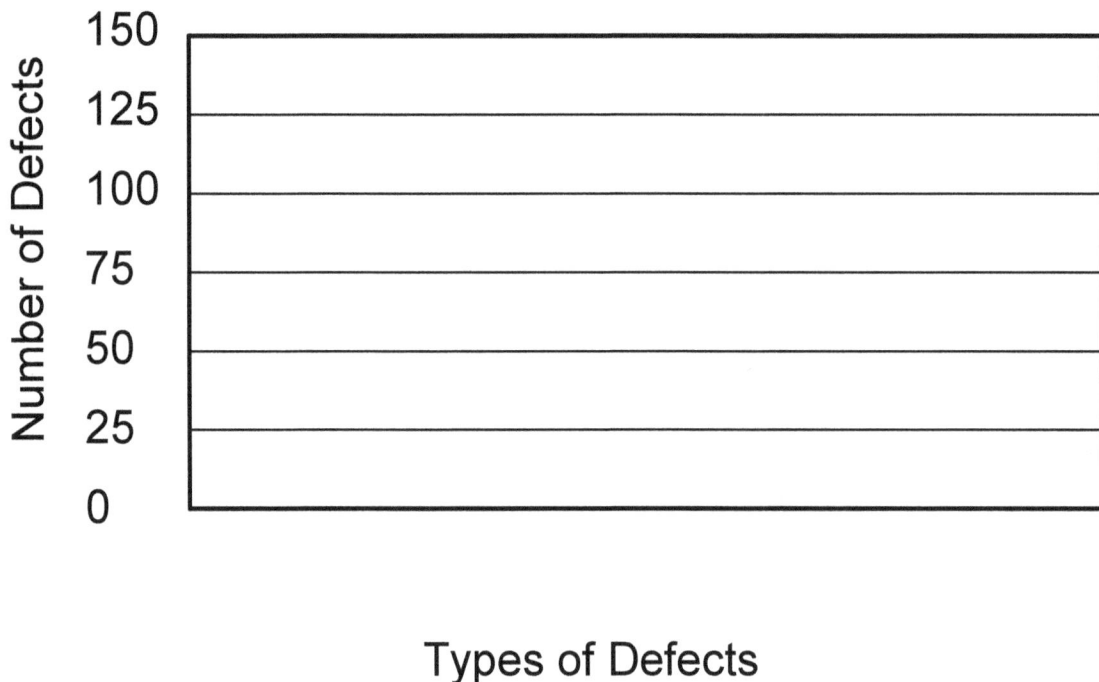

Number of Defects

150
125
100
75
50
25
0

Types of Defects

PMP Scrimmage® Curriculum, Edition 3.01   *Page 206*
www.tapuniversity.com
TECHNOLOGY
AS PROMISED

Exercise 91. Scatter Plot

Plot the number of defects against the years of the team member's experience. For example, for the first team member with 1 year of experience, make a dot where "1" would be on the x-axis and where "26" would be on the y-axis. What conclusions can you draw from this data?

Years of Experience	Number of Defects
1	26
1	29
1	24
2	21
2	24
2	23
2	20
2	17
2	22
2	23
3	22
3	17
4	12
5	9
5	8
7	3
8	2
8	3

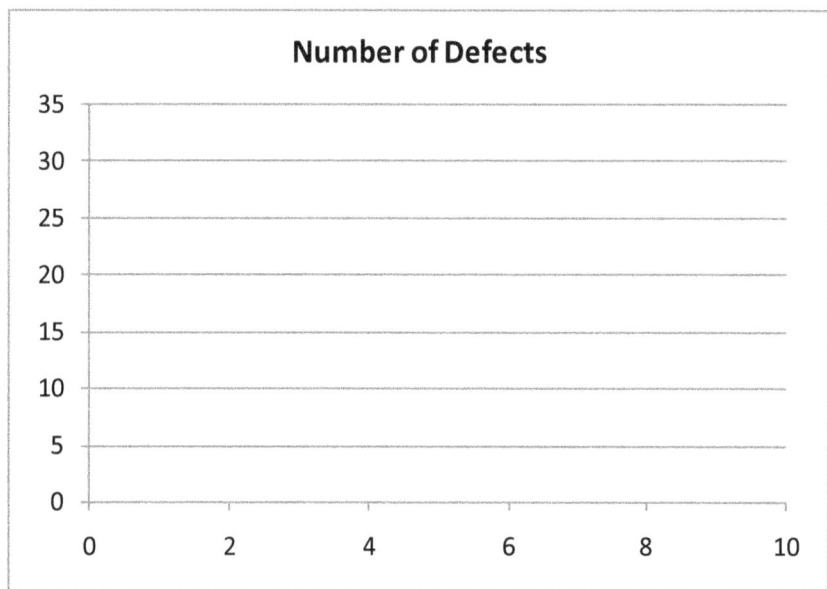

Number of Defects

Exercise 92. Report Performance – Forecasting

Forecasting is one of the tools and techniques of the Report Performance process. There are several categories of forecasting methods. This exercise uses the multiple regression method. In this example, a rabbitry (farm that raises rabbit) is trying to predict how many show rabbits they will sell in a given month. They are trying to predict the number of rabbits sold using these predictors: number of dollars spent on advertising that month, number of awards won at rabbit shows, and the number of shows during that month in the state. Using multiple regression, they were able to calculate the following formula that predicts how many show rabbits they will sell in a month:

Number of Show Rabbits Sold =
2.34 + (Advertising Dollars x .0528) + (Awards Won x 2.19) – (Shows in State x .186)

Help them to calculate how many rabbits they can expect to sell in the following circumstances. The first is done already.

1. If for a given month, they spend $0 on advertising, won 2 awards, and there was 1 show in the state, how many show rabbits can they expect to sell?

   2.34 + (0 x .0528) + (2 x 2.19) – (1 x .186) = 6.534 Rabbits

2. If for a given month, they spend $10 on advertising, won 2 awards, and there was 1 show in the state, how many show rabbits can they expect to sell?

3. If for a given month, they spend $100 on advertising, won 4 awards, and there were 2 shows in the state, how many show rabbits can they expect to sell?

Exercise 93. *Report Performance – Variance Analysis*

Variance Analysis is a tool and technique of the Report Performance process. Variance Analysis compares the planned performance to the actual performance. It may involve earned value. Here are graphs showing the progress of two different projects. The first chart is showing percentage of work completed in 8 months; the second chart is showing earned value over 8 weeks. Compare planned to actual performance, and write a couple sentences explaining the progress in order to report performance on each project.

PROJECT #1

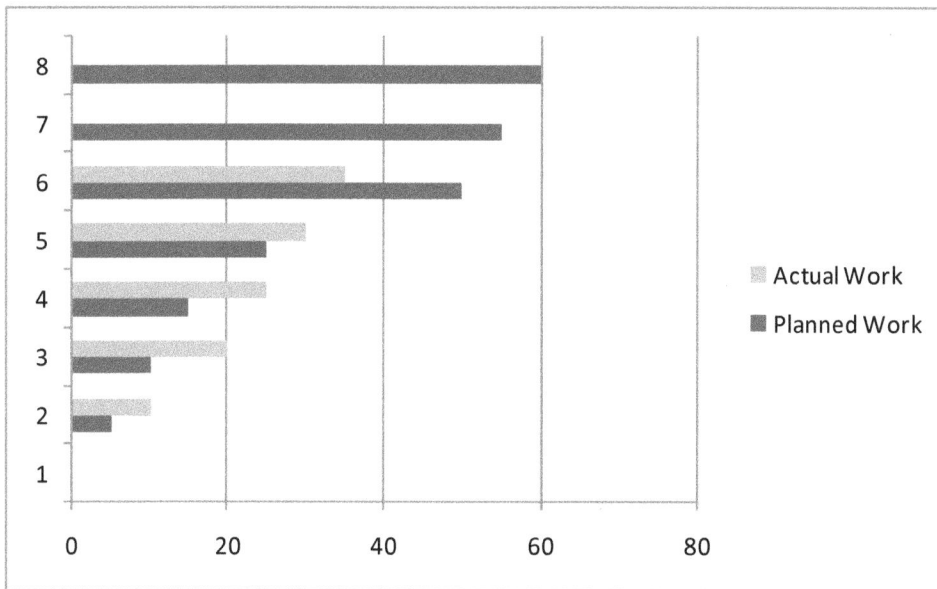

_____

_____

_____

_____

_____

PROJECT #2

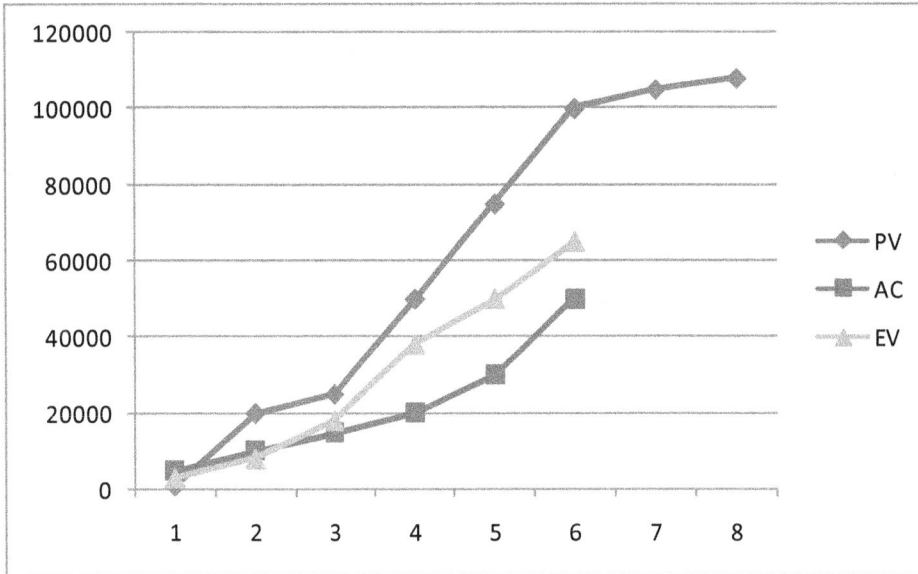

_____

_____

_____

_____

_____

TECHNOLOGY
AS PROMISED

Exercise 94. Administer Procurements

Procurement Documentation is an output of the Administer Procurements process. The Procurement Contract is part of this documentation. Fill in the blanks below of this simplified Procurement Contract for your company to obtain needed services from Sir Viss Inc. which provides an array of services. First determine the service you need. The services you request could be a consultation, someone to mow the company lawn, someone to bring in fresh doughnuts to your team every morning, etc. Decide how you will pay Sir Viss—will it be a lump sum or will there be a payment schedule? Will it be Fixed Price or Time & Materials contract? Will there be an Incentive Fee?

SERVICES AGREEMENT

THIS AGREEMENT for the performance of services is executed on the
_____ day of _____, 20_____ and made effective as of the _____ day of
_____, 20_____, between _____ ("_____") and
Sir Viss Inc. ("Sir Viss").

The parties hereto mutually agree as follows:

Article I   Agreement Description
This Agreement supersedes any and all earlier versions of this agreement. The contractual terms and conditions of this Agreement may be changed only through formal written amendments to this Agreement.

Article II   Description of Services

Sir Viss shall _____

_____

_____

_____

_____

Article III Compensation

_____

_____

_____

_____

IN WITNESS WHEREOF, the parties hereto have executed this Agreement as of the date and year first above written.

TECHNOLOGY
AS PROMISED

Exercise 95. Thirty Questions on Nine Processes

Answer these thirty questions on the nine processes listed below.

Direct and Manage Project Execution
Perform Quality Assurance
Monitor and Control Project Work
Perform Integrated Change Control
Verify Scope
Control Scope
Control Schedule
Perform Quality Control
Monitor and Control Risks

1. The majority of the budget is spent during this process:
2. The work of the project is performed during this process:
3. Process that performs the quality activities from the quality plan:
4. An independent review by trained auditors or third-parties to identify poor processes:
5. Examines process improvement from an organizational and technical perspective:
6. Quality audits are performed during this process:
7. This process monitors all the process groups:
8. In some organizations this is established to review change requests:
9. The process where all change requests are processes and either approved or denied:
10. Describes product, tracks product changes, and verifies product requirements:
11. The three activities of Configuration Management:
12. Documented procedures on how to submit changes and manage change requests:
13. Process that formalizes the acceptance of the project meeting objectives:
14. The only tool and technique of this process is "Inspection":
15. Process that specifically controls changes to the project scope:
16. Process determining schedule status, if changes occurred, and influencing changes:
17. Chart with two bars for each activity showing approved schedule and actual status:
18. Defines how changes to the schedule are made and managed:
19. Tools and techniques of Perform Quality Control are listed as a tool of this process:
20. Process seeing if work meets quality standards from the quality management plan:
21. A type of bar chart that ranks orders important effects by their frequency:
22. A line chart that illustrates whether process is in or out of control:
23. A line chart that displays a variable over time without illustrating control limits:
24. Relationship between problem and causes, also called fishbone/ Ishikawa diagram:
25. Examining a run chart or control chart for patterns in the data:
26. Examining a subset of something to make inferences about the whole:
27. A chart showing the relationship of two variables through dots:
28. Process that identifies and responds to new risks as they occur:
29. Audits focused on implementation and effective use of risk strategies:
30. An unplanned response to a negative risk event:

Chapter 7 - Close'er Up

There are two remaining processes that support project closing – Close Project or Phase and Close Procurements. Closing up your project happens in two important ways:

1. When the project is complete and the results of that project are transferred to operations (or day to day production support), and/or
2. When the project completes a phase and is approved to move forward (organizations that utilize a phased, milestone of stage gate review and move forward process).

Close Project or Phase (4.6)

This was called Close Project in the third edition PMBOK®. The Close Project or Phase process is the final process within the Project Integration Knowledge Area.

The closure procedures can be as straight forward as a punch down list for a new home or as intricate and complex as a refueling tanker final acceptance test (that can take over three years). The Organizational Process Assets Updates places all of that wonderful project information and artifacts into an accessible electronic or manual repository.

Close Procurements (12.4)

This process was called Contract Closure in the third edition PMBOK®. Contract closure directly supports and can be considered a subset of the Close Project process. It also provides a process to update contract-specific close out information such as formal acceptance forms or early termination.

Procurement Audits have taken on increasing importance as they fall under global financial regulatory authorities (European Union Standards and Sarbanes Oxley in the United States). No longer a superficial review at the end; procurement audits need to assess whether any material deviations have occurred with the performing organization.

The major output is the Closed Procurements. Lessons learned, each deliverables acceptance or rejection, and contract files are then appended to the Organizational Process Assets.

You are now **DONE!**

Now get back to the other 11.2 projects and change requests on your plate. That is the average number of things or stuff that project managers must juggle based on TAPUniversity research of over 160 project managers in 2006-07.

Chapter 7 Exercises

Exercise 96. Project Close-Out

This exercise reviews the four formal close-out methods for a project.

1. Project Knock Your Socks Off delivered all the agreed-upon deliverables, and these deliverables have been accepted by the stakeholders. Which of the four formal close-out methods is being described?

Addition　　　　　Starvation　　　　　Integration　　　　　Extinction

2. Project Check Up on Quality was meant to be a six-month monitoring process for defects. However, it was so useful at finding and leading to the correction of defects, it has been decided that it should become a permanent part of the process. Which of the four formal close-out methods is being described?

Addition　　　　　Starvation　　　　　Integration　　　　　Extinction

3. Jacki started managing a project a year ago that began with a team of ten people. One by one, her team members were pulled away for projects that were considered more important to the organization. Now nothing is being accomplished on this project because there is no team. Which of the four formal close-out methods is being described?

Addition　　　　　Starvation　　　　　Integration　　　　　Extinction

4. Sallie was managing a project that concerned making specific modifications to a product ordered by a large customer. The customer cancelled the order, so there are no funds and no reasons to continue the project.

Which of the four formal close-out methods is being described?

Addition　　　　　Starvation　　　　　Integration　　　　　Extinction

5. Which of the four formal close-out methods is considered the best ending for a project?

Addition　　　　　Starvation　　　　　Integration　　　　　Extinction

6. Which method is how your last project ended?

Addition　　　　　Starvation　　　　　Integration　　　　　Extinction

Exercise 97. Sample Project Post Mortem for Internet Portal (stage gate report after completion of the design)

Was the scope of the project met? **YES – DESIGN IS COMPLETE!**

Plus / Delta

What went well	What could have been improved
<ul><li>**Maintained timeline**</li><li>**Hit major objectives**</li><li>**Received Feedback**</li></ul>	<ul><li>**Usability study and testing was delayed due to additional contract letting**</li></ul>

What were the project highlights? - **getting it done**/lowlights? - **our ability to jump through the procurement hoops.**

What was effectiveness of the project metrics used to monitor progress (schedule, cost, risk, communication, quality, and scope)? **Very effective – however – that's not typically the case. It's driven more by the project's importance.**

Did the escalation plan need to be invoked? Yes or no. If yes, what was the reason? What was the result?

What three things will you take away from this project and incorporate in the next one?
1. **When we focus on perceived important project – we make things happen.**
2. **We need to bring that to the next project.**
3. **Plus we've been able to cut through a lot of normally choking red tape to make stuff happen.**

What is the team's opinion of how the project was managed? **Effective although QC/ Testing is a bit concerned about aggressiveness of schedule.**

What is the client's opinion of how the project was managed? **Sales force has high favorability (4.8 on a 5.0 scale), but operations was less favorable (3.9 on a 5.0 scale).**

Exercise 97. Project Post Mortem

Now it's your turn.

For your selected project, was the scope of the project met? Yes or No

Plus/Delta

What went well	What could have been improved

What were the project highlights/lowlights?

What was effectiveness of the project metrics used to monitor progress (schedule, cost, risk, communication, quality, and scope)?

Did the escalation plan need to be invoked? Yes or No. If yes, what was the reason? What was the result?

What three things will you take away from this project and incorporate in the next one?

What is the team's opinion of how the project was managed?

What is the client's opinion of how the project was managed?

Exercise 98. Close Procurements for the Banana Farm

The outputs of the Close Procurements process are Closed Procurements and Organizational Assets Updates. The Organizational Assets Updates include Deliverable Acceptance, which is formal written notice that the deliverables have been accepted or rejected.

You have just taken over as the Project Manager for a struggling local agricultural project whose purpose is to develop a new type of banana tree. While looking through the files to familiarize yourself with the project, you notice that there are daily invoices from a company called Fair Weather Friend. Your team informs you that they have been hired to perform ancient rituals this past week to cause the weather to be warmer, which should improve the growth of the bananas, but the contract with them has expired yesterday. For the Closed Procurements output, write a brief formal notice that the contract is now closed. For the Deliverable Acceptance, write a brief formal notice on whether or not you have accepted their deliverables based on the weather over the last week.

Closed Procurements
_____

_____

_____

_____

_____

_____

Deliverable Acceptance
_____

_____

_____

_____

_____

_____

TECHNOLOGY
AS PROMISED

Exercise 99. Where Did I Come From?

It's important to know which process the key outputs come from. For each output, write which process created it.

Output	Process
Project Scope Statement	
Change Request Status Update	
Activity List	
Project Schedule	
Project Management Plan	
Requirements Management Plan	
Work Breakdown Structure	
Cost Performance Baseline	
Project Charter	
Scope Baseline	
Deliverables	
Quality Management Plan	
Final Product, Service, or Result Transition	
Accepted Deliverables	
Selected Sellers	
Stakeholder Register	
Risk Register	
Human Resource Plan	
Team Performance Assessments	

Exercise 100. Process Sort

This exercise is a quick way to learn which process groups and knowledge areas all the processes belong to. Cut out the process names on the next page. Study the process table in the PMBOK®, then without looking at the table place all the processes in a square. When done, use the process table again to see how many you got right. Repeat this until you are able to correctly sort all the processes. If studying in a group, this is a good competitive game. You may wish to store the process pieces in an envelope when done.

	Integration	Scope	Time	Cost	Quality	Human Resource	Communications	Risk	Procurement
Closing									
Monitoring and Controlling									
Executing									
Planning									
Initiating									

Cut out the process names to use for the Process Sort exercise.

Acquire Project Team	Administer Procurements	Close Project or Phase	Close Procurements	Collect Requirements	Conduct Procurements
Control Costs	Control Schedule	Control Scope	Create Work Breakdown Structure	Define Activities	Define Scope
Determine Budget	Develop Human Resource Plan	Develop Project Charter	Develop Project Management Plan	Develop Project Team	Develop Schedule
Direct and Manage Project Execution	Distribute Information	Estimate Activity Durations	Estimate Activity Resources	Estimate Costs	Identify Risks
Identify Stakeholders	Manage Project Team	Manage Stakeholders Expectations	Monitor and Control Project Work	Monitor and Control Risks	Perform Integrated Change Control
Perform Qualitative Risk Analysis	Perform Quality Assurance	Perform Quality Control	Perform Quantitative Risk Analysis	Plan Communications	Plan Procurements
Plan Risk Management	Plan Risk Responses	Plan Quality	Report Performance	Sequence Activities	Verify Scope

TECHNOLOGY
AS PROMISED

Exercise 101. Inputs, Tools and Techniques, and Outputs

Practice writing the inputs, tools and techniques, and outputs to the 42 processes. Look at the inputs, tools and techniques, and outputs for a process, and then write as much as you can remember. Look again, and fill in those you missed. Don't try to memorize all the inputs, tools and techniques, but use this to learn the key ones and to learn patterns. Make as many photocopies of this sheet as you wish.

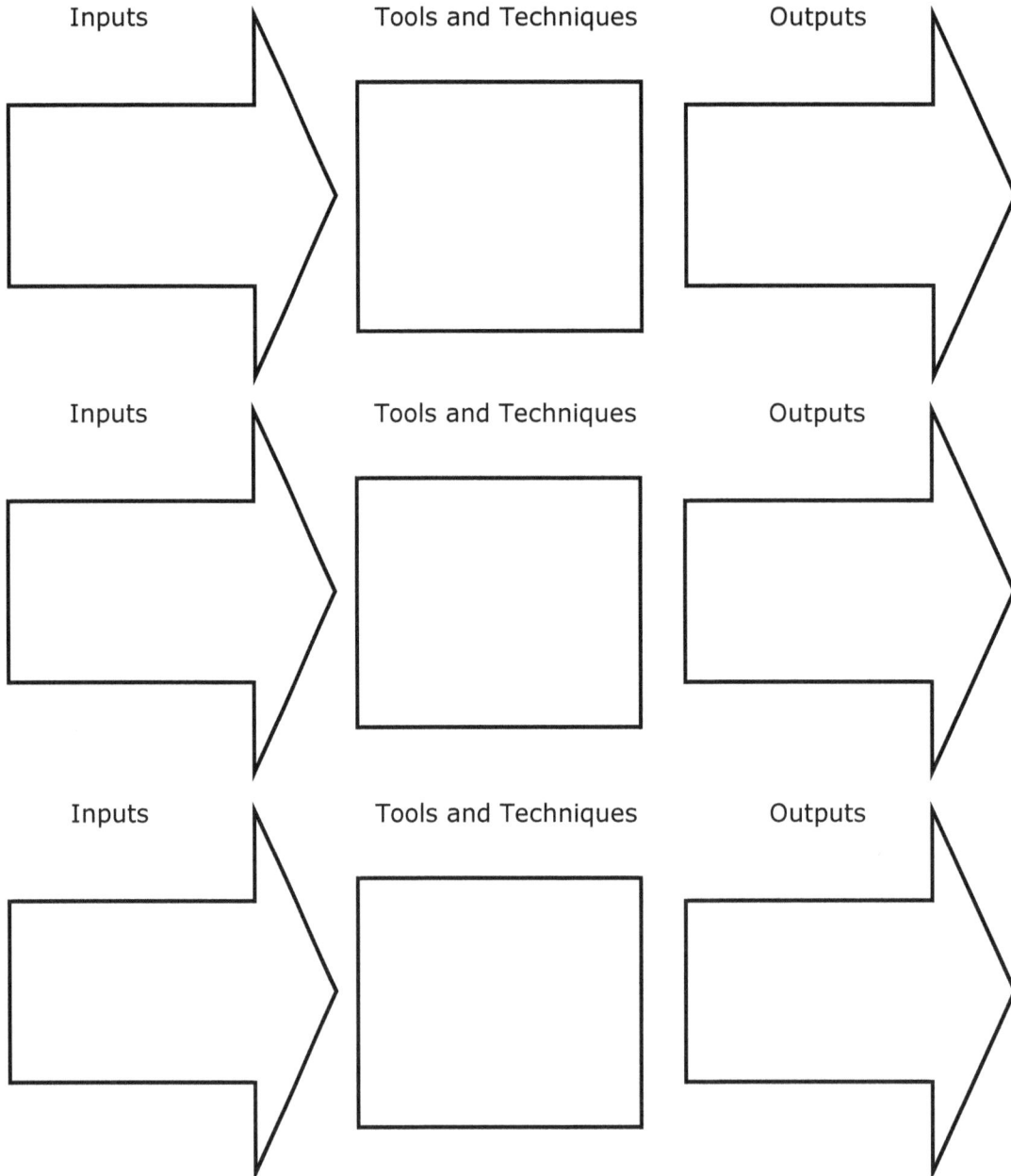

Inputs   Tools and Techniques   Outputs

Inputs   Tools and Techniques   Outputs

Inputs   Tools and Techniques   Outputs

TECHNOLOGY
AS PROMISED

Exercise 102. Integration Inputs, Tools and Techniques, and Outputs

This exercise provides practice identifying the inputs, tools and techniques, and outputs of the Integration Area processes. First study the inputs, tools and techniques, and outputs for the Integration processes. For each input, put and "I" under the processes it is an input to. Put a "T" if it's a tool and technique and an "O" if it's an output. There is a hint after each—for example "4 Inputs" means that this is an input to four of the processes, so you'll be writing 4 "I's." Consider making photocopies of this exercise if you want to try it again.

	Develop Project Charter	Develop Project Management Plan	Direct and Manage Project Execution	Monitor and Control Project Work	Perform Integrated Change Control	Close Project or Phase
Enterprise Environmental Factors (4 Inputs)						
Organizational Process Assets (6 Inputs)						
Expert Judgment (6 Tools)						
Accepted Deliverables (1 Input)						
Approved Change Requests (1 Input)						
Business Case (1 Input)						
Change Requests (2 Outputs, 1 Input)						
Change Request Status Update (1 Output)						
Change Control Meetings (1 Tool)						
Contract (1 Input)						
Deliverables (1 Output)						
Final Product, Service, or Result Transition (1 Output)						
Forecasts (1 Input)						
Outputs from Planning Processes (1 Input)						
Organizational Process Assets (Updates) (1 Output)						
Performance Reports (1 Input)						
Project Statement of Work (1 Input)						
Project Charter (1 Input, 1 Output)						
Project Scope Statement (1 Input)						
Project Management Information System (1 Tool)						
Project Management Plan Updates (3 Outputs)						
Project Documents Updates (3 Outputs)						
Project Management Plan (1 Output, 3 Inputs)						
Work Performance Data (1 Input, 1 Output)						

Exercise 103. Scope Inputs, Tools and Techniques, and Outputs

This exercise provides practice identifying the inputs, tools and techniques, and outputs of the Scope Area processes. First study the inputs, tools and techniques, and outputs for the Scope processes. For each input, put and "I" under the processes it is an input to. Put a "T" if it's a tool and technique and an "O" if it's an output. There is a hint after each—for example "4 Inputs" means that this is an input to four of the processes, so you'll be writing 4 "I's." Consider making photocopies of this exercise if you want to try it again.

	Collect Requirements	Define Scope	Create WBS	Verify Scope	Control Scope
Accepted Deliverables (1 Output)					
Alternatives Identification (1 Tool)					
Change Requests (2 Outputs)					
Decomposition (1 Tool)					
Expert Judgment (1 Tool)					
Facilitated Workshops (2 Tools)					
Focus Groups (1 Tool)					
Group Creativity Techniques (1 Tool)					
Group Decision Making Techniques (1 Tool)					
Inspection (1 Tool)					
Interviews (1 Tool)					
Observations (1 Tool)					
Organizational Process Assets (2 Inputs)					
Organizational Process Assets Updates (1 Output)					
Product Analysis (1 Tool)					
Project Charter (2 Inputs)					
Project Document Updates (2 Outputs)					
Project Management Plan (1 Input)					
Project Management Plan Updates (1 Output)					
Project Scope Statement (1 Tool, 1 Input)					
Prototypes (1 Tool)					
Questionnaires and Surveys (1 Tool)					
Replanning (1 Tool)					
Requirements Management Plan (1 Output)					
Requirements Traceability Matrix (1 Output, 2 Inputs)					
Scope Baseline (1 Output, 1 Input)					
Stakeholder Register (1 Input)					
Stakeholder Requirements Documentation (1 Output, 4 Inputs)					
Validated Deliverables (1 Input)					
Variance Analysis (1 Tool)					
Work Breakdown Structure (1 Output)					
Work Performance Data (1 Input)					
Work Performance Measurements (1 Output)					
WBS Dictionary (1 Output)					

PMP Scrimmage® Curriculum, Edition 3.01   *Page 224*
www.tapuniversity.com
TECHNOLOGY
AS PROMISED

Exercise 104. Time Inputs and Outputs

This exercise provides practice identifying the inputs and outputs of the Time Area processes. First study the inputs and outputs for the Time processes. For each input, put and "I" under the processes it is an input to and an "O" if it's an output. There is a hint after each—for example "4 Inputs" means that this is an input to four of the processes, so you'll be writing 4 "I's." Consider making photocopies of this exercise if you want to try it again.

	Define Activities	Sequence Activities	Estimate Activity Resources	Estimate Activity Durations	Develop Schedule	Control Schedule
Activity Attributes (1 Output, 4 Inputs)						
Activity Duration Estimates (1 Output, 1 Input)						
Activity List (1 Output, 4 Inputs)						
Activity Resource Requirements (1 Output, 2 Inputs)						
Change Requests (1 Output)						
Enterprise Environmental Factors (4 Inputs)						
Milestone List (1 Output, 1 Input)						
Organizational Process Assets (5 Inputs)						
Organizational Process Assets Updates (1 Output)						
Project Document Updates (5 Outputs)						
Project Management Plan (1 Input)						
Project Management Plan Updates (1 Output)						
Project Schedule (1 Output, 1 Input)						
Project Schedule Network Diagrams (1 Output, 1 Input)						
Project Scope Statement (3 Inputs)						
Resource Breakdown Structure (1 Output)						
Resource Calendars (3 Inputs)						
Schedule Baseline (1 Output)						
Schedule Data (1 Output)						
Scope Baseline (1 Input)						
Work Performance Data (1 Input)						
Work Performance Measurements (1 Output)						

Exercise 105. Cost Inputs, Tools and Techniques, and Outputs

This exercise provides practice identifying the inputs, tools and techniques, and outputs of the Cost Area processes. First study the inputs, tools and techniques, and outputs for the Cost processes. For each input, put and "I" under the processes it is an input to. Put a "T" if it's a tool and technique and an "O" if it's an output. There is a hint after each—for example "4 Inputs" means that this is an input to four of the processes, so you'll be writing 4 "I's." Consider making photocopies of this exercise if you want to try it again.

	Estimate Costs	Determine Budget	Control Costs
Activity Cost Estimates (1 Output, 1 Input)			
Analogous Estimating (1 Tool)			
Basis of Estimates (1 Output, 1 Input)			
Bottom-Up Estimating (1 Tool)			
Change Requests (1 Output)			
Contracts (1 Input)			
Cost Aggregation (1 Tool)			
Cost of Quality (1 Tool)			
Cost Performance Baseline (1 Output, 1 Input)			
Earned Value Measurement (1 Tool)			
Enterprise Environmental Factors (1 Input)			
Expert Judgment (1 Tool)			
Forecasted Completion (1 Output)			
Forecasting (1 Tool)			
Funding Limit Reconciliation (1 Tool)			
Historical Relationships (1 Tool)			
Human Resource Plan (1 Input)			
Organizational Process Assets (3 Inputs)			
Organizational Process Assets Updates (1 Output)			
Parametric Estimating (1 Tool)			
Project Document Updates (3 Outputs)			
Project Management Estimating Software (1 Tool)			
Project Management Plan Updates (1 Output)			
Project Management Software (1 Tool)			
Project Funding Requirements (1 Output, 1 Input)			
Project Schedule (2 Inputs)			
Project Status Performance Reviews (1 Tool)			
Reserve Analysis (2 Tools)			
Resource Calendars (1 Input)			
Risk Register (1 Input)			
Scope Baseline (2 Inputs)			
To-complete Performance Index (1 Tool)			
Work Performance Data (1 Input)			
Work Performance Measurements (1 Output)			
Variance Analysis (1 Tool)			
Vendor Bid Analysis (1 Tool)			

Exercise 106. Quality Inputs, Tools and Techniques, and Outputs

This exercise provides practice identifying the inputs, tools and techniques, and outputs of the Quality Area processes. First study the inputs, tools and techniques, and outputs for the Quality processes. For each input, put and "I" under the processes it is an input to. Put a "T" if it's a tool and technique and an "O" if it's an output. There is a hint after each—for example "4 Inputs" means that this is an input to four of the processes, so you'll be writing 4 "I's." Consider making photocopies of this exercise if you want to try it again.

	Plan Quality	Perform Quality Assurance	Perform Quality Control
Additional Quality Planning Tools (1 Tool)			
Approved Change Requests (1 Input)			
Approved Change Request Review (1 Tool)			
Benchmarking (1 Tool)			
Cause and Effect Diagram (1 Tool)			
Change Requests (2 Outputs)			
Control Charts (2 Tools)			
Control Measurements (1 Output)			
Cost-benefit Analysis (1 Tool)			
Cost of Quality (1 Tool)			
Cost Performance Baseline (1 Input)			
Deliverables (1 Input)			
Design of Experiments (1 Tool)			
Enterprise Environmental Factors (1 Input)			
Flowcharting (2 Tools)			
Histogram (1 Tool)			
Inspection (1 Tool)			
Organizational Process Assets (2 Inputs)			
Organizational Process Assets Updates (2 Outputs)			
Pareto Chart (1 Tool)			
Process Analysis (1 Tool)			
Process Improvement Plan (1 Output, 1 Input)			
Project Document Updates (3 Outputs)			
Project Management Plan Updates (2 Outputs)			
Proprietary Quality Management Methodologies (1 Tool)			
Quality Audits (1 Tool)			
Quality Checklists (1 Output, 1 Input)			
Quality Control Measures (1 Input)			
Quality Management Plan (1 Output, 2 Inputs)			
Quality Metrics (1 Output, 2 Inputs)			
Quality Planning & Quality Control T & T (1 Tool)			
Risk Register (1 Input)			
Run Chart (1 Tool)			
Scatter Diagram (1 Tool)			
Schedule Baseline (1 Input)			
Scope Baseline (1 Input)			
Stakeholder Register (1 Input)			
Statistical Sampling (2 Tools)			
Validated Changes (1 Output)			
Validated Deliverables (1 Output)			
Work Performance Data (1 Input)			
Work Performance Measurement (1 Input)			

Exercise 107. Human Resource Inputs, Tools and Techniques, and Outputs

This exercise provides practice identifying the inputs, tools and techniques, and outputs of the Human Resource Area processes. First study the inputs, tools and techniques, and outputs for the Human Resource processes. For each input, put and "I" under the processes it is an input to. Put a "T" if it's a tool and technique and an "O" if it's an output. There is a hint after each—for example "4 Inputs" means that this is an input to four of the processes, so you'll be writing 4 "I's." Consider making photocopies of this exercise if you want to try it again.

	Develop Human Resource Plan	Acquire Project Team	Develop Project Team	Manage Project Team
Acquisition (1 Tool)				
Activity Resource Requirements (1 Input)				
Change Requests (1 Output)				
Co-Location (1 Tool)				
Conflict Management (1 Tool)				
Interpersonal Skills (1 Tool)				
Issue Log (1 Tool)				
Enterprise Environmental Factors (2 Inputs)				
Enterprise Environmental Factor Updates (2 Outputs)				
Ground Rules (1 Tool)				
Human Resource Plan (1 Output, 3 Inputs)				
Interpersonal Skills (1 Tool)				
Negotiation (1 Tool)				
Networking (1 Tool)				
Observation and Conversation (1 Tool)				
Organization Charts and Position Descriptions (1 Tool)				
Organizational Process Assets (3 Inputs)				
Organizational Process Assets Updates (1 Output)				
Organizational Theory (1 Tool)				
Performance Reports (1 Input)				
Pre-Assignment (1 Tool)				
Project Management Plan Updates (2 Outputs)				
Project Performance Appraisals (1 Tool)				
Project Staff Assignments (1 Output, 2 Inputs)				
Recognition and Rewards (1 Tool)				
Resource Calendars (1 Output, 1 Input)				
Team-Building Activities (1 Tool)				
Team Performance Assessments (1 Output, 1 Input)				
Training (1 Tool)				
Virtual Teams (1 Tool)				

Exercise 108. Communications Inputs, Tools and Techniques, and Outputs

This exercise provides practice identifying the inputs, tools and techniques, and outputs of the Communications Area processes. First study the inputs, tools and techniques, and outputs for the Communications processes. For each input, put and "I" under the processes it is an input to. Put a "T" if it's a tool and technique and an "O" if it's an output. There is a hint after each—for example "4 Inputs" means that this is an input to four of the processes, so you'll be writing 4 "I's." Consider making photocopies of this exercise if you want to try it again.

	Identify Stakeholders	Plan Communications	Distribute Information	Manage Stakeholder Expectations	Report Performance
Change Log (1 Input)					
Change Requests (2 Outputs)					
Communication Methods (4 Tools)					
Communication Models (1 Tool)					
Communication Requirements Analysis (1 Tool)					
Communications Management Plan (1 Output, 2 Inputs)					
Communication Technology (1 Tool)					
Enterprise Environmental Factors (2 Inputs)					
Expert Judgment (1 Tool)					
Forecasting Methods (1 Tool)					
Information Distribution Tools (1 Tool)					
Interpersonal Skills (1 Tool)					
Issue Log (1 Input)					
Management Skills (1 Tool)					
Organizational Process Assets (5 Inputs)					
Organizational Process Assets Updates (3 Outputs)					
Performance Reports (1 Input, 1 Output)					
Procurement Document Package (1 Input)					
Project Charter (1 Input)					
Project Document Updates (2 Outputs)					
Project Management Plan (1 Input)					
Project Management Plan Updates (1 Output)					
Reporting Systems (1 Tool)					
Stakeholder Analysis (1 Tool)					
Stakeholder Management Strategy (1 Output, 2 Inputs)					
Stakeholder Register (1 Output, 2 Inputs)					
Variance Analysis (1 Tool)					
Work Performance Data (1 Input)					
Work Performance Measurements (1 Input)					

PMP Scrimmage® Curriculum, Edition 3.01   Page 229
www.tapuniversity.com
TECHNOLOGY
AS PROMISED

Exercise 109. Risk Inputs and Outputs

This exercise provides practice identifying the inputs and outputs of the Risk Area processes. First study the inputs and outputs for the Risk processes. For each input, put and "I" under the processes it is an input to and an "O" if it's an output. There is a hint after each—for example "4 Inputs" means that this is an input to four of the processes, so you'll be writing 4 "I's." Consider making photocopies of this exercise if you want to try it again.

	Plan Risk Management	Identify Risks	Perform Quantitative Risk Analysis	Perform Qualitative Risk Analysis	Plan Risk Responses	Monitor & Control Risks
Activity Cost Estimates (1 Input)						
Activity Duration Estimates (1 Input)						
Change Requests (1 Output)						
Communications Management Plan (1 Input)						
Cost Management Plan (3 Inputs)						
Enterprise Environmental Factors (2 Inputs)						
Organizational Process Assets (4 Inputs)						
Organizational Process Assets Updates (1 Output)						
Other Project Documents (1 Input)						
Performance Reports (1 Input)						
Project Document Updates (2 Outputs)						
Project Management Plan Updates (2 Outputs)						
Project Scope Statement (2 Inputs)						
Quality Management Plan (1 Input)						
Risk Management Plan (1 Output, 5 Inputs)						
Risk Register (1 Output, 4 Inputs)						
Risk Register Updates (4 Outputs)						
Risk Related Contract Decisions (1 Output)						
Schedule Management Plan (3 Inputs)						
Scope Baseline (1 Input)						
Stakeholder Register (1 Input)						
Work Performance Data (1 Input)						

Exercise 110. Procurement Inputs, Tools and Techniques, and Outputs

This exercise provides practice identifying the inputs and outputs of the Procurement Area processes. First study the inputs and outputs for the Procurement processes. For each input, put and "I" under the processes it is an input to and an "O" if it's an output. There is a hint after each—for example "4 Inputs" means that this is an input to four of the processes, so you'll be writing 4 "I's." Consider making photocopies of this exercise if you want to try it again.

	Plan Procurements	Conduct Procurements	Administer Procurements	Close Procurements
Activity Cost Estimates (1 Input)				
Activity Resource Requirements (1 Input)				
Approved Change Requests (1 Input)				
Change Requests (3 Outputs)				
Closed Procurements (1 Output)				
Cost Performance Baseline (1 Input)				
Enterprise Environmental Factors (1 Input)				
Make-or-buy Decisions (1 Output, 1 Input)				
Organizational Process Assets (2 Inputs)				
Organizational Process Assets Updates (2 Outputs)				
Performance Reports (1 Input)				
Procurement Award (1 Output)				
Procurement Documentation (1 Output, 1 Input)				
Procurement Document Packages(1 Output, 1 Input)				
Procurement Documents (1 Input)				
Procurement Management Plan (1 Output, 3 Inputs)				
Procurement Statements of Work (1 Output)				
Project Documents (1 Input)				
Project Document Updates (1 Output)				
Project Management Plan Updates (2 Outputs)				
Project Schedule (1 Input)				
Qualified Seller List (1 Input)				
Resource Calendars (1 Output)				
Risk Register (1 Input)				
Risk-related Contract Decisions (1 Input)				
Scope Baseline (1 Input)				
Selected Sellers (1 Output, 1 Input)				
Seller Proposals (1 Input)				
Source Selection Criteria (1 Output, 1 Input)				
Stakeholder Requirements Documentation (1 Input)				
Teaming Agreements (2 Inputs)				
Work Performance Data (1 Input)				

Exercise 111. Code of Ethics

For these two scenarios, describe how you should handle the situation. Reference the section of the PMI Code of Ethics and Professional Conduct that supports your decision.

1. Your project manager friend, Cindy, is a PMP in your organization who is overseeing opening a store in Chile. Two of your team members have told you that they are positive that Cindy has been compromising the quality of her project in order that she can secretly redirect a portion of the project's funds to support a relief effort for a nearby impoverished village in Chile. What do you do?

2. You are reviewing several dozen proposals that vendors have submitted. To your surprise, your cousin Randy has submitted a proposal and you believe it is truly the most innovative and cost-effective. What do you do?

Chapter 8　　- Appendices

Appendix 1 – Exercise solutions
Appendix 2 – Sample, real world project plan

Appendix 1: Solutions to Exercises

Exercise 1 Projects, Programs, and Ongoing Operations

A. Using your knowledge of Projects, Programs, and Ongoing Operations, identify each below.

1. Stuffed Friends Inc. is going to develop a new set of stuffed animals—a talking donkey and elephant that are to be on the shelves by Election Day.

   Project   Program   Ongoing Operations

2. Stuffed Friends Inc. has implemented a new policy to use a flame thrower at the end of every week to burn out the extra cotton stuffing in the machines so nothing becomes jammed from a build-up of cotton.

   Project   Program   **Ongoing Operations**

3. Sarah has been assigned to develop the new Flame Thrower Policy and make sure the new procedures are implemented smoothly.

   Project   Program   Ongoing Operations

4. Three new Stuffed Friends stores are being opened in Africa as part of a campaign to increase their market share overseas. A different project manager is being assigned to construct and build each store.

   Project   **Program**   Ongoing Operations

5. The talking elephant and donkey were so successful during the current election; that they will be produced again just before the next election.

   Project   Program   **Ongoing Operations**

C. Thinking of a current or past workplace, what would be an example of each of the following?

1. Project

2. Program

3. Ongoing Operations

Exercise 2. Why Do Projects Come Into Existence?

Why did this project come into existence?	Market demand	Organizational need	Customer request	Technological advance	Legal requirement
1. Because Stuffed Friends Inc. is crowded in its current headquarters, they are beginning a project to construct a larger building that will better suit their needs.		x			
2. A new synthetic fur-like fabric has been developed that is able to withstand fire, repels insects, has a pleasant odor, and is machine-washable. Stuffed Friends authorizes a project to gradually replace all their old stuffed animal fabric with this revolutionary fabric.				x	
3. A project has already been begun to redesign the unpopular stuffed shark toy. Customers have been complaining that the sharp glass teeth have been causing deep cuts, and asked that a cuddlier version be manufactured.			x		
4. Stuffed Friends Inc. needs a research report and implementation plan to change the stuffing of its toys to a flame-retardant material in order to comply with new federal consumer safety guidelines.					x
5. The Opossum Fancier Association has requested ten thousand stuffed opossum toys be manufactured for its most loyal members. A project manager has been assigned to develop and launch this new project.			x		
6. Due to a recent trend in Green products, Stuffed Friends Inc. has authorized a project that will develop a feasibility report on creating a line of biodegradable native rainforest animals completely from recycled products.	x				
7. Unfortunately, a small project needs to be launched immediately to discreetly discontinue the jellyfish stuffed toy. Although the engineers had convinced marketing that a toy that produces a realistic electric shock would be successful, the Consumer Protection Agency deemed it unsafe.					x

Exercise 4. Practicing Process Patterns

The best way to learn the organization of the processes is to look for patterns. Using the table of 42 processes in chapter 1, answer the questions below.

1. Which is the only Knowledge Area that has processes in all five Process Groups? *Integration*

2. Which two Knowledge Areas have processes in four of the five Process Groups? *Communications and Procurement*

3. Which is the only Process Group that has processes in all nine Knowledge Areas? *Planning*

4. The three Quality processes all have what word in their name? *Quality*

5. The six Risk processes all have what word in their name? *Risk(s)*

6. The four Procurement processes all have what word in their name? *Procurement*

7. The six Time processes all have one of which two words in their name? *Activities or Schedule*

8. If the word "Team" is in a process name, which Knowledge Area and Process Group must it be in? *The Executing Process Group and the Human Resource Knowledge Area*

9. If the word "Manage" is in a process name, which Process Group must it be in? *Executing*

10. If the work "Plan" is in a process name, which Process Group must it be in? *Planning*

11. If the work "Define" or "Estimate" is in a process name, which Process Group must it be in? *Planning*

12. If the work "Close" is in a process name, which Process Group must it be in? *Closing*

Exercise 6. Organizational Types

	Functional	Weak Matrix	Balanced Matrix	Strong Matrix	Projectized	Composite
1. Amy works at Aviary Architects where part of her job involves coordinating projects. Her team involves people from different departments and she has only limited authority over them.		X				
2. Ben is a project manager at Boats n' Barges. He has complete control over the project budget and has the reputation for firing team members who call their products "ships." His team members do not also have functional managers to report to, and Ben reports directly to the CEO.					X	
3. Christine is a project manager at Comical Calendars. She has moderate authority over her team and she makes joint decisions about her team members with their functional managers. She is completely responsible for the project budget and has full-time administrative staff for the project.				X		
4. Diane works at Dazzling Diamonds. Although the company has a rigid hierarchy and established procedures, when a serious rhinestone mishap occurred, Diane was given the project to correct the situation. The situation was serious enough that she was given a high degree of authority over some of the best employees to form a team that was largely exempt from the standard reporting structure.						X
5. Ernie is a project manager at Sesame Seeds. Although he works on projects full-time, his team members and administrative staff only work on projects part-time.			X			
6. Flora works at Fancy Fabrics as a project manager. She and the functional managers jointly control the project budget.			X			
7. George is a project manager at the corporate headquarters of Greasy Grub, a new fast-food chain. The CEO was formerly in the military and insists on a strict chain of command throughout the company. George occasionally coordinates a project that runs into difficulties because he has no authority over the team or resources.	X					
8. Harriet is a consultant at Hockey Help, a small sports consulting group. The company is set up so that each consultant mainly runs their own projects and has complete authority over their own team. Although the team members are assigned to only one consultant, there are a few administrative staff members in the company that provide services such as billing to all the consultants.					X	
9. Iris coordinates projects at Irritating In-laws, an old, well-established, large psychological counseling business. Her team only works on her projects a few hours a week and she has no authority over them. She must submit paperwork to her team's functional managers before assigning them tasks.	X					
10. Jake is a project manager at Just Jerky, a company specializing in unique meat products. His team members have functional managers although he does have a good deal of authority over the team. Jake reports to a Manager of Project Managers.				X		

Exercise 7. Stakeholders

Read the following paragraph and then identify the common stakeholders.

Jamie is an executive at Sugar-Laden Cereals. She has an idea for a new brand of cereal that is in the shape of little stalks of sugar cane. Jamie approves a project charter which names Kathy as responsible for this project. Kathy wants James and George to be on her team and to help with the more important decisions. George suggests that they sign a contract with Great Ingredients to obtain the sugar cane they need for this new cereal that they are unable to buy from their current supplier. James tells Kathy that Luis in the production department would be good to have on the team as he could be assigned to developing the shape of the cereal. Kathy negotiates with Luis' boss, Chester, to have him assigned part-time to this project. While working on her WBS, Kathy realizes she does not have the most recent template approved by Sugar-Laden Cereals. Kathy goes to the office where Katy works managing the paperwork for all projects across the organization, and Katy provides her with the most recent template. After six months, the project is a success, and shoppers are buying the new cereal in grocery stores across the globe.

Who works in the PMO? Katy
Who is the Project Manager? Kathy
Who is the project Sponsor? Jamie
Who is a Functional Manager? Chester
Who is on the Project Management Team? James and George
Who is a Project Team Member (but not on the Project Management Team)? Luis
Who are the Customers? Shoppers at grocery stores
Who is a Vendor? Great Ingredients

Exercise 9. Benefit-to-Cost and Payback Period

Practice calculating the Benefit-to-Cost and Payback Period for the following opportunities.

1. Fred believes his idea of starting a Jackalope farm will bring in $500,000. He calculates his expenses at $250,000.
          What is the benefit-to-cost ratio? **$500,000/$200,000 = 2.0**
          Based on this, should he take this opportunity? **Yes – ratio over 1.0**

2. Lily finds that a full-page advertisement in a national journal will cost her $4,000. She estimates that it will bring her $3,500 in business.
          What is the benefit-to-cost ratio? **$3,500/$4,000 = 0.875**
          Based on this, should she take this opportunity? **No – ratio under 1.0**

3. Wilma knows the gas station that has the cheapest gas around will take her 10 miles out of her way which will cost her $2 in gas. The gas there is 25 cents per gallon cheaper, and she needs ten gallons. Because she is bored, she decides her time is worth nothing and should not be a factor.
          What is the benefit-to-cost ratio? **($.25 * 10)/$2.00 = 1.25**
          Based on this, should she drive to the cheapest gas station? **Yes – ratio over 1.0**

4. Rebecca thinks that her backyard garden will produce $500 in vegetables each year. Her expenses in the first year will be $980 as she needs to buy tools. Each year after that, she expects to pay only $20 in seeds.
          What is the Payback Period? **2 years (at $1000)**

5. Jack's proposed project will earn nothing for three years, and after that he thinks it will earn $20,000 per fiscal quarter. It will cost $60,000 every year.
          What is the Payback Period? **12 years (at $720,000)**

6. Jill's idea for manufacturing a needed part in-house is calculated to cost $5000 per month. The first year will not produce savings, but after that the savings should be $90,000 per year.
          What is the Payback Period? **3 years (at $180,000)**

Exercise 10 NPV - Solution

Year	Inflow		Outflow		Discount Rate			Present Value
0 (	$0	-	$200,000)	/	$1.10^0 =$	1.00	=	-$200,000
1 (	$150,000	-	$35,000)	/	$1.10^1 =$	1.10	=	$104,545
2 (	$150,000	-	$35,000)	/	$1.10^2 =$	1.21	=	$95,041
3 (	$150,000	-	$35,000)	/	$1.10^3 =$	1.33	=	$86,401

NPV	$85,988

NPV is positive, so the project should be accepted.

Exercise 11 Project Selection Quick Exercise - Solution

	Project A	Project B	Which project would you pick?
1. Net Present Value (what the value of project in today's monetary unit?)	$95,000	$75,000	A
2. Internal Rate of Return (what is the percentage return of the project?)	17%	14.5%	A
3. Payback Period (how long will it take to pay off the cost of the project?)	21 months	18 months	B
4. Benefit Cost Ratio (what is the ratio of NPV benefits to cost?)	2.2	1.8	A

Exercise 12 More on Financial Selection Techniques - Solution

	Project A	Project B
1. The Polar Bear Club is trying to prevent polar bears from injuring themselves by slipping on ice. Project A involves posting signs warning of icy spots and has a benefit-to-cost ratio of 5.1. Project B involves relocating the bears to Florida and has a benefit-to-cost ratio of 1.2.	X	
2. The Chameleon Car Company is experimenting with cars that can change colors. Project A involves developing a special auto body metal and has a payback period of 47 months. Project B involves developing special car paint and has a payback period of 13 months.		X
3. Polly Tishun is running for governor and is contemplating the best strategy to raise campaign funds. Project A focuses upon television ads and has an IRR of 61%. Project B focuses on expensive dinners and has an IRR of 92%.		X
4. Kathy is deciding what type of drink she should sell to supplement the meager allowance she receives from her parents. Project A is to sell lemonade and has a NPV of $25. Project B is to sell chocolate milk and has a NPV of $11.	X	
5. A group of sports enthusiasts are trying to decide between two investments. Project A is to buy a well-known football team which has an IRR of 12% and a benefit-to-cost ratio of 1.5. Project B is to buy a lesser-known baseball team which has an IRR of 10% and a benefit-to-cost ratio of 2.5.	X	
6. Paper Dolls, Inc. is having trouble deciding on a potential new direction. Project A uses plain paper and prints colors with ink on the dolls which would be an investment of $50 K and would return $10 K for the first three months and $5 K every month after that. Project B uses colored paper which would be an investment of $80 K and would return $20 K per month.	7m	X 4m
7. Mutant Veggies, Inc. has to determine which product will be more profitable. Project A is to develop a cross between eggplant and tomatoes "Eggmatoes" and has a payback period of 2 years and a NPV of $2.3 M. Project B is to develop a cross between carrots and broccoli "Carroccolli" and has a payback period of 22 months and a NPV of $2.1 M.	X	
8. Melvin and Maggie are mulling over whether to farm their land with modern machinery or a mule team. Project A, using modern machinery, has a payback period of 25 years and a benefit-to-cost ratio of 1.4. Project B, using a mule team, has a payback period of 2 months and a benefit-to-cost ratio of 53.7.		X
9. Carla is wondering if getting more education would be a good investment. Project A, earning her MBA, has a benefit-to-cost ratio of 3, a NPV of $400 K, and an IRR of 300%. Project B, not getting any more education but working more hours, has a benefit-to-cost ratio of 2.5, a NPV of $200 K, and an IRR of 320%.		X
10. Tropical Treats, a candy store near the equator, is selecting among projects to help cut their operating costs—specifically the outrageous expense of air conditioning. Project A, have the store open during the night when it's cooler instead of the day, has a benefit-to-cost ratio of .83 and a NPV of $ -25 K. Project B, switch the required employee uniform of a sweatshirt with the company's logo to a t-shirt with the company's logo, has a benefit-to-cost ratio of 1.3 and a NPV of $500.		X

Exercise 17. Organizational Process Assets versus Enterprise Environmental Factors

For each, decide whether it is an Organizational Process Asset or an Enterprise Environmental Factor.

	Organizational Process Asset	Enterprise Environmental Factor
Probability and impact matrix	x	
Marketplace conditions		x
Stakeholder risk tolerances		x
Commercial database		x
Lessons learned documentation from old project	x	
Project Management Information Systems		x
Proposal evaluation criteria	x	
Organization's building		x
Strict and formal culture		x
Company's defect management database	x	
WBS template	x	
Employee performance reviews		x
Change control procedures	x	
Time reporting procedures	x	

What do you see as the key differences between Organizational Process Assets and Enterprise Environmental Factors?

Exercise 22. Major Documents.

Although there are commonalities among the major project documents, while identifying which component belongs to which document, notice the different purposes of the documents and the progressive elaboration that occurs with additional documentation.

	Project Charter	Project Management Plan	Scope Statement
Project purpose or justification	X		
Name and responsibility of person authorizing project charter	X		
Assigned project manager with responsibility and authority level	X		
High-level project description	X		
High-level product characteristics	X		
Product scope description			X
Project deliverables			X
High-level requirements	X		
Project boundaries			X
Project management processes chosen by project management team		X	
Selected project life cycle		X	
Summary budget	X		
Cost baseline		X	
Cost management plan and quality management plan		X	
Summary milestone schedule	X		
Schedule baseline		X	
Quality baseline		X	
Description of how work will be executed		X	
Description of how configuration management will be performed		X	
Description of how changes will be monitored and controlled		X	
Need and techniques for stakeholder communication		X	
How integrity of performance measurement baselines maintained		X	
Project assumptions			x
Project constraints			x
Information on key management reviews		X	
Product acceptance criteria			X
Project approval requirements	X		

Exercise 23 Collect Requirements – Group Decision Making Techniques

Group Decision Making Techniques are a tool and technique of the Collect Requirements process. However, they can be applied anytime a group decision needs to be made. The larger the group, the less likely it is that all will agree on something. For this reason, rules may be put into place to determine the group's course of action. For example, if the group will agree to do whatever most of the people want to do, then it is a majority decision. Read the following description of a small town trying to make a decision, and describe what each of the group decision making techniques would look like. The Majority technique is given as an example.

Littleton is a town of exactly 1000 people. They do have a mayor that is trying to help the town reach a decision on whether to allow a weapons research facility that wants to develop radioactive snakes north of their town. Four hundred people live in what is considered "North Littleton," 300 live in "South Littleton," and 300 live in "The Old Mill Area."

1. Unanimity
   If all 1000 townspeople agree, that will be the course of action.

2. Majority
   If 501 or more townspeople agree, that will be the course of action for the town.

3. Consensus
   If 501 or more townspeople agree and the rest agree to accept the decision, that will be the course of action.

4. Plurality
   The largest block of people make the decision, for example, the people in "North Littleton" decide for the whole town.

5. Dictatorship
   If the mayor makes the decision, that will be the course of action for the town.

Exercise 24 Collect Requirements – Questionnaire

Questionnaires are a tool and technique of the Collect Requirements process. Questionnaires are often made, but rarely made well. Critically examine the following questionnaire and mark as many errors as you can find. Check your answers to see how you did.

Opossum Fancier Questionnaire

1. Exactly how much is your income? [sensitive questions should not be at beginning; start with interesting questions]

2. Are you in favor of the annual agenda proposed by the president of the Opossum Fanciers Association? [Assumes knowledge of organization. Should have a filter question beforehand]

3. Should one never not stop to help an injured opossum on the road? [double negative]

4. How many pet opossums do you own? [should be AFTER "do you own pet opossums]
   a. Do you own pet opossums?

5. Have you ever taken a substantial amount of time to seriously consider either in the distant or recent past whether opossums may have several distinct and valuable advantages over other common domestic pets such as dogs, cats, and hamsters? [too long]

6. What makes the best pet? A. Reptiles B. Marsupials C. Insects D. Mammals [marsupials are mammals, so not mutually exclusive categories]

7. How propitious are you towards opossums? [uncommon word]

8. Have you ever done something as disgusting and repulsive as eat an opossum? [leading]

9. Do you support the promotion of opossums as pets and specialized training for veterinarians in their treatment? [double-barreled (two questions in one)]

Exercise 34. Sequence Activities

A. Determine which activity relationship is being described (Finish to Start; Finish to Finish; Start to Start; or Start to Finish).

➢ Becky's mother tells her to start getting up and getting ready for the day so she can finish making all the beds. ***Start to Finish***

➢ Becky's mother is waiting for her to pick out a book so she can read it to her. ***Finish to Start***

➢ Becky's father is waiting for her mother to finish baking her cake so he can finish cleaning up the kitchen. ***Finish to Finish***

➢ Becky and her mother are in the kitchen doing the dishes. Becky is drying the dishes after her mother washes each one. ***Finish to Finish & Start to Start***

B. Think up an example from everyday life of each of the four activity relationships.

➢ **Finish to Start**

➢ **Finish to Finish**

➢ **Start to Start**

➢ **Start to Finish**

Exercise 35 Sequence Activities - Dependencies

The relationship between the sequence of two activities may be described as Mandatory (must be done in that order), Discretionary (order is preferred but not required), and External (relationship with non-project activities).

A. Identify which of these three dependencies is being described.

	Mandatory	Discretionary	External
1. The project team is waiting for the city to issue them a building permit so they can start digging the foundation of their new office building.			X
2. After the team has dug a hole for the foundation, they will pour the cement for the foundation.	x		
3. The team plans on choosing the siding color after choosing the interior paint color.		x	
4. The roofing team is waiting for the hardware store to deliver the shingles so they can start nailing shingles to the roof.			x
5. The painting crew plans on applying a coat of primer before applying the Robin's Egg Blue interior paint.	x		

B. Alternate Terms

What are other terms for Discretionary Dependencies? Other terms for Mandatory Dependencies?

Discretionary: Preferred Logic, Preferential Logic, and Soft Logic

Mandatory: Hard Logic

Exercise 38. PERT and 3-Point Estimate

Murphy has gathered estimates on how many days individual activities will take for his project on reintroducing Jackalopes to South Dakota. PERT is calculated (P+(4xML)+O)/6. Three-point estimates are calculated (P+ML+O)/3. Calculate both PERT and 3-Point Estimate for each activity.

Project Activity	Pessimistic	Most Likely	Optimistic	PERT	3-Point
1. Acquire Breeding Stock	300	100	20	120	140
2. Raise 100 young Jackalopes	200	150	50	142	133
3. Obtain landowners' permission for their release	90	60	3	56	51
4. Release Jackalopes	50	14	5	18	23
5. Monitor Jackalopes in wild	300	100	90	132	163

Exercise 39. Critical Path - Solution

PROJECT: Assemble a $19.50 bookshelf purchased at Shopko for your daughter (Rachael) to hang Barbie accessories and books. Your daughter is the executive sponsor.

SOLUTION: Shortest possible duration is 54 MINUTES. (PATH B to O path)
Alternate path (A, C, L) is 18 MINUTES.
Critical path: B, D, E, F, G, H, I, J, K, M, N and O.

Create a network diagram using the suggested Table below. Determine the activities on the critical path - the series of activities, which determines the earliest completion of the project. Identify the critical path in your diagram by listing the path (i.e. A-B-D-F-G) and mark the path within the network in red or some other fashion.

Activity ID	Activity	Duration (minutes)	Predecessor
A	Read instructions	3	--
B	Group "like" parts together	6	--
C	Verify drawer assembly	3	A
D	Assemble right shelve to bottom shelf	2	B
E	Screw in four screws	3	C,D
F	Place left shelf on bottom shelf	2	E
G	Screw in four more screws	4	F
H	Place in top shelf (with holes pointed in the proper direction)	2	G
I	Find new screw driver in garage	6	H
J	Screw in four more screws	8	I
K	Put middle shelf in.	8	J

L	Place hanging brackets on back	4	C
M	*Screw in hanging brackets*	*6*	*L*
N	*Verify fit*	*5*	*K,M*
O	*Take upstairs to Rachael's room*	*2*	*N*

Exercise 40. Branding Iron Activity Sequencing and Critical Path – Solution

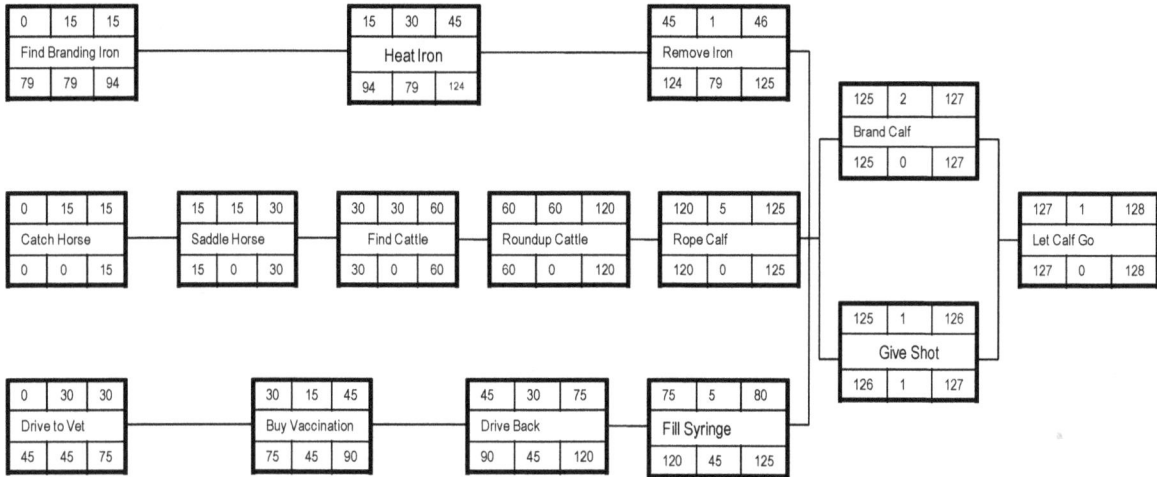

0	15	15
Find Branding Iron		
79	79	94

15	30	45
Heat Iron		
94	79	124

45	1	46
Remove Iron		
124	79	125

125	2	127
Brand Calf		
125	0	127

127	1	128
Let Calf Go		
127	0	128

0	15	15
Catch Horse		
0	0	15

15	15	30
Saddle Horse		
15	0	30

30	30	60
Find Cattle		
30	0	60

60	60	120
Roundup Cattle		
60	0	120

120	5	125
Rope Calf		
120	0	125

125	1	126
Give Shot		
126	1	127

0	30	30
Drive to Vet		
45	45	75

30	15	45
Buy Vaccination		
75	45	90

45	30	75
Drive Back		
90	45	120

75	5	80
Fill Syringe		
120	45	125

Exercise 42. Schedule Bar Chart

A bar chart is a clear way to communicate a project schedule. For this exercise, draw the four horizontal bars representing the activities in the Project Time Frame Area.

Activity	Activity Description	Start Date	Calendar Time	Project Time Frame				
				Year 1	Year 2	Year 3	Year 4	Year 5
1.1	Develop Blueprints	Middle of Year 1	Six months	�largebar				
1.2	Choose Contractors	After Activity 1.1	Nine months		�largebar			
1.3	Building Construction	After Activity 1.2	Two years			�largebar		
1.4	Hiring Employees	Start of Year 4	Fourteen months				�largebar	

Exercise 43. Estimate Costs

1. Analogous Estimating, Parametric Estimating, and Bottom-Up Estimating are three techniques used to estimate costs. Decide which is being used in each scenario.

	Analogous Estimating	Parametric Estimating	Bottom-Up Estimating
Major Motors is building a new car. They think it will cost $20 Million to develop, as that is what the last car cost to develop.	x		
Major Motors has begun a project to specially paint 10 special edition cars with a colorful landscape design. A painting company will supply the workers for $10,000. The black paint will cost $1000, the blue paint will cost $500, the green paint will cost $200, and the white paint will cost $100. The project is estimated to cost $11,800.			X
Major Motors is building a road at its testing facility. The contractor will bill them $50,000 per mile of road. They want a 4-mile round track, so they estimate that this project will cost them $200,000.		X	
Rat-Free Apartments Inc. is building a new apartment building. They are told that the flooring they chose will be $1 per square foot. The apartment building floors will be 20,000 square feet, so they estimate that the flooring will cost $20,000.		X	
Rat-Free Apartments, Inc. is remodeling a particular unit. The flooring will cost $500, the painting will cost $200, and the stove will cost $300. They estimate this project will cost $1000.			X

2. Using one of your current or past projects as an example, how could have you used each of the following estimation techniques?

    Analogous Estimating

    Parametric Estimating

    Bottom-Up Estimating

Exercise 53. Develop Human Resource Plan – Maslow's Hierarchy

Organizational Theory is a tool and technique of the Develop Human Resource Plan process. There are numerous organizational theories which attempt to explain human behavior. A well-known organizational theory is Maslow's Hierarchy of Needs. Maslow proposed that humans are always in a state of need. When a lower-level need is satisfied, humans try to satisfy the need on the next level. This is useful to understand because those with whom we are working have different motivations. Here are five different Project Managers' descriptions of why they want a particular project management job. Write their names next to the level on the pyramid below indicating their level on Maslow's Hierarchy of Needs.

Hope Parsons: *"The requirements of this job mesh perfectly with my natural skills and personality. I truly enjoy managing projects in this industry, and I feel that the completed projects are making the world a better place."*

Katherine Goodwill: *"I really need this job. I'm a single mom who has been unemployed for 8 months now. I haven't been able to pay the rent or electric bill, and I'm barely able to get enough groceries to put meals on the table."*

Jack Thompson: *"I want to work with the project managers and executives at this company. They're the kind of people I want as mentors and friends. I want to be known by others as a project manager at this company."*

Oliver Horents: *"I've been a team member on similar projects, but what I really want to be is the actual project manager. I want people to look at me and know I'm their leader who will get this thing accomplished."*

Michael Woodson: *"I'm interested in this job largely because I know once I'm hired, I'll be able to stay as long as I want. It's a solid industry and the company has never had lay-offs. Also, they have a great retirement plan!"*

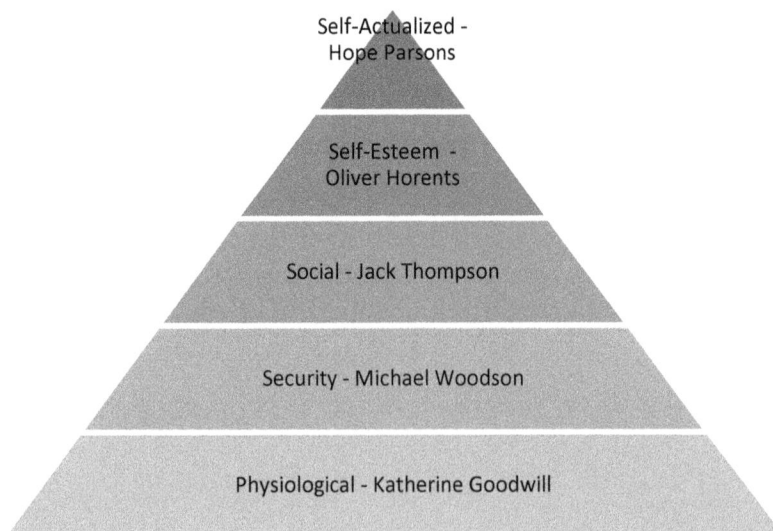

Self-Actualized - Hope Parsons

Self-Esteem - Oliver Horents

Social - Jack Thompson

Security - Michael Woodson

Physiological - Katherine Goodwill

Exercise 55. Communication Formula

Using the Communication Formula, calculate the paths of communication. Try to do it with the formula memorized.

1. There are 5 people on the team. How many communication paths are there?

10

2. There were 10 people on the team, but 3 left. How many communication paths are there now?

21

3. There were 20 people on the team, but now 10 more have been added. How many more communication paths are there now?

435 – 190 = 245

4. There were 8 people on the team, but then 13 communication paths were removed. How many people are on the team now?

6

5. There are 3 people on team A, 5 people on team B, and 4 people on team C. Everyone on team A and B can communicate with each other and everyone on team B and C can communicate with each other. However, team A and team C are not allowed to communicate with other. How many communication paths are there?

((3+5)x(3+5-1))/2 + ((5+4)x(5+4-1))/2 = 28 + 36 = 64

PMP Scrimmage® Curriculum, Edition 3.01   *Page 257*
www.tapuniversity.com
TECHNOLOGY
AS PROMISED

Exercise 56. Plan Communication – Communication Methods

Identify which of the three communication methods each example represents.

	Interactive	Push	Pull
1. Intranet Site			x
2. Meetings	x		
3. Letter		x	
4. Memo		x	
5. Phone Calls	x		
6. Knowledge Repository			x
7. Report		x	
8. Fax		x	
9. Video Conferencing	x		
10. Hallway Conversation	x		

Exercise 60. Plan Risk Responses – Strategies

Strategies for Negative Risks or Threats and Strategies for Positive Risks or Opportunities are two tools and techniques of the Plan Risk Responses process. The strategies for Negative Risks are: Avoid, Transfer, Mitigate, and Acceptance. The strategies for Positive Risks are: Exploit, Share, Enhance, and Accept.

Which strategy is being used in each of the situations below?

1. Angie wants to get a house cat, but she's worried about the risk of having cat hair all over her furniture. So, she decides that she will get a hairless cat. **Avoid**

2. Angie is worried about the risk of vet bills that could occur if her hairless cat becomes injured, so she buys pet health insurance. **Transfer**

3. Angie's husband says the risk of his friends teasing him is too great if they get a hairless cat. They decide they will get the cat, but try not to tell anyone about it, so it'll be less likely that he gets teased. **Mitigate**

4. When Angie's husband discovers how much he can sell hairless kittens for, he teams up with another hairless cat owner and they develop a scheme to start breeding the two cats, and then raising and selling the hairless kittens. **Share**

Exercise 63. Plan Procurements – Make or Buy Analysis

Make or Buy Analysis is a tool and technique of the Plan Procurements process. Make or Buy Analysis is the process of analyzing all the needed factors to determine whether a good or service is better done in-house, or if it should be bought from another organization or individual.

Edward is beginning to manage a project that includes the development of security footstep identification software. He belongs to an organization of about 200 employees. His organization employs 18 programmers, and although the organization is somewhat under-staffed, because the project is important Edward is allowed to have whichever programmers he wants. Edward is now trying to decide whether he should have the footstep software developed internally, or whether he should hire another organization to develop it. In performing this Make or Buy Analysis, there are many things to consider. Think of several things you would suggest that Edward consider and write them below.

There are many factors to consider, here are only some:
1. *Do the current programmers have the necessary expertise?*
2. *How much would it cost to hire a new programmer with this expertise?*
3. *How much would it cost to train a current programmer?*
4. *How much would it cost to hire another company?*
5. *How much will it cost to update the software internally?*
6. *How long would it take to find a company to make the software?*
7. *How long would it take to negotiate a contract with another company?*
8. *How long would it take to hire another programmer?*
9. *How long would it take to train a current programmer?*
10. *Will the other company give up all rights to the software?*
11. *Are there any materials/technology that would need to be purchased if done in-house?*
12. *Will there be a need for this type of expertise in the future?*
13. *How will taking current programmers away from their current projects affect the company?*
14. *Which constraint is the biggest concern—resources, time, or budget?*

Exercise 65. Identify Contract Types – Solution

Mark the box that best describes the type of agreement—Time and Materials (T&M), Cost Plus Fixed Fee (CPFF), Cost Plus Percentage of Cost (CPF) (CPPC), Cost Plus Incentive (CPIF) or Fixed Price.

	T&M	CPFF	CPF	CPIF	Fixed
1. Andrea said that she would clean Andy's hamster cage for a year, but Andy has to reimburse her for the shavings plus pay her $50.		X			
2. Andrea's mother is paying her 2 cents a minute to pick "bouquets" of dandelions from the yard.	X				
3. Antonio is reimbursing his daughter for a weekly planner and set of pens in return for her reminding him 3 days in advance of his wife's birthday and their anniversary. Additionally, if his daughter goes above and beyond the contract and finds out what his wife actually wants, Antonio pays his daughter ten dollars. This contract has a strict confidentiality clause.				X	
4. Antonio pays his niece twice the cost of her gas in return for driving his daughter to her weekly electric guitar lessons.			X		
5. Andy offered his sister five dollars to take the blame for teaching the family dog to retrieve the neighbors' newspapers.					X
6. Antonio told his daughter he would pay her 5 cents each time she played "Jingle Bells" repeatedly on her electric guitar while his in-laws stopped by.	X				
7. Andy's mother needed a cake mix, frosting, butter, pork rinds, and eggs to make her locally-famous Piggy Cake, so she sent Andy to the grocery store. She agreed to pay him 3 times whatever the total cost of the groceries was.			X		
8. Antonio paid his daughter five dollars to teach him how to attach photos to his emails.					X
9. Tired of hearing his co-workers brag about the fish they catch, Antonio tells his children to go buy themselves fishing poles, cell phones, and a camera and he'll pay them back. If they catch a fish larger than 20 pounds, he'll give them $100 if they call him so he can drive down to the river and get his picture taken with the fish.				X	
10. Antonio's wife, Ashley, is tired of hearing him complain about the gas mileage he gets with his van. She pays their son for the cost of gas plus $20 for buying cans of gasoline and sneaking gas into the van daily for three months while it's in the garage at night.		X			

Exercise 66. Plan Procurements - Contract Types

The different types of contracts each have advantages and disadvantages that make some more suitable for certain situations. Contract Types are a tool and technique of the Plan Procurements process. For each situation, circle the type of contract (Fixed Price, Cost Reimbursable, or Time & Materials) you would suggest.

1. Mary is a project manager working on procuring some needed services. Her budget is very tight, and she needs to know what the exact cost will be.

Fixed Price   Cost Reimbursable   Time & Materials

2. Ryan needs a subject matter expert for the skyscraper project he is working on. One of his team members found a professor at a local university who teaches a course on skyscraper construction, and he does consulting at the rate of $150/hour. Ryan isn't sure how many hours of consultation he'll need during the duration of the project.

Fixed Price   Cost Reimbursable   **Time & Materials**

3. Crystal is leading a software development project. They've run into a difficult part in the programming that no one on her team has the expertise to do. One of the programmers mentions that his friend has the needed expertise. Crystal talks to the expert programmer who states that he is unsure how long the work would take, but he's willing to be paid a set price per line of code.

Fixed Price   Cost Reimbursable   **Time & Materials**

4. Paul has a very precise description of the machine he wants developed for his project. The scope statement is detailed, and even the exact brand of materials that he wants used for the project are specified. In the past, he has ordered similar machines from Custom Machines for You, so he knows what this one should cost.

Fixed Price   Cost Reimbursable   Time & Materials

5. Janet has found a contractor that she believes will do an excellent job. However, neither she nor they have a very good idea of the scope of the project. As they work on the project, there will be plenty of progressive elaboration.

Fixed Price   **Cost Reimbursable**   Time & Materials

Exercise 68. Direct and Manage Project Execution – Change Requests

One of the inputs to the Direct and Manage Project Execution process is Approved Change Requests. In the course of implementing these change requests, new Change Requests may arise. These Change Requests are categorized into four types—Corrective Actions, Preventive Actions, Defects, and Updates. Identify the type of Change Request listed below.

	Corrective Actions	Preventive Actions	Defects	Updates
1. The Quack Factory has not been meeting its daily quota for making a batch of special rubber ducks. A request has been submitted to speed up one of the major steps of the process by reducing time allowed for the paint to dry.	X			
2. Most of the ducks coming off of the line had the orange paint from their bills smeared all over their wings. A request has been submitted to increase the drying time between colors to fix this problem.			X	
3. The paint drying time for the ducks is now so long, that they are overheating and some of their heads are melting off. Because of this, a request has been submitted to lower the temperature of the dryer.			X	
4. Now that they are almost ready to ship some ducks, the shipping process activities are better understood, so have been added to the WBS.				X
5. Individuals have been assigned as responsible for specific shipping process activities, so the WBS Dictionary can be revised to include these names.				X
6. Rumors have been flying that the cost of raw rubber will be doubling within the next three months. So a request has been submitted to buy as much rubber as possible now.		X		
7. The cost of this special batch of ducks is starting to exceed budget. To save on materials cost, a request has been submitted to decrease their size to about the size of a dime.	X			

Exercise 76. Manage Project Team – Resolving Conflict

Conflict can be resolved by forcing, smoothing, compromise, confrontation and withdrawal. Which method is being described in the following scenarios?

	Forcing	Smoothing	Compromise	Confrontation	Withdrawal
1. Samantha and Hal are arguing why the project has fallen behind schedule. They decide they better gather data on the possible reasons since neither is certain they really know what the problem is.				x	
2. Margie is fighting with her mother about her poor grades. Margie's father tells them that grades aren't important and they calm down a little.		x			
3. We'll switch to neon-colored paper clips for all our reports. Why? Because I'm the boss and I say so.	x				
4. Paul and Mary disagree on whether or not to buy a new car. Every time Mary wants to discuss it, Paul runs out of the room.					x
5. Paul wants to buy a black truck and Mary thinks they should get a white car. They decide to get a white truck.			x		
6. Which only leads to a temporary solution?		x			
7. Which never results in resolution?					x
8. Which is considered the best method to resolve conflict?				x	

Exercise 84. Earned Value Scrimmage - Solution

Earned value assignment - Project 4th of July Fireworks
Project Facts:
Total Project Budget $28,000
Planned Duration - 10 days
Planned Resource usage -- four people, four hours per day OR 160 hours total
Resource usage estimate confidence – 98 percent -(you have several years experience in doing this)
Material cost -- $12,000
Resource cost -- $16,000 or **$100.00** per hour (*widgets*)
Project start date June 25.
Project completion date July 4, 1100pm

Project Status Date -- July 3, 5:00pm
Actual Expenditures (AC) as of July 3 -- $26,500
Planned Budget (PV) as of July 3 -- $26,000
Budget variance -$(500.00)
Number of hours planned for project completion on July 3 at 5:00pm -- 140.
Actual hours of project completed **150.** -- no delays. Everything's on track.
Material cost has been spent and is sunk **$12,000**

1. Compute the Earned Value Amount $27,000

2. Complete the following table.

Planned	Earned	Cost	Variances		Performance Index	
Budget $	**EARNED VALUE $**	**Actual Cost $**	**Cost Variance $**	**Schedule $**	**CPI**	**SPI**
PV	**EV**	**AC**	**(EV-AC)**	**(EV-PV)**	**EV/AC**	**EV/PV**
26,000	27,000	$26,500	500	1,000	1.02	1.04

3. What's the EAC (estimate at completion)? Use the formula for everything's on track, no need for corrective action.
   short cut formula = -- (28,000/1.02) =*27450*
   LONG Formula 26,500+ ((28,000-27,000)/1.02)) = 26,500 + 980.40 = *27,480*

4. What's the ETC (estimate to completion)? (28,000 - 27,000)/1.02 = *$980.40*

5. Your Chief Financial Officer has been breathing down your neck because the fireworks are $500.00 over budget. You're feeling pretty good about that based on earned value. Why and what would you share with your CFO so he doesn't explode. **Chill**

Exercise 85. Earned Value Basics

The first step in mastering Earned Value is memorizing what the acronyms stand for. Next to the acronym, write out what it stands for.

BAC	*Budget at Completion*
AC	*Actual Cost*
PV	*Planned Value*
EV	*Earned Value*
CV	*Cost Variance*
CPI	*Cost Performance Index*
SV	*Schedule Variance*
SPI	*Schedule Performance Index*
EAC	*Estimate At Completion*
ETC	*Estimate To Completion*
VAC	*Variance At Completion*

Next, write the acronym next to its description.

EV	Amount budgeted for the work *performed* so far. It can be calculated as BAC * (work completed / total work).
SV	How close to schedule the project is in terms of cost. A negative number means the project is behind schedule and a positive number means the project is ahead of schedule. It is calculated EV – PV.
BAC	Amount of money budgeted for the entire project.
VAC	How much over or under budget the whole project will be. It is calculated BAC – EAC.
AC	Amount of money actually spent.
ETC (typical)	What will be spent to finish remaining project or activity. It is calculated ETC = (BAC – EV) / CPI. (This is algebraically equivalent to ETC = EAC - AC).
PV	Amount budgeted for work *scheduled* so far. It can be calculated as BAC * (time passed / total time scheduled).
EAC (flawed)	What will be spent on the whole project or activity. It is calculated AC + ETC.
CV	How the actual spending differs from the amount budgeted. A negative number means you are over budget and a positive number means you are under budget. It is calculated EV - AC.
SPI	The percentage of the planned rate you are progressing. A number more than 1 means good performance and a number less than 1 means poor performance. It is calculated EV / PV.
CPI	How much value you are getting from every dollar spent. A number greater than 1 indicates good performance and a number less than 1 indicates poor performance. It is calculated EV / AC.

Exercise 86. Earned Value Practice – Solution

Budget at Completion (BAC) is the amount of money budgeted for the entire project.
Actual Cost (AC) is the amount of money actually spent.
Planned Value (PV) is the amount budgeted for work *scheduled* so far.
It can be calculated as PV = BAC * (time passed / total time scheduled).
Earned Value (EV) is the amount budgeted for the work *performed* so far.
It can be calculated as EV = BAC * (work completed / total work).

A. Joshua and Jolene are remodeling three rooms in their home and decided they can spend $15,000 and take three months on this project. They planned to spend the same amount of time and money on each of the three rooms. They have just finished remodeling the first room (the kitchen) which took two months and cost $7,000.

    1. What is the BAC?_____ $15,000
    2. What is the AC?_____ $7,000
    3. What is the PV?_____ $10,000
    4. What is the EV?_____ $5,000

B. Felicia is spending ten days in Hawaii on vacation and decided she can spend $200 a day in her quest to obtain 20 stunning souvenirs that will make all her friends jealous. However, after the first day she spent $500 on 10 souvenirs.

    1. What is the BAC?_____ $2,000
    2. What is the AC?_____ $500
    3. What is the PV?_____ $200
    4. What is the EV?_____ $1,000

C. Damian needs to drive 1000 miles in 20 hours in order to get to the annual Friends of the Manatees convention. He has $300 he can spend to get there. After 5 hours, he has driven 250 miles and spent $100 on gas and snacks.

    1. What is the BAC?_____ $300
    2. What is the AC?_____ $100
    3. What is the PV?_____ $75
    4. What is the EV?_____ $75

More Formulas

Cost Variance (CV) is how the actual spending differs from the amount budgeted. A negative number means you are over budget and a positive number means you are under budget. It is calculated CV = EV - AC.

Cost Performance Index (CPI) is how much value you are getting from every dollar spent. A number greater than 1 indicates good performance and a number less than 1 indicates poor performance. It is calculated CPI = EV / AC.

Schedule Variance (SV) is how close to schedule the project is in terms of cost. A negative number means the project is behind schedule and a positive number means the project is ahead of schedule. It is calculated SV = EV – PV.

Schedule Performance Index (SPI) is the percentage of the planned rate you are progressing. A number more than 1 means good performance and a number less than 1 means poor performance. It is calculated SPI = EV / PV.

A. Meagan has $500 and 5 days to make 1000 party mints. It's the end of the third day and she has used $400 and made 900 mints.

1. What is the BAC?_____	$500
2. What is the AC?_____	$400
3. What is the PV?_____	$300
4. What is the EV?_____	$450
6. What is the CV? _____	$50
7. What is the CPI? _____	1.125
8. What is the SV? _____	$150
9. What is the SPI? _____	1.5
10. Is she under, over, or exactly on-budget?_____	$50 under
11. Is she progressing slow, fast, or exactly on-schedule?_____	1.5 times faster

B. Five-year-old Molly has a neighbor whose yard is full of fireflies at night. The neighbor kid will let her run around and catch as many as she can for a dollar an hour. Molly wants to catch 50 fireflies in a jar and her father gives her two dollars to do so. After one hour, Molly has caught 40 fireflies and gives the neighbor kid the first dollar before starting on her second hour.

1. What is the BAC?_____	$2
2. What is the AC?_____	$1
3. What is the PV?_____	$1
4. What is the EV?_____	$1.60
6. What is the CV? _____	$.60
7. What is the CPI? _____	1.60
8. What is the SV? _____	$.60
9. What is the SPI? _____	1.60
10. Is she under, over, or exactly on-budget?_____	$ .60 under
11. Is she progressing slow, fast, or exactly on-schedule?_____	1.6 times faster

And Yet More Formulas!

Estimate At Completion when assumptions flawed (EAC) is what will be spent on the whole project or activity. It is calculated EAC = AC + ETC.

*Estimate At Completion with typical variation (EAC) is what will be spent on the whole project or activity. It is calculated EAC = AC + ((BAC – EV) / CPI). (This is algebraically equivalent to EAC = BAC / CPI).

Estimate At Completion with atypical variation (EAC) is what will be spent on the whole project or activity. It is calculated EAC = AC + BAC – EV.

*Estimate To Completion with typical variation (ETC) is what will be spent to finish remaining project or activity. It is calculated ETC = (BAC – EV) / CPI. (This is algebraically equivalent to ETC = EAC - AC).

*Estimate To Completion with atypical variation (ETC) is what will be spent to finish remaining project or activity. It is calculated ETC = BAC – EV.

Variance At Completion (VAC) is how much over or under budget the whole project will be. It is calculated VAC = BAC – EAC.

A. April and Andy are building an addition to their home. They have $30,000 to spend on the project and want it completed in 100 days. It is now the end of day 75 and they have spent $25,000. They believe the addition is exactly halfway completed.

1. What is the BAC?_____	$30,000
2. What is the AC?_____	$25,000
3. What is the PV?_____	$22,500
4. What is the EV?_____	$15,000
6. What is the CV? _____	$-10000
7. What is the CPI? _____	.60
8. What is the SV? _____	$-7500
9. What is the SPI? _____	.66
10. Are they under, over, or exactly on-budget?_____ $ 10,000 over	
11. Are they progressing slow, fast, or exactly on-schedule?_____ .66 slower	
12. What is EAC for typical variation?_____	$50,000
13. What is ETC for typical variation?_____	$25,000

Practice

A. PV = 10; AC = 8; EV = 12.
   1. What is CV?_____   4   Are you over, **under**, or on Budget?
   2. What is CPI? _____   1.5
   3. What is SV? _____   2   Are you behind, **ahead**, or on Schedule
   4. What is SPI? _____   1.2

B. PV = 500; AC = 600; EV = 550.
   1. What is CV?_____   -50   Are you **over**, under, or on Budget?
   2. What is CPI? _____   .92
   3. What is SV? _____   50   Are you behind, **ahead**, or on Schedule?
   4. What is SPI? _____   1.1

C. PV = 3000; AC = 2000; EV = 8000.
   1. What is CV?_____   6000   Are you over, **under**, or on Budget?
   2. What is CPI? _____   4
   3. What is SV? _____   5000   Are you behind, **ahead**, or on Schedule?
   4. What is SPI? _____   2.67

D. PV = 20,000; AC = 50,000; EV = 40,000.
   1. What is CV?_____-10000   Are you **over**, under, or on Budget?
   2. What is CPI? _____   .80
   3. What is SV? _____20000   Are you behind, **ahead**, or on Schedule
   4. What is SPI? _____   2

E. PV = 300; AC = 300; EV = 250.
   1. What is CV?_____   -50   Are you **over**, under, or on Budget?
   2. What is CPI? _____   .83
   3. What is SV? _____   -50   Are you **behind**, ahead, or on Schedule?
   4. What is SPI? _____   .83

F. PV = 7; AC = 10; EV = 7.
   1. What is CV?_____   -3   Are you **over**, under, or on Budget?
   2. What is CPI? _____   .70
   3. What is SV? _____   0   Are you behind, ahead, or **on Schedule**
   4. What is SPI? _____   1

G. PV = 600; AC = 580; EV = 650.
   1. What is CV?_____   70   Are you over, **under**, or on Budget?
   2. What is CPI? _____   1.12
   3. What is SV? _____   50   Are you behind, **ahead**, or on Schedule?
   4. What is SPI? _____   1.08

Exercise 89. Control Chart - Solution

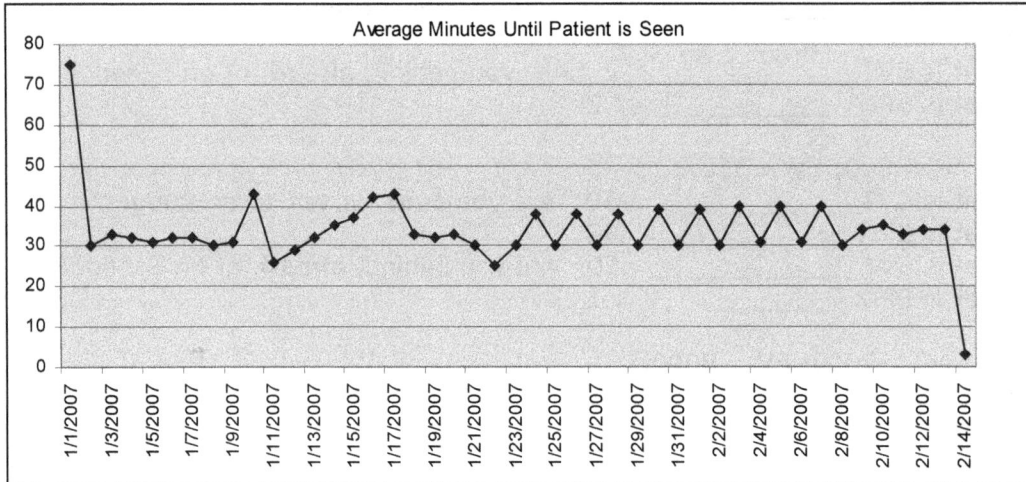

Average Minutes Until Patient is Seen

	Precise	Graph
mean	33.84	34
std	8.89	9
1std above	42.73	43
2 std	51.62	52
3 std	60.50	61
1 std below	24.96	25
2 std below	16.07	16
3 std below	7.19	7

Where is the "Shift"? (The first set of 8 starting Jan 2—they are all under mean)
Where is the "Trend"? (The upwards trend of 8 starting January 11)
Where is the "Pattern"? (Up/down cycle starting January 23)
Where is the process out of control? (The first and last days are more than 3 std away from mean. Note dates).

Exercise 90. Pareto Diagram - Solution

Complaint Type	Missing a Skill	Way it is Dressed	Delivered Late	Biting	Other
Number of Complaints	70	50	8	5	12
Total Complaints	70	120	128	133	145

Rent-A-Monkey Complaints

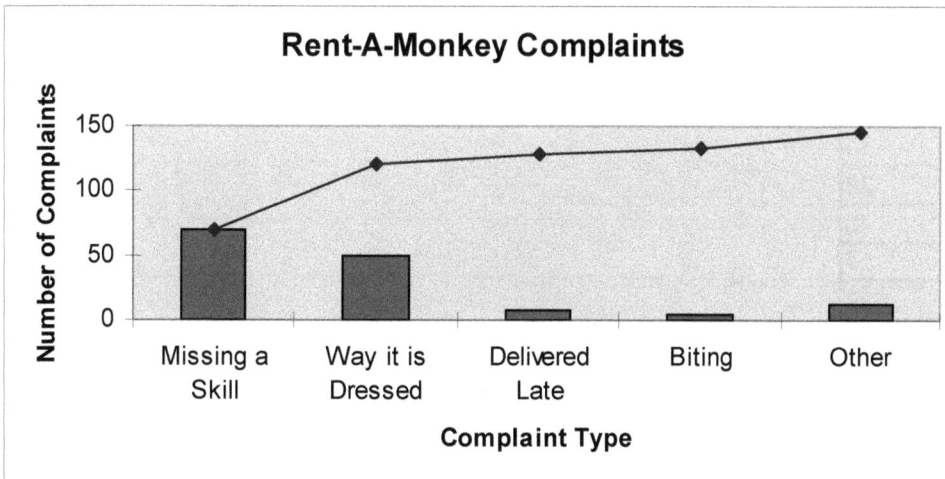

Exercise 91. Scatter Plot

Plot the number of defects against the years of the team member's experience. For example, for the first team member with 1 year of experience, make a dot where "1" would be on the x-axis and where "26" would be on the y-axis. What conclusions can you draw from this data?

The data shows that the more years of experience a team member has, the fewer defects they make.

Years of Experience	Number of Defects
1	26
1	29
1	24
2	21
2	24
2	23
2	20
2	17
2	22
2	23
3	22
3	17
4	12
5	9
5	8
7	3
8	2
8	3

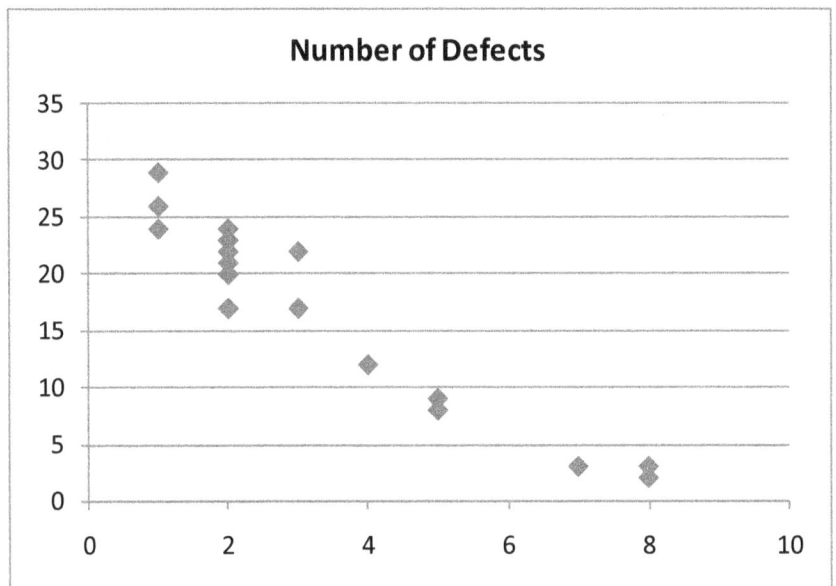

Number of Defects

TECHNOLOGY
AS PROMISED

Exercise 92. Report Performance – Forecasting

Forecasting is one of the tools and techniques of the Report Performance process. There are several categories of forecasting methods. This exercise uses the multiple regression method. In this example, a rabbitry (farm that raises rabbit) is trying to predict how many show rabbits they will sell in a given month. They are trying to predict the number of rabbits sold using these predictors: number of dollars spent on advertising that month, number of awards won at rabbit shows, and the number of shows during that month in the state. Using multiple regression, they were able to calculate the following formula that predicts how many show rabbits they will sell in a month:

Number of Show Rabbits Sold =
2.34 + (Advertising Dollars x .0528) + (Awards Won x 2.19) – (Shows in State x .186)

Help them to calculate how many rabbits they can expect to sell in the following circumstances. The first is done already.

1. If for a given month, they spend $0 on advertising, won 2 awards, and there was 1 show in the state, how many show rabbits can they expect to sell?

   2.34 + (0 x .0528) + (2 x 2.19) – (1 x .186) = 6.534 Rabbits

2. If for a given month, they spend $10 on advertising, won 2 awards, and there was 1 show in the state, how many show rabbits can they expect to sell?

   9.066 Rabbits

3. If for a given month, they spend $100 on advertising, won 4 awards, and there were 2 shows in the state, how many show rabbits can they expect to sell?

   16.008 Rabbits

Exercise 95. Thirty Questions on Nine Processes

1. The majority of the budget is spent during this process: Direct and Manage Project Execution
2. The work of the project is performed during this process: Direct and Manage Project Execution
3. Process that performs the quality activities from the quality plan: Perform Quality Assurance
4. An independent review performed by trained auditors or third-parties to identify poor processes: Quality Audit
5. Examines process improvement from an organizational and technical perspective: Process Analysis
6. Quality audits are performed during this process: Perform Quality Assurance
7. This process monitors all the process groups: Monitor and Control Project Work
8. In some organizations this is established to review change requests: Configuration Control Board
9. The process where all change requests are processes and either approved or denied: Perform Integrated Change Control
10. Describes product, tracks product changes, and verifies that product requirements are met: Configuration Management
11. The three activities of Configuration Management: Configuration Identification, Configuration Status Accounting, Configuration Verification and Auditing
12. Documented procedures describing how to submit changes and manage change requests: Change Control System
13. Process that formalizes the acceptance of the project meeting objectives and completeness of work: Verify Scope
14. The only tool and technique of this process is "Inspection": Verify Scope
15. Process that specifically controls changes to the project scope: Control Scope
16. Process that determines project schedule status, whether changes have occurred, and influencing these changes: Control Schedule
17. Chart with two bars for each activity showing approved schedule and actual status: Schedule comparison bar charts
18. Defines how changes to the schedule are made and managed: Schedule Change Control System
19. The tools and techniques of Perform Quality Control are listed as a tool of this process: Perform Quality Assurance
20. Process that monitors work to see if it meets quality standards from the quality management plan: Perform Quality Control.
21. A type of bar chart that ranks orders important effects by their frequency: Pareto chart
22. A line chart that displays a process over time and illustrates whether process is in or out of control: Control chart
23. A line chart that displays a variable over time without illustrating control limits: Run Chart
24. Shows the relationship between a problem and causes and is also called fishbone and Ishikawa diagram: Cause-and-effect diagram.
25. Examining a run chart or control chart for patterns in the data: Trend Analysis
26. Examining a subset of something to make inferences about the whole: Statistical sampling
27. A chart showing the relationship of two variables through dots: Scatter Diagram
28. Process that identifies and responds to new risks as they occur: Monitor and Control Risks
29. Audits focused on implementation and effective use of risk strategies: Risk audit
30. An unplanned response to a negative risk event: workaround

Exercise 96. Project Close-Out

This exercise reviews the four formal close-out methods for a project.

1. Project Knock Your Socks Off delivered all the agreed-upon deliverables, and these deliverables have been accepted by the stakeholders. Which of the four formal close-out methods are being described?

Addition   Starvation   Integration   **Extinction**

2. Project Check Up on Quality was meant to be a six-month monitoring process for defects. However, it was so useful at finding and leading to the correction of defects, it has been decided that it should become a permanent part of the process. Which of the four formal close-out methods are being described?

Addition   Starvation   Integration   Extinction

3. Jacki started managing a project a year ago that began with a team of ten people. One by one, her team members were pulled away for projects that were considered more important to the organization. Now nothing is being accomplished on this project because there is no team. Which of the four formal close-out methods are being described?

Addition   Starvation   **Integration**   Extinction

4. Sallie was managing a project that concerned making specific modifications to a product ordered by a large customer. The customer cancelled the order, so there are no funds and no reasons to continue the project.

Which of the four formal close-out methods are being described?

Addition   **Starvation**   Integration   Extinction

5. Which of the four formal close-out methods is considered the best ending for a project?

Addition   Starvation   Integration   **Extinction**   ·

6. Which method is how your last project ended?

Addition   Starvation   Integration   Extinction

Exercise 99. Where Did I Come From?

It's important to know which process the key outputs come from. For each output, write which process created it.

Output	Process
Project Scope Statement	Define Scope
Change Request Status Update	Perform Integrated Change Control
Activity List	Define Activities
Project Schedule	Develop Schedule
Project Management Plan	Develop Project Management Plan
Requirements Management Plan	Collect Requirements
Work Breakdown Structure	Create Work Breakdown Structure
Cost Performance Baseline	Determine Budget
Project Charter	Develop Project Charter
Scope Baseline	Create Work Breakdown Structure
Deliverables	Direct and Manage Project Execution
Quality Management Plan	Plan Quality
Final Product, Service, or Result Transition	Close Project or Phase
Accepted Deliverables	Verify Scope
Selected Sellers	Conduct Procurements
Stakeholder Register	Identify Stakeholders
Risk Register	Identify Risks
Human Resource Plan	Develop Human Resource Plan
Team Performance Assessments	Develop Project Team

TECHNOLOGY
AS PROMISED

Exercise 102. Integration Area Inputs, Tools and Techniques, and Outputs

This exercise provides practice identifying the inputs, tools and techniques, and outputs of the Integration Area processes. First study the inputs, tools and techniques, and outputs for the Integration processes. For each input, put and "I" under the processes it is an input to. Put a "T" if it's a tool and technique and an "O" if it's an output. There is a hint after each—for example "4 Inputs" means that this is an input to four of the processes, so you'll be writing 4 "I's". Consider making photocopies of this exercise if you want to try it again.

	Develop Project Charter	Develop Project Management Plan	Direct and Manage Project Execution	Monitor and Control Project Work	Perform Integrated Change Control	Close Project or Phase
Enterprise Environmental Factors (4 Inputs)	I	I	I	I		
Organizational Process Assets (6 Inputs)	I	I	I	I	I	I
Expert Judgment (6 Tools)	T	T	T	T	T	T
Accepted Deliverables (1 Input)						I
Approved Change Requests (1 Input)			I			
Business Case (1 Input)	I					
Change Requests (2 Outputs, 1 Input)			O	O	I	
Change Request Status Update (1 Output)					O	
Change Control Meetings (1 Tool)					T	
Contract (1 Input)	I					
Deliverables (1 Output)			O			
Final Product, Service, or Result Transition (1 Output)						O
Forecasts (1 Input)				I		
Outputs from Planning Processes (1 Input)		I				
Organizational Process Assets (Updates) (1 Output)						O
Performance Reports (1 Input)				I		
Project Statement of Work (1 Input)	I					
Project Charter (1 Input, 1 Output)	O	I				
Project Scope Statement (1 Input)		I				
Project Management Information System (1 Tool)			T			
Project Management Plan Updates (3 Outputs)			O	O	O	
Project Documents Updates (3 Outputs)			O	O	O	
Project Management Plan (1 Output, 3 Inputs)		O	I	I		I
Work Performance Data (1 Input, 1 Output)			O	I		

Exercise 103. Scope Inputs, Tools and Techniques, and Outputs

This exercise provides practice identifying the inputs, tools and techniques, and outputs of the Scope Area processes. First study the inputs, tools and techniques, and outputs for the Scope processes. For each input, put and "I" under the processes it is an input to. Put a "T" if it's a tool and technique and an "O" if it's an output. There is a hint after each—for example "4 Inputs" means that this is an input to four of the processes, so you'll be writing 4 "I's". Consider making photocopies of this exercise if you want to try it again.

	Collect Requirements	Define Scope	Create WBS	Verify Scope	Control Scope
Accepted Deliverables (1 Output)				O	
Alternatives Identification (1 Tool)		T			
Change Requests (2 Outputs)				O	O
Decomposition (1 Tool)			T		
Expert Judgment (1 Tool)		T			
Facilitated Workshops (2 Tools)	T	T			
Focus Groups (1 Tool)	T				
Group Creativity Techniques (1 Tool)	T				
Group Decision Making Techniques (1 Tool)	T				
Inspection (1 Tool)				T	
Interviews (1 Tool)	T				
Observations (1 Tool)	T				
Organizational Process Assets (2 Inputs)		I	I		
Organizational Process Assets Updates (1 Output)					O
Product Analysis (1 Tool)		T			
Project Charter (2 Inputs)	I	I			
Project Document Updates (2 Outputs)		O	O		
Project Management Plan (1 Input)					I
Project Management Plan Updates (1 Output)					O
Project Scope Statement (1 Tool, 1 Input)		O	I		
Prototypes (1 Tool)	T				
Questionnaires and Surveys (1 Tool)	T				
Replanning (1 Tool)					T
Requirements Management Plan (1 Output)	O				
Requirements Traceability Matrix (1 Output, 2 Inputs)	O			I	I
Scope Baseline (1 Output, 1 Input)			O	I	
Stakeholder Register (1 Input)	I				
Stakeholder Requirements Documentation (1 Output, 4 Inputs)	O	I	I	I	I
Validated Deliverables (1 Input)				I	
Variance Analysis (1 Tool)					T
Work Breakdown Structure (1 Output)			O		
Work Performance Data (1 Input)					I
Work Performance Measurements (1 Output)					O
WBS Dictionary (1 Output)			O		

Exercise 104. Time Inputs and Outputs

This exercise provides practice identifying the inputs and outputs of the Time Area processes. First study the inputs and outputs for the Time processes. For each input, put and "I" under the processes it is an input to and an "O" if it's an output. There is a hint after each—for example "4 Inputs" means that this is an input to four of the processes, so you'll be writing 4 "I's". Consider making photocopies of this exercise if you want to try it again.

	Define Activities	Sequence Activities	Estimate Activity Resources	Estimate Activity Durations	Develop Schedule	Control Schedule
Activity Attributes (1 Output, 4 Inputs)	O	I	I	I	I	
Activity Duration Estimates (1 Output, 1 Input)				O	I	
Activity List (1 Output, 4 Inputs)	O	I	I	I	I	
Activity Resource Requirements (1 Output, 2 Inputs)			O	I	I	
Change Requests (1 Output)						O
Enterprise Environmental Factors (4 Inputs)	I		I	I	I	
Milestone List (1 Output, 1 Input)	O	I				
Organizational Process Assets (5 Inputs)	I	I	I	I	I	I
Organizational Process Assets Updates (1 Output)						O
Project Document Updates (5 Outputs)		O	O	O	O	O
Project Management Plan (1 Input)						I
Project Management Plan Updates (1 Output)						O
Project Schedule (1 Output, 1 Input)					O	I
Project Schedule Network Diagrams (1 Output, 1 Input)		O			I	
Project Scope Statement (3 Inputs)		I		I	I	
Resource Breakdown Structure (1 Output)			O			
Resource Calendars (3 Inputs)			I	I	I	
Schedule Baseline (1 Output)					O	
Schedule Data (1 Output)					O	
Scope Baseline (1 Input)	I					
Work Performance Data (1 Input)						I
Work Performance Measurements (1 Output)						O

TECHNOLOGY
AS PROMISED

Exercise 105. Cost Inputs, Tools and Techniques, and Outputs

This exercise provides practice identifying the inputs, tools and techniques, and outputs of the Cost Area processes. First study the inputs, tools and techniques, and outputs for the Cost processes. For each input, put and "I" under the processes it is an input to. Put a "T" if it's a tool and technique and an "O" if it's an output. There is a hint after each—for example "4 Inputs" means that this is an input to four of the processes, so you'll be writing 4 "I's". Consider making photocopies of this exercise if you want to try it again.

	Estimate Costs	Determine Budget	Control Costs
Activity Cost Estimates (1 Output, 1 Input)	O	I	
Analogous Estimating (1 Tool)	T		
Basis of Estimates (1 Output, 1 Input)	O	I	
Bottom-Up Estimating (1 Tool)	T		
Change Requests (1 Output)			O
Contracts (1 Input)		I	
Cost Aggregation (1 Tool)		T	
Cost of Quality (1 Tool)	T		
Cost Performance Baseline (1 Output, 1 Input)		O	I
Earned Value Measurement (1 Tool)			T
Enterprise Environmental Factors (1 Input)	I		
Expert Judgment (1 Tool)		T	
Forecasted Completion (1 Output)			O
Forecasting (1 Tool)			T
Funding Limit Reconciliation (1 Tool)		T	
Historical Relationships (1 Tool)		T	
Human Resource Plan (1 Input)	I		
Organizational Process Assets (3 Inputs)	I	I	I
Organizational Process Assets Updates (1 Output)			O
Parametric Estimating (1 Tool)	T		
Project Document Updates (3 Outputs)	O	O	O
Project Management Estimating Software (1 Tool)	T		
Project Management Plan Updates (1 Output)			O
Project Management Software (1 Tool)			T
Project Funding Requirements (1 Output, 1 Input)		O	I
Project Schedule (2 Inputs)	I	I	
Project Status Performance Reviews (1 Tool)			T
Reserve Analysis (2 Tools)	T	T	
Resource Calendars (1 Input)		I	
Risk Register (1 Input)	I		
Scope Baseline (2 Inputs)	I	I	
To-complete Performance Index (1 Tool)			T
Work Performance Data (1 Input)			I
Work Performance Measurements (1 Output)			O
Variance Analysis (1 Tool)			T
Vendor Bid Analysis (1 Tool)	T		

Exercise 106. Quality Inputs, Tools and Techniques, and Outputs

This exercise provides practice identifying the inputs, tools and techniques, and outputs of the Quality Area processes. First study the inputs, tools and techniques, and outputs for the Quality processes. For each input, put and "I" under the processes it is an input to. Put a "T" if it's a tool and technique and an "O" if it's an output. There is a hint after each—for example "4 Inputs" means that this is an input to four of the processes, so you'll be writing 4 "I's". Consider making photocopies of this exercise if you want to try it again.

	Plan Quality	Perform Quality Assurance	Perform Quality Control
Additional Quality Planning Tools (1 Tool)	T		
Approved Change Requests (1 Input)			I
Approved Change Request Review (1 Tool)			T
Benchmarking (1 Tool)	T		
Cause and Effect Diagram (1 Tool)			T
Change Requests (2 Outputs)		O	O
Control Charts (2 Tools)	T		T
Control Measurements (1 Output)			O
Cost-benefit Analysis (1 Tool)	T		
Cost of Quality (1 Tool)	T		
Cost Performance Baseline (1 Input)	I		
Deliverables (1 Input)			I
Design of Experiments (1 Tool)	T		
Enterprise Environmental Factors (1 Input)	I		
Flowcharting (2 Tools)	T		T
Histogram (1 Tool)			T
Inspection (1 Tool)			T
Organizational Process Assets (2 Inputs)	I		I
Organizational Process Assets Updates (2 Outputs)		O	O
Pareto Chart (1 Tool)			T
Process Analysis (1 Tool)		T	
Process Improvement Plan (1 Output, 1 Input)	O	I	
Project Document Updates (3 Outputs)	O	O	O
Project Management Plan Updates (2 Outputs)		O	O
Proprietary Quality Management Methodologies (1 Tool)	T		
Quality Audits (1 Tool)		T	
Quality Checklists (1 Output, 1 Input)	O		I
Quality Control Measures (1 Input)		I	
Quality Management Plan (1 Output, 2 Inputs)	O	I	I
Quality Metrics (1 Output, 2 Inputs)	O	I	I
Quality Planning & Quality Control T & T (1 Tool)		T	
Risk Register (1 Input)	I		
Run Chart (1 Tool)			T
Scatter Diagram (1 Tool)			T
Schedule Baseline (1 Input)	I		
Scope Baseline (1 Input)	I		
Stakeholder Register (1 Input)	I		
Statistical Sampling (2 Tools)	T		T
Validated Changes (1 Output)			O
Validated Deliverables (1 Output)			O
Work Performance Data (1 Input)		I	
Work Performance Measurement (1 Input)			I

TECHNOLOGY
AS PROMISED

Exercise 107. Human Resource Inputs, Tools and Techniques, and Outputs

This exercise provides practice identifying the inputs, tools and techniques, and outputs of the Human Resource Area processes. First study the inputs, tools and techniques, and outputs for the Human Resource processes. For each input, put and "I" under the processes it is an input to. Put a "T" if it's a tool and technique and an "O" if it's an output. There is a hint after each—for example "4 Inputs" means that this is an input to four of the processes, so you'll be writing 4 "I's". Consider making photocopies of this exercise if you want to try it again.

	Develop Human Resource Plan	Acquire Project Team	Develop Project Team	Manage Project Team
Acquisition (1 Tool)		T		
Activity Resource Requirements (1 Input)	I			
Change Requests (1 Output)				O
Co-Location (1 Tool)			T	
Conflict Management (1 Tool)				T
Interpersonal Skills (1 Tool)				T
Issue Log (1 Tool)				T
Enterprise Environmental Factors (2 Inputs)	I	I		
Enterprise Environmental Factor Updates (2 Outputs)			O	O
Ground Rules (1 Tool)			T	
Human Resource Plan (1 Output, 3 Inputs)	O	I	I	I
Interpersonal Skills (1 Tool)			T	
Negotiation (1 Tool)		T		
Networking (1 Tool)	T			
Observation and Conversation (1 Tool)				T
Organization Charts and Position Descriptions (1 Tool)	T			
Organizational Process Assets (3 Inputs)	I	I		I
Organizational Process Assets Updates (1 Output)				O
Organizational Theory (1 Tool)	T			
Performance Reports (1 Input)				I
Pre-Assignment (1 Tool)		T		
Project Management Plan Updates (2 Outputs)		O		O
Project Performance Appraisals (1 Tool)				T
Project Staff Assignments (1 Output, 2 Inputs)		O	I	I
Recognition and Rewards (1 Tool)			T	
Resource Calendars (1 Output, 1 Input)		O	I	
Team-Building Activities (1 Tool)			T	
Team Performance Assessments (1 Output, 1 Input)			O	I
Training (1 Tool)			T	
Virtual Teams (1 Tool)		T		

TECHNOLOGY
AS PROMISED

Exercise 108. Communications Inputs, Tools and Techniques, and Outputs

This exercise provides practice identifying the inputs, tools and techniques, and outputs of the Communications Area processes. First study the inputs, tools and techniques, and outputs for the Communications processes. For each input, put and "I" under the processes it is an input to. Put a "T" if it's a tool and technique and an "O" if it's an output. There is a hint after each—for example "4 Inputs" means that this is an input to four of the processes, so you'll be writing 4 "I's". Consider making photocopies of this exercise if you want to try it again.

	Identify Stakeholders	Plan Communications	Distribute Information	Manage Stakeholder Expectations	Report Performance
Change Log (1 Input)				I	
Change Requests (2 Outputs)				O	O
Communication Methods (4 Tools)		T	T	T	T
Communication Models (1 Tool)		T			
Communication Requirements Analysis (1 Tool)		T			
Communications Management Plan (1 Output, 2 Inputs)		O	I	I	
Communication Technology (1 Tool)		T			
Enterprise Environmental Factors (2 Inputs)	I	I			
Expert Judgment (1 Tool)	T				
Forecasting Methods (1 Tool)					T
Information Distribution Tools (1 Tool)			T		
Interpersonal Skills (1 Tool)				T	
Issue Log (1 Input)				I	
Management Skills (1 Tool)				T	
Organizational Process Assets (5 Inputs)	I	I	I	I	I
Organizational Process Assets Updates (3 Outputs)			O	O	O
Performance Reports (1 Input, 1 Output)			I		O
Procurement Document Package (1 Input)	I				
Project Charter (1 Input)	I				
Project Document Updates (2 Outputs)		O		O	
Project Management Plan (1 Input)					I
Project Management Plan Updates (1 Output)				O	
Reporting Systems (1 Tool)					T
Stakeholder Analysis (1 Tool)	T				
Stakeholder Management Strategy (1 Output, 2 Inputs)	O	I		I	
Stakeholder Register (1 Output, 2 Inputs)	O	I		I	
Variance Analysis (1 Tool)					T
Work Performance Data (1 Input)					I
Work Performance Measurements (1 Input)					I

Exercise 109. Risk Inputs and Outputs

This exercise provides practice identifying the inputs and outputs of the Risk Area processes. First study the inputs and outputs for the Risk processes. For each input, put and "I" under the processes it is an input to and an "O" if it's an output. There is a hint after each—for example "4 Inputs" means that this is an input to four of the processes, so you'll be writing 4 "I's". Consider making photocopies of this exercise if you want to try it again.

	Plan Risk Management	Identify Risks	Perform Quantitative Risk Analysis	Perform Qualitative Risk Analysis	Plan Risk Responses	Monitor & Control Risks
Activity Cost Estimates (1 Input)		I				
Activity Duration Estimates (1 Input)		I				
Change Requests (1 Output)						O
Communications Management Plan (1 Input)	I					
Cost Management Plan (3 Inputs)	I	I		I		
Enterprise Environmental Factors (2 Inputs)	I	I				
Organizational Process Assets (4 Inputs)	I	I	I	I		
Organizational Process Assets Updates (1 Output)						O
Other Project Documents (1 Input)		I				
Performance Reports (1 Input)						I
Project Document Updates (2 Outputs)					O	O
Project Management Plan Updates (2 Outputs)					O	O
Project Scope Statement (2 Inputs)	I		I			
Quality Management Plan (1 Input)		I				
Risk Management Plan (1 Output, 5 Inputs)	O	I	I	I	I	I
Risk Register (1 Output, 4 Inputs)		O	I	I	I	I
Risk Register Updates (4 Outputs)			O	O	O	O
Risk Related Contract Decisions (1 Output)					O	
Schedule Management Plan (3 Inputs)	I	I		I		
Scope Baseline (1 Input)		I				
Stakeholder Register (1 Input)		I				
Work Performance Data (1 Input)						I

Exercise 110. Procurement Inputs, Tools and Techniques, and Outputs

This exercise provides practice identifying the inputs and outputs of the Procurement Area processes. First study the inputs and outputs for the Procurement processes. For each input, put and "I" under the processes it is an input to and an "O" if it's an output. There is a hint after each—for example "4 Inputs" means that this is an input to four of the processes, so you'll be writing 4 "I's". Consider making photocopies of this exercise if you want to try it again.

	Plan Procurements	Conduct Procurements	Administer Procurements	Close Procurements
Activity Cost Estimates (1 Input)	I			
Activity Resource Requirements (1 Input)	I			
Approved Change Requests (1 Input)			I	
Change Requests (3 Outputs)	O	O	O	
Closed Procurements (1 Output)				O
Cost Performance Baseline (1 Input)	I			
Enterprise Environmental Factors (1 Input)	I			
Make-or-buy Decisions (1 Output, 1 Input)	O	I		
Organizational Process Assets (2 Inputs)	I	I		
Organizational Process Assets Updates (2 Outputs)			O	O
Performance Reports (1 Input)			I	
Procurement Award (1 Output)		O		
Procurement Documentation (1 Output, 1 Input)			O	I
Procurement Document Packages(1 Output, 1 Input)	O	I		
Procurement Documents (1 Input)			I	
Procurement Management Plan (1 Output, 3 Inputs)	O	I	I	I
Procurement Statements of Work (1 Output)	O			
Project Documents (1 Input)		I		
Project Document Updates (1 Output)		O		
Project Management Plan Updates (2 Outputs)		O	O	
Project Schedule (1 Input)	I			
Qualified Seller List (1 Input)		I		
Resource Calendars (1 Output)		O		
Risk Register (1 Input)	I			
Risk-related Contract Decisions (1 Input)	I			
Scope Baseline (1 Input)	I			
Selected Sellers (1 Output, 1 Input)		O	I	
Seller Proposals (1 Input)		I		
Source Selection Criteria (1 Output, 1 Input)	O	I		
Stakeholder Requirements Documentation (1 Input)	I			
Teaming Agreements (2 Inputs)	I	I		
Work Performance Data (1 Input)			I	

Appendix 2: Sample "Real World" Project Management Plan

Through its consulting services and through the practical delivery of adjunct faculty, Technology As Promised has archived several real world examples of delivering projects with the WEMSHA, PMBOK® based approach. While it would not be appropriate to share plans that impinge on intellectual property or competitive advantage for our clients; this project plan is in the public domain and approved by the then unemployment insurance director for the State of Nebraska for disclosure.

Shared here is a public sector, procurement based project from 2003–2004. Its mission was to implement a modernized unemployment insurance benefit payment system. This was Phase two of a four phase project for which TAPUniversity faculty, David Kohrell, was selected to develop the methodology. The results of that project have been detailed in two IBM Rational Edge articles and, more importantly, was implemented by the State of Nebraska and TCS America in August of 2006.

Those articles and similar material form the foundation for the next "Complete" workbook – The Complete Business Analysis Workbook.

As you review this real world plan, you'll see that the PMBOK® is not followed to the letter of the law. For example, the Risk Management section reflects best practice from a Federal best practice source and Microsoft Solutions Framework. The overall texture and "spirit" of the PMBOK® and WEMSHA PM Workbook approach was followed to get the vendor selection completed.

DRAFT

Department of Labor
Benefit System Modernization
Project Plan

Date of Publication: 11/12/2003

Project Charter and Scope

	Project Charter
	Scope Statement

The project mission, objectives and scope are from the project charter approved in principle on August 27, 2003.

Mission

	Project Charter
	Scope Statement

The mission of this project is to bring the tools that comprise the benefit payment system into the twenty first century to serve Nebraska's employers, workforce, and Workforce Development team members.

Objectives

	Project Charter
	Scope Statement

The BPS Project will follow the Strategic Technical Architecture Roadmap (STAR) 1.0. Specifically, BPS will meet the following objectives:

- *Define the business requirements in a manner in which they can be turned into system specifications by January 5, 2004.*
- *Define the enhanced information reporting capabilities via an "enterprise data/reporting warehouse" by January 5, 2004.*
- *Develop a Request for Proposal and select a vendor to complete the BPS Implementation phase of the project by May 1, 2004.*

Scope

	Project Charter
	Scope Statement

The principal scope of this project is to deliver, within the identified project budget and time constraints, a modernized Benefits Payment System which equals or exceeds the functionality, reliability, security, efficiency, and overall capabilities of the current system.

A modernized Benefits Payment System is generally understood to be that which 1) is built upon an integrated data model, using a relational database system, 2) employs n-tier, component-based, computing architecture based on .NET or J2EE technology, and 3) is highly integrated, among internal and external systems, using loosely-coupled, standards-based transaction architecture.

It includes and excludes the following items.

In Scope:

	Project Charter
	Scope Statement

Major business functions involved in BPS:
- Claims intake, initial and continued claims
- Monetary eligibility determinations
- Non-monetary eligibility and adjudication
- Payment, employer charging and Trust Fund management
- Appeals
- Overpayments
- Fraud and abuse detection
- Internal security

Features and functions
- Federal reporting, program measures and validation
- Management information reports
- Internal and external interfaces
- Analyze, design, build, and test data models to accommodate the above business functions
- Analyze, design, build and test views/screens, forms, reports and all output to support the business functions
- Analyze, design, build and test back-end processes
- Analyze, design, build and test the internal and external system interfaces needed to obtain and exchange data
- Develop technical and user operating documentation
- Integration with Call Center GUI and Neb Dial
- Explore tax modernization opportunities in the Requirements and RFP
- Explore Document management, imaging, workflow and COLD opportunities in the Requirements and RFP.
- Integration with Initial Claims

Out of Scope:

- Developing Call Center GUI features
- Developing Neb-Dial features
- Developing Internet Initial claims features

Communication Plan

Project Charter	
Scope Statement	

Principles

The communication plan for the BPS Modernization Project 2020 follows these foundational principles. Communication should be:

- Brief – it is respectful of competing time demands and need for brevity.
- Affirming – it focuses on success, issues, and events. It does not personalize issues. It respects a person's intelligence and desire to learn.
- Reliable – it is accurate and trustworthy.
- Secure – it is protected from unwarranted intrusion.
- Open – it's inclusive and available to the project team, stakeholders and members of the organization.
- Accessible – it is available in multiple ways and venues that support all learning styles (visual, kinesthetic and auditory).
- Persistent – it is available for immediate project use and for future projects in archival form for future projects.

Lack of communicating progress barriers is a common risk for information technology projects. This is also called "going dark". The principles listed above and elements contained in the remainder of this document help ensure that all of the news is shared, good or bad. Problems and conflict are resolved by bringing issues out into the sunlight and dealing with them.

Audience

The responsibility assignment matrix identifies audiences by their role. It is located on page 4. The section provides some additional explanation.

There are five stakeholder groups to consider.

Core Team

The core team originates and participates in daily work effort. It is a team of peers with responsibilities assigned based on role. People involved in this role produce and guide the project deliverables. They are most closely tied to project's task and have the greatest ability and availability to get things done. They are accountable for delivering the product, in the BPS 2020 Project Phase two, that product is the request for proposal or resources as well as supporting documentation (use cases, requirements and UML).

This team will meet almost daily throughout the project and during the Joint Application Requirements (JAD) sessions each day.

Steering Committee

The steering committee is held accountable for the project's results. The executive sponsor and IT sponsor hold a special accountability role in terms of signing off that project deliverables are complete and meet project charter and plan expectations. This group provides the authority for achieving the BPS 2020 Project mission and objectives.

This group meets once a week.

Requirements Validation Team

All members of OUI will be involved in the project in some way.

Each JAD session benefits from specific subject area expertise in addition to core team members – e.g. Appeals and Legal. For those sessions one to two members of the Requirements Validation Team will be included in the JAD session.

All OUI associates will have access to project progress, updates and requirements documentation that is stored in Quick Place.

Other State Agencies

It is anticipated that the Departments of Information Management Services, Administrative Services (purchasing) and Communications will have a direct role in reviewing and critiquing RFI and RFP/RFR material.

United States Department of Labor

The United States Department of Labor is included in project communication via the grant reporting cycle.

Responsibility Assignment Matrix (RAM) – A Communications View

	Project Charter
	Scope Statement

Work Breakdown Structure element (high level) People	Charter the project	Approve the project plans	Release an request for information (RFI)	Define and capture requirements for new BPS	Release a Request for Proposal (RFP)	Close out Phase 2 *Begin Phase 3 of BPS project.*
Exec. Sponsor	SIGNOFF	SIGNOFF	SIGNOFF	SIGNOFF	SIGNOFF	SIGNOFF
Steering Committee Member	ACCOUNTABLE	ACCOUNTABLE	ACCOUNTABLE	ACCOUNTABLE	ACCOUNTABLE	ACCOUNTABLE
Information Technology Sponsor	PARTICIPANT	PARTICIPANT	SIGNOFF	SIGNOFF	SIGNOFF	SIGNOFF
Core Team (CT)	PARTICIPANT	PARTICIPANT	PARTICIPANT	PARTICIPANT (daily during JAD)	PARTICIPANT	PARTICIPANT
Requirements Validation Team (RVT)	INFORMED	INFORMED	INFORMED	PARTICIPANT	INFORMED	INFORMED
Project Director	ACCOUNTABLE	ACCOUNTABLE	ORIGINATOR	ACCOUNTABLE	ORIGINATOR	PARTICIPANT
Project Manager	ORIGINATOR	ORIGINATOR	PARTICIPANT	ORIGINATOR	PARTICIPANT	ORIGINATOR
BPS user		INFORMED	INFORMED	PARTICIPANT (weekly)	INFORMED	INFORMED
Workforce Development Associate (in addition to ECT)		INFORMED	INFORMED	INFORMED	INFORMED	INFORMED
State IMS		INFORMED	REVIEWER	INFORMED	REVIEWER	INFORMED
State DOC		INFORMED	REVIEWER	INFORMED	REVIEWER	INFORMED
State Purchasing			REVIEWER	INFORMED	SIGNOFF	INFORMED
US Department of Labor			INFORMED	INFORMED	INFORMED	INFORMED

RAM Legend

Responsibility	Time Involved	Update frequency	Information needed from others for review	Information produced for others	Inherited responsibilities
P = participant	10 – 30 hours per week	Daily	Source documents	Feedback, provision of source material and creation of new source document	I

O = originator	30 – 40 hours per week	Daily	Source documentation and SME expertise	Project artifacts and documents including plans, requests for information / proposal and requirements analysis / UML.	P, I, A
S = sign off	2 – 10 hours per week	Daily - weekly	Formal project documents and deliverables – interim and final	Executive updates to stakeholders within NWD and outside NWD	P, I, R, A
A= accountable	4 – 10 hours per week	Daily - weekly	Formal project documents and deliverables – interim and final	Feedback to project core team in email, web survey or written form	P, I, R,
R = reviewer	4 – 10 hours per week	Daily - weekly	Formal project documents and deliverables – final drafts	Comments and changes to draft project documents	P,I
I = informed and input	1 – 2 hours per week	Weekly	Extracts of formal project documents and complete documents. Project status updates that can be read in less than 5 minutes.	Feedback to project management role	

Content and Distribution

	Project Charter
	Scope Statement

Electronic Storage
Project documents (charter, plans, requirements, etc) are stored electronically in the shared network folder
S:\BPS Modernization ProjectS:\BPS Modernization Project and in the Lotus QuickPlace intranet site.

Within the shared network folder and Lotus QuickPlace intranet site, the most recent documents will be displayed. All other documents are stored in an archived directory.

Printed Storage
A printed document of record for documents that have been approved and signed off by the Steering Committee and/or Executive and IT sponsors are stored at NWD records repository located in the BPS project room, 310.

Distribution of information

Email groups

Email is used for informal discussions, communication to all NWD employees, meeting reminders and announcing completed tasks, documents, and milestones.

Email groups will be created based on responsibility assignment matrix role (e.g. Steering Committee and Core Team).

Emails directed at the project coordination team (director and manager) will be responded to within two hours of receipt. The response will contain either the solution or a working solution and response time for next step.

Intranet – QuickPlace
Formal approval of milestones, in process requirements, and request for information / proposal are stored in QuickPlace.

Meetings and Updates

Project Charter	
Scope Statement	

Meetings

Meetings are scheduled in advanced via recurring meeting request in MS Outlook.

- Steering Committee meetings, subject to change, are held each Wednesday from 3:00pm CDT/CST to 4:30pm CDT/CST in conference room 310.
- Core team meetings occur daily in the BPS 2020 Project Office, room 310.
- A introduction and kick off meeting for the core team is scheduled for August 26, 2003
- A kick off meeting or update to the Requirements Validation Team (RVT) should occur one to two weeks prior to the start of the JAD sessions.

Meeting results will be compiled and published within four hours of conclusion.

Updates

Updates to the broader NWD workforce and associates will focus on tangible project results and application to users of BPS. In person, large group updates from project coordination, steering committee or core team will be made available on a twice-monthly basis. Monthly updates will be provided by project coordination, steering committee or core team in locations to be determined.

Escalation

	Project Charter
	Scope Statement

In order to ensure that an issue (or risk event or action item) does not hamper forward progress, the following are some escalation guidelines. **Resolution is defined as either a solution or plan of action.**

1. Within the context of the core team, an issue that is not resolved by the core team within four hours is logged and escalated to the Steering Committee via email.
2. Within the context of the core team, an issue that is not resolved by the core team within twenty-four hours is logged and escalate to the Executive Sponsor in person.
3. Within the context of the Steering Committee, an issue that is not resolved by the committee within seventy-two hours is logged and escalated to the Commissioner of Labor via email.

Change Control

	Project Charter
	Scope Statement

There are two types of change that need management during the life of the project: 1) changes to the scope of the project and 2) changes in requirements. The requirements change management will be established as Rational Requisite and model tools are deployed in early October of 2003. Changes to the scope of the project are addressed in the following sections beginning with a discussion on the Constraint Triangle.

Constraint Triangle

The Theory of Constraints establishes that projects are implemented most effectively when the following three factors are balanced and pressured. This diagram helps explain the concept.

Project cost, quality, and risk are impacted proportionally by the schedule, resource, and requirements. **For example, a project with a high requirements demand and limited resources over a short duration will have a high risk for project failure, potential for poor quality, and longer term cost of ownership.** Pressure can be applied to one side of the triangle, but not all three before increasing risk, harming quality, or driving up cost.

Change control steps

The BPS 2020 project change control process will balance the constraint triangle by evaluating each change request at the steering committee level. The change control steps are:

Step 1: Requester documents desired change using the project change request form contained in QuickPlace.
The form contains the following data elements:
1. Name of requestor
2. Date of change
3. Purpose of change
4. Type of change – more requirements, shorter time frame, resource loss
5. Description of change.

A sample form is located at the QuickPlace website.

Step 2: Requester forwards change request to the Steering Committee via email group / or QuickPlace menu item

Step 3: Project Manager reviews change request and advises the Steering Committee of the following
- Change type and constraint area impacted – schedule, requirements, or resources or all three
- Impact of change on quality, risk or cost

Step 4: Steering committee reviews change request and project manager's review at next available steering committee meeting

Alternate route -- for changes suggested during and/or by Steering Committee, go to Step 3.

Risk Management Plan

	Project Charter
	Scope Statement

Definition

Risk involves uncertain events that have not occurred yet. The result of those events may be positive or negative. In general, the result is perceived to be negative. Risk management is the art and science of managing those future, unknown events.

Risk Management Approach

Effective risk management occurs when relevant project risks are identified, analyzed, and prioritized. The art is in identifying enough risks to ensure reliability and validity without overwhelming the process and stalling action.

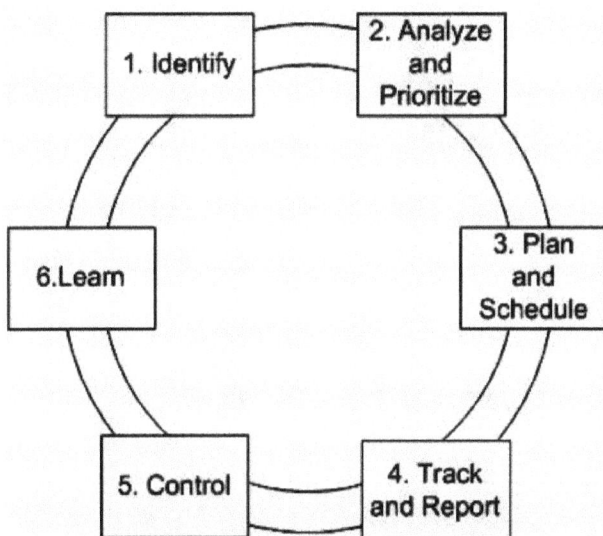

The Information Technology Support Center (ITSC) produced a thorough and well written risk management document, *UI Modernization Risk Guidebook*, in 2001. It was based on work with Indiana, Ohio, and Wisconsin. There are sixty-four risks noted that guidebook. Several are applicable to Phase Two or Phase Three. This is recommended reading for a deeper insight into risk management for the BPS2020 project.

Microsoft utilizes aggressive risk management in many of its products. The Microsoft Solutions Framework provides a good model for risk identification, prioritization and management. As the chart below illustrates, the task is to identify as many risks as possible and then trim them down to a manageable size.

The approach recommended for the BPS Modernization Project is:

1. **Organize risks into Phase Two (requirements and RFP) and Phase Three (construction of new system in house or through a vendor).**
5.
6. **Review ITSC risks for similar and/or applicable risks to Nebraska.**
7. **Compile the raw list of risks.**
8. **Analyze risks statements to determine which phase they belong in, what other risks they are like, severity of impact if the risk occurs and probability the risk event will occur.**
9. **Prioritize top 5 to 10 risks and actively manage each one through acceptance, transfer, mitigation, or avoidance.**

Risk Management – Phase Two

There are risks associated with accomplishing the objectives noted in the Project Charter. These are generally process risks. There are also risks with accomplishing the overall BPS

2020 Modernization mission of delivering a new system by 2005/6. Those risks will be addressed more thoroughly in Phase Three. Many of the Phase Three risk can be identified now. A factor in successfully managing risk is lead time. By considering some Phase Three risks now, time works for the project teams and not against.

Phase Two

Phase Two risks concern process. The purpose is fundamentally
1. to identify and analyze all relevant requirements and
1. to develop a RFI/RFP that encapsulates those requirements and selects a solution to implement them.

Risks associated with either one involve review processes that take longer than planned or missing a key requirement. Neither one is trivial. The foundation for success is laid during this phase and some risks, such as missing a key requirement, may not trigger until late in the project at a much higher cost.

The following page contains a risk assessment table first used in the Project Charter – it fills in the blanks and clarifies.

Phase Two Risk Management Table – Updated 11-12-2003

	Short Name	Risk Description	Charter Risk Assessment (High, Med, Low)	Size of Loss	Probability of Loss	Risk Exposure (P*I) Matrix	Priority	Management Strategy (avoid, transfer, mitigate, accept)	Person responsible
	Off Shore – policy considerations	Selecting a vendor with offshore resources as a primary workforce introduces potential policy constraints and considerations							
	Off Shore – "silver bullet syndrome"	Vendor may purport cost savings from off shore in proposal, hidden costs of business analysts and project management overhead							
	Performance	How will State NWD, DOL be assured the vendor will							

	bond	deliver as promised?							
A	Missed requirement	The time afforded to gather requirements is compressed (yet not unrealistic). The project team is employing use of Joint Application Development techniques and Use Cases in the requirements step of the development lifecycle – that means the core team will not validate requirements through prototypes as they progress.	Medium	30 days	50%	15 days	High	Mitigate this through consistent facilitation creation of story boards in Visio along side use cases visual recording of walkthroughs validation with extended NWD associates – primarily field staff appropriate incentives to core team members for finding "what's missing"	David Kohrell
A	RFP process	The project schedule **is** aggressive in terms of review and authorization process for release of an RFP within the State of Nebraska	High	60 days				Mitigate this risk through front loading of administrative tasks for an RFI e.g., meetings with DAS Purchasing and IMS	Mitch Ummel
A	RFP escalating commitment	Rejecting all vendors in favor of an RFR may prove difficult at the RFP phase due to sunk investment of time and cost.	Medium					Structure RFP to allow separation of technical and cost Determine probability of match at the conclusion of RFI	Steering committee
C	Fast track time schedule	The Phase 2 schedule has been compressed or fast tracked to select a vendor or staff augmentation company. This will allow for a faster delivery of Phase	Medium	20 days	50%	10 days	Medium	Mitigate through precision of communication strategy. This will be seen in early alerts of project slippage	David Kohrell

TECHNOLOGY
AS PROMISED

		3 and implementation of new BPS system. The fast track schedule will press the communication among stakeholders						and proactive communication strategy	
C	RFI process	The project schedule **may be** aggressive in terms of review and authorization processes for release of an RFI within the State of Nebraska	Mediu m	1 0 d a y s	50%	5 days	Mediu m	Mitigate this risk through front loading of administrative tasks for an RFI e.g., meetings with DAS Purchasing and IMS	Mitch Ummel
C	Getting Rational Requisite and training	The project will use Rational Requisite which is new to NWD. Aka Rational Requisite as a tool and RUP in general beginning September 10 may prove difficult. ADDRESSED – TRAINING SET SEPT 22 -- 24	Mediu m	2 0	25%	5 days	Mediu m	Mitigate software procurement through trial and education versions of Rational Requisite. Accept training risk and schedule at next best available date(s) in September	Mitch Ummel

Quality Plan

	Project Charter
	Scope Statement

Quality planning for a project involves –

    1) Ensuring the product(s) developed function properly and as specified – this is akin to quality control and

    2) Ensuring that the project objectives are met – this is akin to quality assurance.

Phase Two, the focus of this project plan, concerns more process than final product. The final product is a set of requirements, a request for proposal, and selected vendor or solution. The quality plan concentrates on quality assurance tasks to ensure the

TECHNOLOGY
AS PROMISED

objectives are met. If those objectives are met, then the stage is set for a successful BPS system.

There is a direct tie in from Phase Two to Three; the selected solution is most evident. Additionally, the use cases generated during the JAD sessions will serve as test cases for the selected vendor and/or solution (or the inputs to quality control of the new BPS).

With that background, Phase Two quality assurance steps are:

Step 1. Review and feedback of various project activities including

1. project tracking data on a weekly basis by the steering committee and core team.
2. requirements by core team, requirements validation team, steering committee and OUI staff
3. request for information and proposal by roles identified in the RAM.

Step 2. Milestone reviews by core team and steering committee.

1. Measure what went well and what could be improved.
2. Measure project process performance (earned value, schedule variance, etc.) compared to previous milestone and median of entire project.
3. Distribute web surveys that measure and validate team member ownership and involvement; establish benchmark team ownership index.
4. Determine what action needs to occur for next milestone.
5. Determine what learning is applicable to future projects.
6. Use of QuickPlace to establish a unique intranet presence that fosters the shared communication.
7. Use of meetings, briefings and informal discussions to communicate project specifics such as use cases for an application or status of RFI responses.
8. Use of email newsletters to push information to appropriate groups as defined in the Communications Plan.

Resource and staffing plan

Phase Two

Staffing for Phase Two consists of two contractors, core team members, steering committee members, and OUI staff. There may be need to hire additional expertise in Rational Requisite document creation and management (technical writer). The competencies and talent needed for that role parallel a business analyst and include focus, strategic thinking, oral communication, writing, and technical acumen.

TECHNOLOGY
AS PROMISED

Phase Three

Staffing for Phase Three will require more people. How many people and what competencies and talent are needed will be determined based on whether the path taken is a request for proposal or request for resources. Some practical guidance can be offered in this document. The BPS modernization is more than a small scale to medium scale project. Based on requirements known at publication of this document, the total person hours needed for the project are over 100,000.

WBS – Work Breakdown Structure

	Project Charter
	Scope Statement

The responsibility assignment matrix provides a high level view of the work break down structure. A fully developed WBS is contained below.

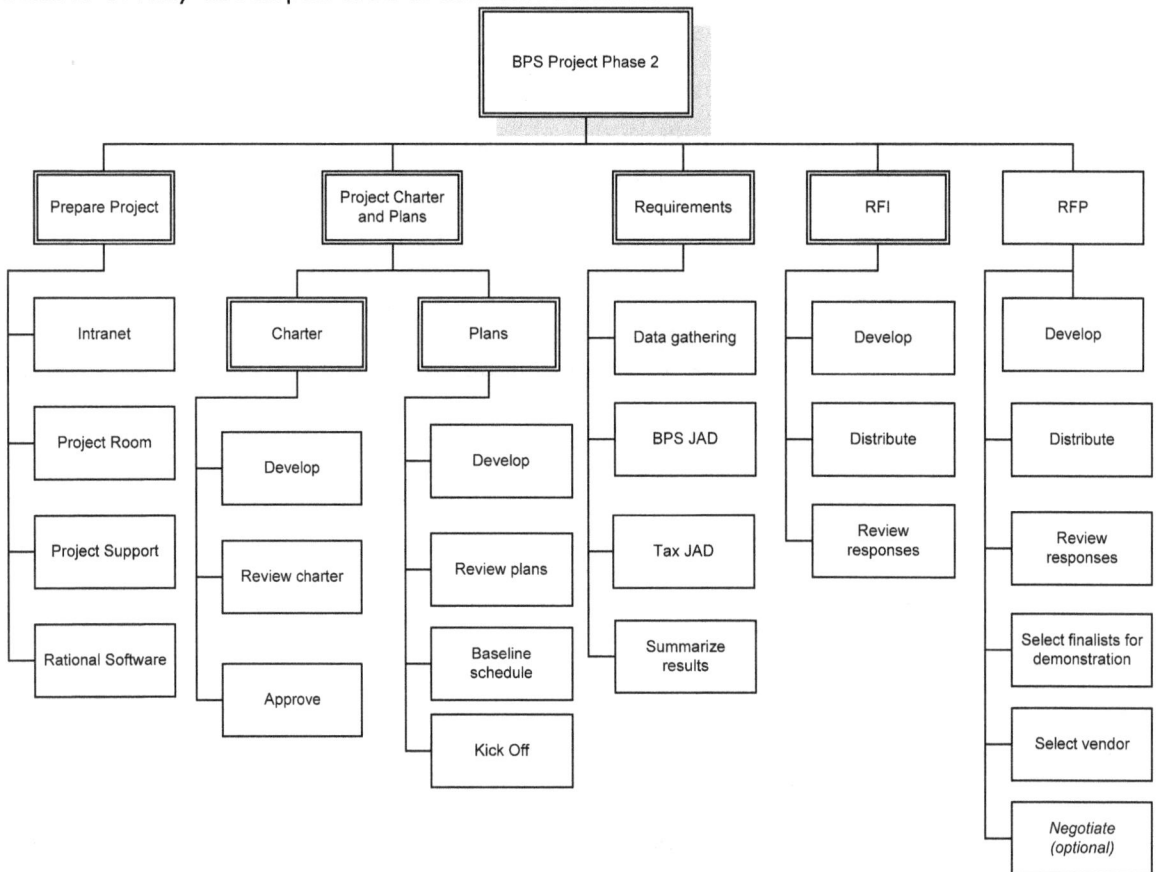

Phase Two Schedule

	Project Charter
	Scope Statement

The following is an extract of project schedule. It contains the first and second level of the work breakdown structure as depicted on the previous page. A snapshot of the scheduler (also called a baseline) will be taken on September 3 to provide a reference point for project performance. The schedule will be updated on a daily basis.

ID	WBS	Task Name	Duration	Start	Finish
0	0	RFP Phase Project Plan	201 days	Wed 7/30/03	Fri 5/28/04
1	1	Project Startup	1 day	Wed 7/30/03	Wed 7/30/03
2	2	Project Phase Planning and Environmer Prep	24 days	Thu 7/31/03	Wed 9/10/03
8	3	Adopt Project Charter and Plans	15.5 days	Mon 8/18/03	Tue 9/9/03
26	4	Release a Request for Information	32 days	Wed 9/10/03	Thu 10/23/03
31	5	Define and validate high level requirements	51.45 days	Tue 9/9/03	Fri 11/21/03
62	6	Release RFP	157 days	Thu 10/2/03	Thu 5/27/04
85	7	Perform project support activities	152.25 days	Wed 8/13/03	Wed 3/31/04
140	8	Closeout Project	0 days	Fri 5/28/04	Fri 5/28/04

Phase Two Budget

	Project Charter
	Scope Statement

Summary

Phase 2 budget	$378,430.00
Phase 3 budget	$6,444,488.00
Phase 2 and 3 budget	$6,822,918.00

Glossary of Terms and Acronyms

Common Acronyms

AC Actual Cost *of Work Performed*
AD Activity Description
ADM Arrow Diagramming Method
AF Actual Finish date
AOA Activity-On-Arrow
AON Activity-On-Node
AS Actual Start date
BAC Budget At Completion
CCB Change Control Board
CPFF Cost Plus Fixed Fee
CPIF Cost Plus Incentive Fee
CPI Cost Performance Index
CPM Critical Path Method
CV Cost Variance
DD Data Date
DU Duration
EAC Estimate At Completion
EF Early Finish date
ES Early Start date
ETC Estimate (or Estimated) To Complete (or Completion)
EV Earned Value
FF Free Float or Finish-to-Finish
FFP Firm Fixed Price
FPIF Fixed Price Incentive Fee
FS Finish-to-Start
GERT Graphical Evaluation and Review Technique
IFB Invitation For Bid
LF Late Finish date
LOE Level Of Effort
LS Late Start date
MPM Modern Project Management
OBS Organization(al) Breakdown Structure
PC Percent Complete
PDM Precedence Diagramming Method
PERT Program Evaluation and Review Technique
PF Planned Finish date
PM Project Management or Project Manager
PMBOK Project Management Body of Knowledge
PMP Project Management Professional
PV Planned Value
PS Planned Start date
QA Quality Assurance
QC Quality Control

RAM Responsibility Assignment Matrix
RDU Remaining Duration
RFP Request For Proposal
RFQ Request For Quotation
SDLC System Development Lifecycle
SF Scheduled Finish date or Start-to-Finish
SOW Statement Of Work
SPI Schedule Performance Index
SS Scheduled Start date or Start-to-Start
SV Schedule Variance
TC Target Completion date
TF Total Float or Target Finish date
TS Target Start date
TQM Total Quality Management
WBS Work Breakdown Structure

GLOSSARY

Accountability Matrix. See responsibility assignment matrix.
Activity. An element of work performed during the course of a project. An activity normally has an expected duration, an expected cost, and expected resource requirements. Activities are often subdivided into tasks.
Activity Definition. Identifying the specific activities that must be performed in order to produce the various project deliverables.
Activity Description (AD). A short phrase or label used in a project network diagram. The activity description normally describes the scope of work of the activity.
Activity Duration Estimating. Estimating the number of work periods which will be needed to complete individual activities.
Activity-On-Arrow (AOA). See Arrow Diagramming Method.
Activity-On-Node (AON). See Precedence Diagramming Method.
Actual Cost. Total costs incurred (direct and indirect) in accomplishing work during a given time period. Referred to as Actual Cost (AC) since 2000 Edition of the PMBOK®. (In the 1996 PMBOK® and other project management references it may be referred to as ACWP or actual cost of work performed. See also Earned Value.
Actual Finish Date (AF). The point in time that work actually ended on an activity. (Note: in some application areas, the activity is considered "finished" when work is "substantially complete.")
Actual Start Date (AS). The point in time that work actually started on an activity.
Administrative Closure. Generating, gathering, and disseminating information to formalize project completion.
Application Area. A category of projects that have common elements not present in all projects. Application areas are usually defined in terms of either the product of the project (i.e., by similar technologies or industry sectors) or the type of customer (e.g., internal vs. external, government vs. commercial). Application areas often overlap.
Arrow. The graphic presentation of an activity. See also Arrow Diagramming Method.

Arrow Diagramming Method (ADM). A network diagramming technique in which activities are represented by arrows. The tail of the arrow represents the start and the head represents the finish of the activity (the length of the arrow does not represent the expected duration of the activity). Activities are connected at points called nodes (usually drawn as small circles) to illustrate the sequence in which the activities are expected to be performed. See also Precedence Diagramming Method.

As-of Date. See Data Date.

Backward Pass. The calculation of late finish dates and late start dates for the uncompleted portions of all network activities. Determined by working backwards through the network logic from the project's end date. The end date may be calculated in a forward pass or set by the customer or sponsor. See also Network Analysis.

Bar Chart. A graphic display of schedule-related information. In the typical bar chart, activities or other project elements are listed down the left side of the chart, dates are shown across the top, and activity durations are shown as date-placed horizontal bars. Also called a Gantt chart.

Baseline. The original plan (for a project, a work package, or an activity), plus or minus approved changes. Usually used with a modifier (e.g., cost baseline, schedule baseline, performance measurement baseline).

Baseline Finish Date. See scheduled Finish Date.

Baseline Start Date. See scheduled Start Date.

Budget At Completion (BAC). The estimated total cost of the project when done.

Budget Estimate. See Estimate.

Budgeted Cost of Work Performed (BCWP). The sum of the approved cost estimates (including any overhead allocation) for activities (or portions of activities) completed during a given period (usually project-to-date). Referred to as Earned Value alone since 2000 Edition of the PMBOK®. See also Earned Value.

Budgeted Cost of Work Scheduled (BCWS). The sum of the approved cost estimates (including any overhead allocation) for activities (or portions of activities) scheduled to be performed during a given period (usually project-to-date). Referred to as Planned Value alone since 2000 Edition of the PMBOK®. See also Earned Value.

Calendar Unit. The smallest unit of time used in scheduling the project. Calendar units are generally in hours, days, or weeks, but can also be in shifts or even in minutes. Used primarily in relation to project management software.

Change Control Board (CCB). A formally constituted group of stakeholders responsible for approving or rejecting changes to the project baselines.

Change in Scope. See Scope Change.

Chart of Accounts. Any numbering system used to monitor project costs by category (e.g., labor, supplies, materials). The project chart of accounts is usually based upon the corporate chart of accounts of the primary performing organization. See also code of accounts.

Charter. See Project Charter.

Code of Accounts. Any numbering system used to uniquely identify each element of the work breakdown structure. See also Chart of Accounts.

Communications Planning. Determining the information and communications needs of the project stakeholders.

TECHNOLOGY
AS PROMISED

Concurrent Engineering. An approach to project staffing that, in its most general form, calls for implementers to be involved in the design phase. Sometimes confused with fast tracking.

Contingencies. See Reserve and Contingency Planning.

Contingency Allowance. See Reserve.

Contingency Planning. The development of a management plan that identifies alternative strategies to be used to ensure project success if specified risk events occur.

Contingency Reserve. A separately planned quantity used to allow for future situations which may be planned for only in part (sometimes called "known unknowns"). For example, rework is certain; the amount of rework is not. Contingency reserves may involve cost, schedule, or both. Contingency reserves are intended to reduce the impact of missing cost or schedule objectives. Contingency reserves are normally included in the project's cost and schedule baselines.

Contract. A contract is a mutually binding agreement which obligates the seller to provide the specified product and obligates the buyer to pay for it. Contracts generally fall into one of three broad categories:

- Fixed price or lump sum contracts-
  this category of contract involves a fixed total price for a well-defined product. Fixed price contracts may also include incentives for meeting or exceeding selected project objectives such as schedule targets.
- Cost reimbursable contracts-
  this category of contract involves payment (reimbursement) to the contractor for its actual costs. Costs are usually classified as direct costs (costs incurred directly by the project, such as wages for members of the project team) and indirect costs (costs allocated to the project by the performing organization as a cost of doing business, such as salaries for corporate executives). Indirect costs are usually calculated as a percentage of direct costs. Cost reimbursable contracts often include incentives for meeting or exceeding selected project objectives such as schedule targets or total cost.
- Unit price contracts-
  the contractor is paid a preset amount per unit of service (e.g., $70 per hour for professional services or $1.08 per cubic yard of earth removed) and the total value of the contract is a function of the quantities needed to complete the work.

Contract Administration. Managing the relationship with the seller.

Contract Close-out. Completion and settlement of the contract, including resolution of all outstanding items.

Control. The process of comparing actual performance with planned performance, analyzing variances, evaluating possible alternatives, and taking appropriate corrective action as needed.

Control Charts. Control charts are a graphic display of the results, over time and against established control limits, of a process. They are used to determine if the process is "in control" or in need of adjustment.

Corrective Action. Changes made to bring expected future performance of the project into line with the plan.

Cost Budgeting. Allocating the cost estimates to individual project components.

TECHNOLOGY
AS PROMISED

Cost Control. Controlling changes to the project budget.

Cost Estimating. Estimating the cost of the resources needed to complete project activities.

Cost of Quality. The costs incurred to ensure quality. The cost of quality includes quality planning, quality control, quality assurance, and rework.

Cost Performance Index (CPI). The ratio of budgeted costs to actual costs (BCWP/ACWP). CPI is often used to predict the magnitude of a possible cost overrun using the following formula: original cost estimate/CPI = projected cost at completion. See also Earned Value.

Cost Plus Fixed Fee (CPFF) Contract. A type of contract where the buyer reimburses the seller for the seller's allowable costs (allowable costs are defined by the contract) plus a fixed amount of profit (fee).

Cost Plus Incentive Fee (CPIF) Contract. A type of contract where the buyer reimburses the seller for the seller's allowable costs (allowable costs are defined by the contract), and the seller earns its profit if it meets defined performance criteria.

Cost Variance (CV).

1. Any difference between the estimated cost of an activity and the actual cost of that activity.
2. In earned value, EV less AC. Crashing. Taking action to decrease the total project duration after analyzing a number of alternatives to determine how to get the maximum duration compression for the least cost.

Critical Activity. Any activity on a critical path. Most commonly determined by using the critical path method. Although some activities are "critical" in the dictionary sense without being on the critical path, this meaning is seldom used in the project context.

Critical Path. In a project network diagram, the series of activities which determines the earliest completion of the project. The critical path will generally change from time to time as activities are completed ahead of or behind schedule. Although normally calculated for the entire project, the critical path can also be determined for a mile-stone or subproject. The critical path is usually defined as those activities with float less than or equal to a specified value, often zero. See Critical Path Method.

Critical Path Method (CPM). A network analysis technique used to predict project duration by analyzing which sequence of activities (which path) has the least amount of scheduling flexibility (the least amount of float). Early dates are calculated by means of a forward pass using a specified start date. Late dates are calculated by means of a backward pass starting from a specified completion date (usually the forward pass is calculated by the project's early finish date).

Current Finish Date. The current estimate of the point in time when an activity will be completed.

Current Start Date. The current estimate of the point in time when an activity will begin.

Data Date (DD). The point in time that separates actual (historical) data from future (scheduled) data. Also called as-of date.

Definitive Estimate. See Estimate.

Deliverable. Any measurable, tangible, verifiable outcome, result, or item that must be produced to complete a project or part of a project. Often used more narrowly in reference to an external deliverable, this is a deliverable that is subject to approval by the project sponsor or customer. See logical relationship.

Dummy Activity. An activity of zero duration used to show a logical relationship in the arrow diagramming method. Dummy activities are used when logical relationships cannot be completely or correctly described with regular activity arrows. Dummies are shown graphically as a dashed line headed by an arrow.

Duration (DU). The number of work periods (not including holidays or other non-working periods) required to complete an activity or other project element. Usually expressed as workdays or workweeks. Sometimes incorrectly equated with elapsed time. See also effort.

Duration Compression. Shortening the project schedule without reducing the project scope. Duration compression is not always possible and often requires an increase in project cost.

Early Finish Date (EF). In the critical path method, the earliest possible point in time on which the uncompleted portions of an activity (or the project) can finish based on the net-work logic and any schedule constraints. Early finish dates can change as the project progresses and changes are made to the project plan.

Early Start Date (ES). In the critical path method, the earliest possible point in time on which the uncompleted portions of an activity (or the project) can start, based on the net-work logic and any schedule constraints. Early start dates can change as the project progresses and changes are made to the project plan.

Earned Value (EV).

1. A method for measuring project performance. It compares the amount of work that was planned with what was actually accomplished to determine if cost and schedule performance is as planned. See also actual cost of work performed, budgeted cost of work scheduled, budgeted cost of work performed, cost variance, cost performance index, schedule variance, and schedule performance index.
2. The budgeted cost of work performed for an activity or group of activities.

Earned Value Analysis. See definition (1) under earned value.
The number of labor units required to complete an activity or other project element. Usually expressed as staff hours, staff days, or staff weeks. Should not be confused with duration.

Estimate. An assessment of the likely quantitative result. Usually applied to project costs and durations and should always include some indication of accuracy (e.g., ± x percent). Usually used with a modifier (e.g., preliminary, conceptual, feasibility). Some application areas have specific modifiers that imply particular accuracy ranges (e.g., order-of-magnitude estimate, budget estimate, and definitive estimate in engineering and construction projects).

Estimate At Completion (EAC). The expected total cost of an activity, a group of activities, or of the project when the defined scope of work has been completed. Most Techniques for forecasting EAC include some adjustment of the original cost estimate based on project performance to date. Also shown as "estimated at completion." Often shown as EAC = Actuals-to-date + ETC. See also Earned Value and Estimate to Complete.

Estimate To Complete (ETC). The expected additional cost needed to complete an activity, a group of activities, or the project. Most techniques for forecasting ETC include some adjustment to the original estimate based on project performance to date. Also called "estimated to complete." See also Earned Value and Estimate at Completion.

Event-on-Node. A network diagramming technique in which events are represented by boxes (or nodes) connected by arrows to show the sequence in which the events are to occur. Used in the original Program Evaluation and Review Technique.

Exception Report. Document that includes only major variations from plan (rather than all variations).

Expected Monetary Value. The product of an event's probability of occurrence and the gain or loss that will result. For example, if there is a 50 percent probability that it will rain, and rain will result in a $100 loss, the expected monetary value of the rain event is $50 (.5 x $100).

Fast Tracking. Compressing the project schedule by overlapping activities that would normally be done in sequence, such as design and construction. Sometimes confused with concurrent engineering.

Finish Date. A point in time associated with an activity's completion. Usually qualified by one of the following: actual, planned, estimated, scheduled, early, late, baseline, target or current.

Finish-to-Finish (FF). See Logical Relationship.

Finish-to-Start (FS). See Logical Relationship.

Firm Fixed Price (FFP) Contract. A type of contract where the buyer pays the seller a set amount (as defined by the contract) regardless of the seller's costs.

Fixed Price Contract. See Firm Fixed Price Contract.

Fixed Price Incentive Fee (FPIF) Contract. A type of contract where the buyer pays the seller a set amount (as defined by the contract), and the seller can earn an additional amount if it meets defined performance criteria.

Float. The amount of time that an activity may be delayed from its early start without delaying the project finish date. Float is a mathematical calculation and can change as the project progresses and changes are made to the project plan. Also called slack, total float, and path float. See also Free Float.

Forecast Final Cost. See Estimate at Completion.

Forward Pass. The calculation of the early start and early finish dates for the uncompleted portions of all network activities. See also Network Analysis and Backward Pass.

Fragnet. See Subnet.

Free Float (FF). The amount of time an activity can be delayed without delaying the early start of any immediately following activities. See also Float.

Functional Manager. A manager responsible for activities in a specialized department or function (e.g., engineering, manufacturing, marketing).

Functional Organization. An organization structure in which staff are grouped hierarchically by specialty (e.g., production, marketing, engineering, and accounting at the top level; with engineering, further divided into mechanical, electrical, and others).

Gantt Chart. See Bar Chart.

Grade. A category or rank used to distinguish items that have the same functional use (e.g., "hammer") but do not share the same requirements for quality (e.g., different hammers may need to withstand different amounts of force).

Graphical Evaluation and Review Technique (GERT). A network analysis technique that allows for conditional and probabilistic treatment of logical relationships (i.e., some activities may not be performed).

Hammock. An aggregate or summary activity (a group of related activities is shown as one and reported at a summary level). A hammock may or may not have an internal sequence. See also Subproject and Subnet.

Hanger. An unintended break in a network path. Hangers are usually caused by missing activities or missing logical relationships.

Information Distribution. Making needed information available to project stakeholders in a timely manner.

Initiation. Committing the organization to begin a project phase.

Integrated Cost/Schedule Reporting. See Earned Value.

Invitation for Bid (IFB). Generally, this term is equivalent to request for proposal. However, in some application areas it may have a narrower or more specific meaning.

Key Event Schedule. See Master Schedule.

Lag. A modification of a logical relationship which directs a delay in the successor task. For example, in a finish-to-start dependency with a 10-day lag, the successor activity cannot start until 10 days after the predecessor has finished. See also Lead.

Late Finish Date (LF). In the critical path method, the latest possible point in time that an activity may be completed without delaying a specified milestone (usually the project finish date).

Late Start Date (LS). In the critical path method, the latest possible point in time that an activity may begin without delaying a specified milestone (usually the project finish date).

Lead. A modification of a logical relationship which allows an acceleration of the successor task. For example, in a finish-to-start dependency with a 10-day lead, the successor activity can start 10 days before the predecessor has finished. See also Lag.

Level of Effort (LOE). Support-type activity (e.g., vendor or customer liaison) that does not readily lend itself to measurement of discrete accomplishment. It is generally characterized by a uniform rate of activity over a specific period of time.

Leveling. See Resource Leveling.

Life-cycle Costing. The concept of including acquisition, operating, and disposal costs when evaluating various alternatives.

Line Manager.

1. The manager of any group that actually makes a product or performs a service.
2. A functional manager.

Link. See Logical Relationship.

Logic. See Network Logic.

Logic Diagram. See Project Network Diagram.

Logical Relationship. A dependency between two project activities, or between a project activity and a milestone. See also precedence relationship. The four possible types of logical relationships are:

- Finish-to-start: the "from" activity must finish before the "to" activity can start.
- Finish-to-finish: the "from" activity must finish before the "to" activity can finish.
- Start-to-start: the "from" activity must start before the "to" activity can start.
- Start-to-finish: the "from" activity must start before the "to" activity can finish.

Loop. A network path that passes the same node twice. Loops cannot be analyzed using traditional network analysis techniques such as CPM and PERT. Loops are allowed in GERT.

Management Reserve. A separately planned quantity used to allow for future situations which are impossible to predict (sometimes called "unknown unknowns"). Management reserves may involve cost or schedule. Management reserves are intended to reduce the risk of missing cost or schedule objectives. Use of management re-serve requires a change to the project's cost baseline.

Master Schedule. A summary-level schedule which identifies the major activities and key milestones. See also Milestone Schedule.

Mathematical Analysis. See Network Analysis.

Matrix Organization. Any organizational structure in which the project manager shares responsibility with the functional managers for assigning priorities and for directing the work of individuals assigned to the project.

Milestone. A significant event in the project, usually completion of a major deliverable.

Milestone Schedule. A summary-level schedule which identifies the major milestones. See also Master Schedule.

Mitigation. Taking steps to lessen risk by lowering the probability of a risk event's occurrence or reducing its effect should it occur.

Modern Project Management (MPM). A term used to distinguish the current broad range of project management (scope, cost, time, quality, risk, etc.) from narrower, traditional use that focused on cost and time.

Monitoring. The capture, analysis, and reporting of project performance, usually as compared to plan.

Monte Carlo Analysis. A schedule risk assessment technique that performs a project simulation many times in order to calculate a distribution of likely results.

Near-Critical Activity. An activity that has low total float.

Network. See Project Network Diagram.

Network Analysis. The process of identifying early and late start and finish dates for the uncompleted portions of project activities. See also Critical Path Method, Program Evaluation and Review Technique, and Graphical Evaluation and Review Technique.

Network Logic. The collection of activity dependencies that make up a project network diagram.

Network Path. Any continuous series of connected activities in a project network diagram.

Node. One of the defining points of a network; a junction point joined to some or all of the other dependency lines. See also arrow diagramming method and precedence diagramming method.

Order of Magnitude Estimate. See Estimate.

Organizational Breakdown Structure (OBS). A depiction of the project organization arranged so as to relate work packages to organizational units.

Organizational Planning. Identifying, documenting, and assigning project roles, responsibilities, and reporting relationships.

Overall Change Control. Coordinating changes across the entire project.

Overlap. See Lead.

Parametric Estimating. An estimating technique that uses a statistical relationship between historical data and other variables (e.g., square footage in construction, lines of code in software development) to calculate an estimate.

Pareto Diagram. A histogram, ordered by frequency of occurrence, that shows how many results were generated by each identified cause.

Path. A set of sequentially connected activities in a project network diagram.

Path Convergence. In mathematical analysis, the tendency of parallel paths of approximately equal duration to delay the completion of the milestone where they meet.

Path Float. See Float.

Percent Complete (PC). An estimate, expressed as a percent, of the amount of work which has been completed on an activity or group of activities.

Performance Reporting. Collecting and disseminating information about project performance to help ensure project progress.

Performing Organization. The enterprise whose employees are most directly involved in doing the work of the project.

PERT Chart. A specific type of project network diagram. See Program Evaluation and Review Technique.

Phase. See project phase.

Planned Finish Date (PF). See Scheduled Finish Date.

Planned Start Date (PS). See Scheduled Start Date.

Precedence Diagramming Method (PDM). A network diagramming technique in which activities are represented by boxes (or nodes). Activities are linked by precedence relationships to show the sequence in which the activities are to be performed.

Precedence Relationship. The term used in the precedence diagramming method for a logical relationship. In current usage, however, precedence relationship, logical relationship, and dependency are widely used interchangeably regardless of the diagramming method in use.

Predecessor Activity.

1. In the arrow diagramming method, the activity which enters a node.
2. In the precedence diagramming method, the "from" activity. Procurement Planning. Determining what to procure and when. Program. A group of related projects managed in a coordinated way. Programs usually include an element of ongoing activity.

Program Evaluation and Review Technique (PERT). An event-oriented network analysis technique used to estimate project duration when there is a high degree of uncertainty with the individual activity duration estimates. PERT applies the critical path method to a weighted average duration estimate. Also given as Program Evaluation and Review Technique.

Project. A temporary endeavor undertaken to create a unique product or service.

Project Charter. A document issued by senior management that provides the project manager with the authority to apply organizational resources to project activities.

Project Communications Management. A subset of project management that includes the processes required to ensure proper collection and dissemination of project information. It consists of communications planning, information distribution, performance reporting, and administrative closure.

Project Cost Management. A subset of project management that includes the processes required to ensure that the project is completed within the approved budget. It consists of resource planning, cost estimating, cost budgeting, and cost control.

Project Human Resource Management. A subset of project management that includes the processes required to make the most effective use of the people involved with the project. It consists of organizational planning, staff acquisition, and team development.

Project Integration Management. A subset of project management that includes the processes required to ensure that the various elements of the project are properly coordinated. It consists of project plan development, project plan execution, and overall change control.

Project Life Cycle. A collection of generally sequential project phases whose name and number are determined by the control needs of the organization or organizations involved in the project.

Project Management (PM). The application of knowledge, skills, tools, and techniques to project activities in order to meet or exceed stakeholder needs and expectations from a project.

Project Management Body of Knowledge (PMBOK), Third Edition. An inclusive term that describes the sum of knowledge within the profession of project management. As with other professions such as law, medicine, and accounting, the body of knowledge rests with the practitioners and academics who apply and advance it. The PMBOK includes proven, traditional practices which are widely applied as well as innovative and advanced ones which have seen more limited use.

Project Management Professional (PMP). An individual certified as such by the Project Management Institute.

Project Management Software. A class of computer applications specifically designed to aid with planning and controlling project costs and schedules.

Project Management Team. The members of the project team who are directly involved in project management activities. On some smaller projects, the project management team may include virtually all of the project team members.

Project Manager (PM). The individual responsible for managing a project.

Project Network Diagram. Any schematic display of the logical relationships of project activities. Always drawn from left to right to reflect project chronology. Often incorrectly referred to as a "PERT chart."

Project Phase. A collection of logically related project activities, usually culminating in the completion of a major deliverable.

Project Plan. A formal, approved document used to guide both project execution and project control. The primary uses of the project plan are to document planning assumptions and decisions, to facilitate communication among stakeholders, and to document approved scope, cost, and schedule baselines. A project plan may be summary or detailed.

Project Plan Development. Taking the results of other planning processes and putting them into a consistent, coherent document.

Project Plan Execution. Carrying out the project plan by performing the activities included therein.

Project Planning. The development and maintenance of the project plan.

TECHNOLOGY
AS PROMISED

Project Procurement Management. A subset of project management that includes the processes required to acquire goods and services from outside the performing organization. It consists of procurement planning, solicitation planning, solicitation, source selection, contract administration, and contract close-out.

Project Quality Management. A subset of project management that includes the processes required to ensure that the project will satisfy the needs for which it was undertaken. It consists of quality planning, quality assurance, and quality control.

Project Risk Management. A subset of project management that includes the processes concerned with identifying, analyzing, and responding to project risk. It consists of risk identification, risk quantification, risk response development, and risk response control.

Project Schedule. The planned dates for performing activities and the planned dates for meeting milestones.

Project Scope Management. A subset of project management that includes the processes required to ensure that the project includes all of the work required, and only the work required, to complete the project successfully. It consists of initiation, scope planning, scope definition, scope verification, and scope change control.

Project Team Members. The people who report either directly or indirectly to the project manager.

Project Time Management. A subset of project management that includes the processes required to ensure timely completion of the project. It consists of activity definition, activity sequencing, activity duration estimating, schedule development, and schedule control.

Projectized Organization. Any organizational structure in which the project manager has full authority to assign priorities and to direct the work of individuals assigned to the project.

Quality Assurance (QA).

1. The process of evaluating overall project performance on a regular basis to provide confidence that the project will satisfy the relevant quality standards.
2. The organizational unit that is assigned responsibility for quality assurance.

Quality Control (QC).

1. The process of monitoring specific project results to determine if they comply with relevant quality standards and identifying ways to eliminate causes of unsatisfactory performance.
2. The organizational unit that is assigned responsibility for quality control.

Quality Planning. Identifying which quality standards are relevant to the project and determining how to satisfy them.

Remaining Duration (RDU). The time needed to complete an activity.

Request for Proposal (RFP). A type of bid document used to solicit proposals from prospective sellers of products or services. In some application areas it may have a narrower or more specific meaning.

Request for Quotation (RFQ). Generally, this term is equivalent to request for proposal. However, in some application areas it may have a narrower or more specific meaning.

PMP Scrimmage® Curriculum, Edition 3.01   *Page 317*
www.tapuniversity.com
TECHNOLOGY
AS PROMISED

Reserve. A provision in the project plan to mitigate cost and/or schedule risk. Often used with a modifier (e.g., management reserve, contingency reserve) to provide further detail on what types of risk are meant to be mitigated. The specific meaning of the modified term varies by application area.

Resource Leveling. Any form of network analysis in which scheduling decisions (start and finish dates) are driven by resource management concerns (e.g., limited resource availability or difficult-to-manage changes in resource levels).

Resource-Limited Schedule. A project schedule whose start and finish dates reflect expected resource availability. The final project schedule should always be resource-limited.

Resource Planning. Determining what resources (people, equipment, materials) are needed in what quantities to perform project activities.

Responsibility Assignment Matrix (RAM). A structure which relates the project organization structure to the work breakdown structure to help ensure that each element of the project's scope of work is assigned to a responsible individual.

Responsibility Chart. See Responsibility Assignment Matrix.

Responsibility Matrix. See Responsibility Assignment Matrix.

Retainage. A portion of a contract payment that is held until contract completion in order to ensure full performance of the contract terms.

Risk Event. A discrete occurrence that may affect the project for better or worse.

Risk Identification. Determining which risk events are likely to affect the project.

Risk Quantification. Evaluating the probability of risk event occurrence and effect.

Risk Response Control. Responding to changes in risk over the course of the project.

Risk Response Development. Defining enhancement steps for opportunities and mitigation steps for threats.

S-Curve. Graphic display of cumulative costs, labor hours, or other quantities, plotted against time. The name derives from the S-like shape of the curve (flatter at the beginning and end, steeper in the middle) produced on a project that starts slowly, accelerates, and then trails off.

Schedule. See Project Schedule.

Schedule Analysis. See Network Analysis.

Schedule Compression. See Duration Compression.

Schedule Control. Controlling changes to the project schedule.

Schedule Development. Analyzing activity sequences, activity durations, and resource requirements to create the project schedule.

Schedule Performance Index (SPI). The ratio of work performed to work scheduled (BCWP/BCWS). See Earned Value.

Schedule Variance (SV).

1. Any difference between the scheduled completion of an activity and the actual completion of that activity.
2. In earned value, EV minus PV.

Scheduled Finish Date (SF). The point in time work was scheduled to finish on an activity. The scheduled finish date is normally within the range of dates delimited by the early finish date and the late finish date.

Scheduled Start Date (SS). The point in time work was scheduled to start on an activity. The scheduled start date is normally within the range of dates delimited by the early start date and the late start date.

Scope. The sum of the products and services to be provided as a project.

Scope Baseline. See Baseline.

Scope Change. Any change to the project scope. A scope change almost always requires an adjustment to the project cost or schedule.

Scope Change Control. Controlling changes to project scope.

Scope Definition. Decomposing the major deliverables into smaller, more manageable components to provide better control.

Scope Planning. Developing a written scope statement that includes the project justification, the major deliverables, and the project objectives.

Scope Verification. Ensuring that all identified project deliverables have been completed satisfactorily.

Should-Cost Estimates. An estimate of the cost of a product or service used to provide an assessment of the reasonableness of a prospective contractor's proposed cost.

Slack. Term used in PERT for float.

Solicitation. Obtaining quotations, bids, offers, or proposals as appropriate.

Solicitation Planning. Documenting product requirements and identifying potential sources.

Source Selection. Choosing from among potential contractors.

Staff Acquisition. Getting the human resources needed assigned to and working on the project.

Stakeholder. Individuals and organizations that are involved in or may be affected by project activities.

Start Date. A point in time associated with an activity's start, usually qualified by one of the following: actual, planned, estimated, scheduled, early, late, target, baseline, or current.

Start-to-Finish. See Logical Relationship.

Start-to-Start. See Logical Relationship.

Statement of Work (SOW). A narrative description of products or services to be supplied under contract.

Subnet. A subdivision of a project network diagram usually representing some form of subproject.

Subnetwork. See Subnet.

Successor Activity.

1. In the arrow diagramming method, the activity which departs a node.
2. In the precedence diagramming method, the "to" activity.

Target Completion Date (TC). An imposed date which constrains or otherwise modifies the network analysis.

Target Schedule. See Baseline.

Task. See Activity.

Team Development. Developing individual and group skills to enhance project performance.

Team Members. See Project Team Members.

Time-Scaled Network Diagram. Any project network diagram drawn in such a way that the positioning and length of the activity represents its duration. Essentially, it is a bar chart that includes network logic.

Target Finish Date (TF). The date work is planned (targeted) to finish on an activity.

Target Start Date (TS). The date work is planned (targeted) to start on an activity.

Total Float (TF). See Float.

Total Quality Management (TQM). A common approach to implementing a quality improvement program within an organization.

Workaround. A response to a negative risk event. Distinguished from contingency plan in that a workaround is not planned in advance of the occurrence of the risk event.

Work Breakdown Structure (WBS). A deliverable-oriented grouping of project elements which organizes and defines the total scope of the project. Each descending level represents an increasingly detailed definition of a project component. Project components may be products or services.

Work Item. See Activity.

Work Package. A deliverable at the lowest level of the work breakdown structure. A work package may be divided into specific actions needed to complete each package.

Sources Cited

i   Project Management Institute, Guide to the Project Management Body of Knowledge, Third Edition (2004).

ii   Adapted from Wikipedia and Investopedia

iii Silverstein, Michael J. (2004). Trading Up. Boston Consulting Group.

iv Zells, Lois. (1992). Object Oriented Project Management, Infotec, Omaha, NE.

v   Practice Standard for Work Breakdown Structures, Second Edition. (2006). Project Management Institute, page 7.

vi Simon, H. A., & Newell, A. (1965). Heuristic problem solving by computer. In M.A. Sass and W.D. Wilkinson (Eds.), Computer augmentation of human reasoning (pp. 25-35). Washington, DC: Spartan Books.